CONTEMPORARY SOCIA

General Editor: ANTHONY GIDDENS

This series aims to create a forum for debate between different theoretical and philosophical traditions in the social sciences. As well as covering broad schools of thought, the series will also concentrate upon the work of particular thinkers whose ideas have had a major impact on social science (these books appear under the sub-series title of 'Theoretical Traditions in the Social Sciences'). The series is not limited to abstract theoretical discussion – it will also include more substantive works on contemporary capitalism, the state, politics and other subject areas.

CONTEMPORARY SOCIAL THEORY

General Editor: ANTHONY GIDDENS

Theoretical Traditions in the Social Sciences

This series introduces the work of major figures in social science to students beyond their immediate specialisms.

Published titles

Barry Barnes, *T. S. Kuhn and Social Science*
Ted Benton, *The Rise and Fall of Structural Marxism*
David Bloor, *Wittgenstein: A Social Theory of Knowledge*
Christopher G. A. Bryant, *Positivism in Social Theory and Research*
Ira J. Cohen, *Structuration Theory: Anthony Giddens and the Constitution of Social Life*
Mark Cousins and Athar Hussain, *Michel Foucault*
Bob Jessop, Nicos Poulantzas, *Marxist Theory and Political Strategy*
William Outhwaite, *New Philosophies of Social Science: Realism, Hermeneutics and Critical Theory*
Julian Roberts, *Walter Benjamin*
Rick Roderick, *Habermas and the Foundations of Critical Theory*
James Schmidt, *Maurice Merleau-Ponty: Between Phenomenology and Structuralism*
Dennis Smith, *Barrington Moore: Violence, Morality and Political Change*
Dennis Smith, *The Chicago School*
Piotr Sztompka, *Robert K. Merton: An Intellectual Profile*

Forthcoming titles

John Forrester, *Jacques Lacan*
Robin Williams, *Erving Goffman*

Series Standing Order

If you would like to receive future titles in this series as they are published, you can make use of our standing order facility. To place a standing order please contact your bookseller or, in case of difficulty, write to us at the address below with your name and address and the name of the series. Please state with which title you wish to begin your standing order. (If you live outside the United Kingdom we may not have the rights for your area, in which case we will forward your order to the publisher concerned.)

Customer Services Department, Macmillan Distribution Ltd, Houndmills, Basingstoke, Hampshire, RG21 2XS, England.

Structuration Theory

Anthony Giddens and the Constitution of Social Life

Ira J. Cohen

MACMILLAN

First published 1989

Published by
MACMILLAN EDUCATION LTD
Houndmills, Basingstoke, Hampshire RG21 2XS
and London
Companies and representatives
throughout the world

Printed in the People's Republic of China

British Library Cataloguing in Publication Data
Cohen, Ira J., *1946–*
Structuration theory: Anthony Giddens and
the constitution of social life.
1. Society. Theories of Giddens, Anthony
I. Title
301'.092'4
ISBN 0–333–37120–8 (hardcover)
ISBN 0–333–37121–6 (paperback)

For R.F.C.

who understands that circumstances received from the past
include means through which a better future is produced.

Contents

Acknowledgements

My initial debt, of course, is to Anthony Giddens. I first became acquainted with him during my informal participation in a series of seminars he conducted on issues arising from his early work in structuration theory at Cambridge during 1976. Notwithstanding the uncommon talent and theoretical acumen he brought to these seminars, I was equally impressed by his tolerance and respect for the views of others. I mention this not simply to draw attention to these virtues, although tolerance and respect indeed are virtues often in short supply in contemporary academic life. I mention it, rather, because Tony Giddens is the general editor of the series in which this book appears, and during the course of my writing it he has consistently remained tolerant of certain unavoidable delays, and respectful of my autonomy as an author, even as I addressed myself to ideas that originate in his work.

I would like to acknowledge Adrian Hayes, Susan Hekman, Jeff Livesay, Chris Prendergast, David Sciulli, and Jon Turner for their encouragement and for their critical comments on various chapters. I am indebted to Malcolm Willison, George Theodorson, and especially Joe Elder, for encouragement and assistance of a different, but no less important, kind. The Research Council of Rutgers University provided financial assistance during the period in which this book was written.

My greatest debt is to Reggie Feiner Cohen for her encouragement and patience, and especially for her support. She will understand when I say that this book truly is 'our everyday thing'.

Plainsboro, New Jersey   Ira J. Cohen

Abbreviated Citations

Abbreviations in the citations refer to the following of Giddens's works:

NRSM   *New Rules of Sociological Method: A Positive Critique of Interpretative Sociologies* (London: Hutchinson/New York: Basic Books, 1976).

SSPT   *Studies in Social and Political Theory* (London: Hutchinson/New York: Basic Books, 1977).

CPST   *Central Problems in Social Theory: Action, Structure and Contradiction in Social Analysis* (London: Macmillan/Berkeley: University of California Press, 1979).

CCHM   *A Contemporary Critique of Historical Materialism: Volume 1: Power, Property, and the State* (London: Macmillan/Berkeley: University of California Press, 1981).

'AI'   'Agency, Institution, and Time–Space Analysis', in *Advances in Social Theory and Methodology: Toward an Integration of Micro- and Macro-Sociologies*, edited by K. Knorr-Cetina and A. V. Cicourel (Boston: Routledge & Kegan Paul, 1981), pp. 161–74.

PCST   *Profiles and Critiques in Social Theory* (London: Macmillan/Berkeley: University of California Press, 1982).

'Commentary' 'Commentary on the Debate', *Theory and Society*, 11: 4 (July 1982), pp. 527–39.

'Interview'   'Historical Materialism Today: An Interview with

Anthony Giddens', *Theory, Culture & Society*, 1: 2 (Autumn 1982), pp. 63–77.

'Comments'   'Comments on the Theory of Structuration', *Journal for the Theory of Social Behavior*, 13 (1983), pp. 75–80.

CS   *The Constitution of Society: Outline of the Theory of Structuration* (Cambridge: Polity Press/ Berkeley: University of California Press, 1984).

NSV   *The Nation-State and Violence: Volume Two of A Contemporary Critique of Historical Materialism* (Cambridge: Polity Press/Berkeley: University of California Press, 1985).

STMS   *Social Theory and Modern Sociology* (Cambridge: Polity Press/Stanford: Stanford University Press, 1987).

Introduction

Structuration theory originates in the writings of Anthony Giddens. I have written this book in the belief that Giddens's reputation is better known than structuration theory, and that some elements of structuration theory are better known than others. That this should be so is not too surprising. Structuration theory addresses the most fundamental, and therefore familiar, problems in the social sciences, but it addresses them in an unconventional way. It is grounded in commonsense, yet departs from and challenges established theoretical positions and traditions.

Structuration theory provides an account of the constitution of social life, the generic qualities of the subject-matter with which the social sciences at large are concerned. But structuration theory departs from prevailing conventions by conceiving the generic qualities of social life prior to the point where epistemological assumptions regarding acceptable forms of knowledge are made. Structuration theory does not propose empirically relevant accounts of substantive circumstances or events, it does not provide a method of theory construction, and it is not a 'grand theory' for the systematic integration of concepts, or the progressive accumulation of social scientific research.

Since all social scientists ultimately are concerned with the production of knowledge it may seem peculiar that structuration theory does not begin with postulates regarding the methods and objectives of theory and research. But structuration theory is designed to address a set of issues that arise before decisions are made on the kinds of knowledge it is appropriate to pursue. Although it is not always acknowledged in completed studies, at the start of their work most social scientists already have made certain assumptions of an ontological nature about the social world which shape their epistemological and methodological decisions, as well as their definitions of empirical problems. These ontological assumptions involve matters such as the nature of social action, social relations, social systems, and the like. Of course these assumptions do not always appear in an ontological form. Some social scientists take them to be self-evident features of the empirical domain to which their inquiries are addressed, others accept them via concepts pre-supposed 'for purposes of analysis', and still others tacitly accept the ontological implications of their epistemological principles. Structuration theory, however, presumes that these ontological assumptions deserve close attention and sustained elaboration. Although it does not develop substantive accounts of the empirical social world in any given socio-historical domain, structuration theory is designed to inform the development of such accounts. That is to say, it provides ontological resources for the formulation of empirically oriented theory and research.

The ontology which structuration theory provides proceeds from an insight that is part of the commonsense shared by social scientists and lay actors alike: all social life is generated in and through social *praxis*; where social *praxis* is defined to include the nature, conditions, and consequences of historically and spatio-temporally situated activities and interactions produced through the agency of social actors. As commonsensical as this insight may seem, in working out its implications structuration theory departs from and challenges alternative traditions of theory and research. For a variety of reasons, many of which involve exigencies associated with the production of knowledge, the centrality of social *praxis* often is forgotten, or insufficiently developed. This is not to say that alternative traditions have nothing to offer, nor that they should be rejected out of hand. To the contrary, Giddens develops structuration theory by way of 'positive critiques' through which he not only underscores the errors of established schools of thought, but through which he also appropriates and reconstructs insights and concepts of enduring value.

The preceding remarks on the ontological status of structuration theory, and the centrality of *praxis* to the account of the constitution of social life it provides, anticipate a more extended discussion of these issues which appears in Chapter 1. For the remainder of this introduction I shall set these matters aside. My purpose in this book is to provide a clarification and explication of the themes and concepts established in structuration theory. Since Anthony Giddens is the founder of structuration theory, it should be evident that this book is based upon his writings. What may not be clear is the exegetical stance I assume toward his works. It is by discussing this stance that I can best indicate what I have tried to accomplish in this book, as well as certain objectives I have chosen not to pursue. This discussion also is important with regard to two expectations readers may have for my treatment of Giddens's works. First, some readers may expect a comprehensive study of Giddens's thought in its entirety. Second, many readers may anticipate a descriptive exposition of the ideas he has advanced. Neither of these expectations is entirely consistent with what readers will actually find in the following pages. Briefly stated, this study is confined to Giddens's writings on structuration theory, and while it does expound his thought in this regard, it also includes explications and extensions of his ideas as well. My remarks here are organised to deal with each point in turn.

Comprehensive studies of the thought of leading theorists make important contributions, and they frequently demand more from their authors than may be readily apparent. Although Giddens is only at the mid-point of his career, I believe that a study of his works along these lines might be quite worthwhile. This is not only because of the intrinsic significance of the themes and topics he develops, but also, and of equal importance, because of the considerable influence he has exercised on the direction social theory has taken over the past two decades as it has moved beyond the limits of the 'orthodox consensus' and classical Marxism. But as valuable as such a study might be it is not my purpose to embark on it here. At an early stage in preparing this book it became obvious that to do justice to the details of structuration theory it would be necessary to treat it as a subject on its own. This is not to say that structuration theory is discontinuous with Giddens's overall project. The reason lies rather in the extraordinary scope of Giddens's ambitions.

In the opening lines of the preface to Giddens's first major work, *Capitalism and Modern Social Theory* (p. vii), Giddens indicated his ambition to move social theory beyond the frameworks inherited from the classical founders of sociology. Even prior to this point, he had set a course in this direction by developing a post-Durkheimian theory of suicide (*SSPT*, ch. 9), as well as an extensive critique of Talcott Parsons's analysis of power (*SSPT*, ch. 10). The diversity of themes in his early works made clear that he did not intend to transform social theory according to a single, dominant principle of thought, or to pursue the strategy of systematic 'grand theory' adopted *inter alia* by Comte, Spencer, Parsons, and Habermas. Instead, more in the manner of Simmel, Weber, Merton, and Mills, Giddens indicated that he would proceed on a variety of intellectual fronts. His subsequent writings have maintained this approach. Drawing upon an erudition few theorists can match, Giddens has addressed an enormous range of issues. His output has been prodigious and he has left few stones unturned.

But if Giddens is not driven by a systematic impulse, nor obsessed by a single *idée fixe*, his efforts to revise the foundations of social theory are not altogether without shape or form. In 1976 (*NRSM*, p. 7; see also *PCST*, p. viii) he divided his overall project into three basic concerns: first, to develop a critical approach to classical theory; second, to develop a post-orthodox and post-Marxist substantive account of the nature and dilemmas of modernity; third, to develop a conceptual reconstruction of the subject-matter of the field. Although structuration theory falls under the last of these headings, a few words should be said on his works under the other headings as well.

Capitalism and Modern Social Theory represents Giddens's most extensive study in classical theory. It probably is his best known book, and at an early date it did more to alter the orthodox reception of Durkheim, Weber, and especially Marx, than perhaps any other single treatise or text. Giddens inaugurated his substantive analysis of modernity in 1973 with the publication of *The Class Structure of Advanced Societies*. It too remains well known and is widely cited today. However, in the intervening years Giddens has refashioned his substantive concerns, and considerably expanded their scale. The basic theme which he pursues in *A Contemporary Critique of Historical Materialism*, and *The Nation-State and Violence* is that the institutions and institutional orders of modernity, including the intrinsically and historically related orders of capitalism and the nation-state, differ profoundly from all previous forms of social life in ways that neither Marxist theories nor theories of 'industrial society' fully appreciate or understand. It should be added here that not all of Giddens's works can be easily categorised under the three headings set forth above. For example, he has produced an extensive essay on positivist philosophy of science and the criticism it has received, and a number of critical commentaries on the thought of Jurgen Habermas as well.

Given the diversity and range of Giddens's themes it should be evident why a choice must be made between dealing with the nature and influence of his works at large, or dealing with structuration theory at length and in detail. Although all of Giddens's arguments and inquiries can be related to structuration theory, and while his substantive analyses of the distinctive qualities of modernity, in particular, both inform and are informed by certain elements of structuration theory, structuration theory *per se* is addressed to an independent agenda of issues. Since I have chosen to adhere to this agenda I have imposed two exegetical limits on my exposition of Giddens's works. First, I have almost entirely set aside Giddens's writings published prior to 1976, the year in which he launched structuration theory in *New Rules of Sociological Method*. This means, *inter alia*, I shall not be concerned with either *Capitalism and Modern Social Theory*, or *The Class Structure of Advanced Societies*. Second, I have confined my use of Giddens's more recent substantive works to issues that directly pertain to structuration theory, although, for reasons indicated in context, the latter portion of Chapter 7 is somewhat an exception in this regard. To readers unfamiliar with Giddens's writings the foregoing limits may appear unduly restrictive. This might be true if Giddens were not such a prolific scholar. In all he has produced three volumes devoted entirely to structuration theory, augmented by works which appear in three collections of essays, and several free-standing publications as well. A list of these works, and the citational abbreviations I employ when referring to them, are included at the beginning of this book.

I earlier said that this book is something more than a straightforward description of Giddens's ideas, and I now want to indicate why and how this is so. Even when attention is limited to Giddens's writings on structuration theory, one still finds that he develops an extensive array of themes, concepts, and 'positive critiques'. Moreover, while he maintains intellectual consistency throughout his works, he is not always careful to explicitly establish lines of continuity as he moves from one topic to another. Lewis Coser (1981, p. 1435) once compared the way in which Giddens develops his ideas to the flight of a honey bee who dips into a wide variety of flowers. Giddens, himself, would appear to agree. In *The Constitution of Society*(p. 163) he describes his overall approach as 'circulating in and out' of a range of connected issues. In the introduction to the same volume (*CS*, p. xxxv) he acknowledges that the book was not particularly easy to write, and proved in some part refractory to the normal ordering of chapters. The same can be said for his other books on structuration theory as well.

In certain respects Giddens's disorganised style results from his aversion to the kind of systematic theory which lends formal coherence to the works of theorists such as Talcott Parsons. As I shall indicate in Chapter 1 (see also Cohen, 1986), I believe that Giddens's aversion to systematic coherence is warranted in light of the nature and purposes of structuration theory itself. But even unsystematised theoretical discourse can be organised to a greater or lesser extent. Giddens most definitely leaves some room for improvement in this regard.

The fact that Giddens only loosely organises the exposition of his themes and concepts is responsible, in part, for the recurrent criticism that he is an 'eclectic' or 'syncretic' scholar. I could not have written this book if I accepted this claim, and while I have not explicitly set out to refute it, I hope that my exposition will put it to rest. Having said this, there can be no denying that the loose exposition of structuration theory in Giddens's works poses a variety of problems. In some instances he turns from one insight to another before the first is fully elaborated; on certain issues his 'circulating' style leaves gaps in his argument. These problems are abetted by the fact that in each major work on structuration theory Giddens develops new themes and ideas, and expands upon those he has previously introduced. To further complicate matters, the connections between various aspects of social life established in his concepts are unorthodox, and require numerous qualifications. As necessary as these qualifications may be, at times they threaten to obscure the nub of what he is trying to say.

Given these problems my strategy in this book is designed not only to make Giddens's ideas on structuration theory accessible as they stand, but also to develop ideas which are implied in his work.

In certain instances this involves little more than expanding upon concepts as they appear in his texts. But on a number of occasions I have ventured beyond this point to introduce insights with which Giddens may or may not agree. The interpretation of structuration theory as an ontology of potentials in Chapter 1, for example, moves beyond anything available in Giddens's texts, and there are extensions of this kind in later chapters as well. I have tried to at least briefly indicate these extensions as they occur. However, readers familiar with Giddens's writings should be able to recognise them without too much trouble.

I also have exercised a free hand in dealing with Giddens's 'positive critiques' of alternative traditions. For example, while I discuss his critique of functionalism in some detail, I set aside his criticism of scholars identified with the French structuralist tradition. Readers also should be alerted to the fact that certain critical backdrops are inspired by, rather than expositions of, the critiques which Giddens provides: for example, the critiques of positivism and theories of action in Chapter 1. Finally, the critique of social morphology presented in Chapter 2 is substantially my own, and here again it is important to note that Giddens may or may not agree with my argument.

The clarifications and extensions I propose are developed from a constructive point of view. Although I do underscore several problems in Giddens's writings, I do not develop a sustained critique. I also have taken a rather selective approach to the critical literature on structuration theory. Criticism, to be effective, must be well-informed. Unfortunately this cannot be said of all of the criticism Giddens has received. Some critics appear to misunderstand his intent, and most of them concentrate upon certain ideas at the expense of others. Overall, only a handful of sophisticated commentaries presently exist, and where they bear upon the issues I address, I have tried to take fundamental points they raise into account (see especially Chapter 6 on the problem of structural constraint). I regret that I am unable to address a number of recent or forthcoming critical works. These include a German monograph by Bernd Kiessling, *Kritik der Giddensschen Sozialtheorie* (1988), and two forthcoming collections of essays, one edited by David Held and John Thompson, and the other by Jon Clark, Sohan Mogdil, and Celia Mogdil.

Whatever liberties I have taken with Giddens's texts, it is my intention that readers come away from this book with a better understanding of his texts on structuration theory than that with which they began. To this end I have tried to organise my presentation of themes in an order that adheres to the logic of his thought. The seven chapters of exposition deal in sequence with four basic themes. Chapter 1, as I have indicated, concerns the ontological status of structuration theory, and the central role of social *praxis* in structuration theory at large. Chapters 2 and 3 establish the nature and significance of Giddens's views on the patterning of social systems in time and space. Chapter 4 and 5 deal with his non-functionalist account of the organisation of social systems. Chapter 5 also includes an analysis of the concepts involved in his account of power and domination. Chapters 6 and 7 are devoted to the structural themes in the ontology of structuration theory. The latter portion of Chapter 7 moves a bit beyond ontology *per se* to consider Giddens's cautiously formulated conception of societal systems, and the conditions conducive to social change. Finally, in the concluding remarks I briefly consider the development of structuration theory beyond the realm of ontological themes. Topics here include the relevance of structuration theory to social research and critical theory.

1

Structuration Theory and Social Praxis

Human beings 'make their own history, but not in circumstances of their own choosing' (Marx, 1963, p. 15; for variations, see Simmel, 1950, pp. 12–13; Vico, 1968, pp. 382–3, para. 1108) is an aphorism that appears more cogent in the preface to most works in social theory than it does in the conclusions. There is, of course, a substantial body of theory and research that illustrates various processes and procedures through which social action is produced; but such works generally neglect the implication of historically inherited collective circumstances in the course and outcome of social conduct, and make no mention of the constitution of social collectivities. Theory and research that capture the contours of collectivities have been a fundamental objective of social science since its inception; but accounts of social action incorporated in such works typically are designed to stress the intrusion of structure or systemic circumstances into the consciousness of actors or the domain in which activity occurs, while the practices through which the production of social life takes place remain unaddressed. The numerous analytical arguments and methodological procedures that have been advanced to ascribe priority to either social action or the properties of collectivities are difficult to sustain when considered in light of two textbook truisms: the existence of collectivities exhibiting specific properties and particular configurations depends upon the transaction of determinate forms of conduct; conversely, social conduct is carried out in different ways in historically specific types of collectivities. The only plausible conclusion once these maxims are conjoined is that properties of collectivities and procedures of action in some way

9

presuppose one another in the reality of social life. To ascribe priority *ab initio* to collectivities or action appears mistaken and misleading when it is recognised that the two are interwoven whenever human beings make their own history.

If it were a simple matter to reconcile action with collectivities, then the division between these themes never would have arisen. But it is especially difficult to embark upon this project given the broad array of issues that must be addressed, a diversity reflected in the disparate array of theories and traditions of research that currently exist on both sides of the divide. It is to the credit of Anthony Giddens that he has accepted the burdens which this project entails in his writings on structuration theory.

While all concepts in structuration theory exhibit Giddens's persistent concern to reconcile social action with the collective dimensions of social life, finding a single concept that lends consistency to his thought is more difficult than it seems. One problem here is that Giddens has not presented a sustained account of the meta-theoretical status of structuration theory, thus leaving it unclear exactly how he intends his concepts to be understood. But a problem of equal, if not greater, importance is the sheer range of issues addressed in structuration theory. For example, in Giddens's early writings it seemed plausible to suggest that one pivotal concept, the duality of structure, stood at the centre of all of his concerns. Yet even in these writings Giddens consistently distinguished the structural properties of social systems, conceived with reference to the duality of structure, from social systems as articulated patterns of social interaction. In subsequent work Giddens's growing involvement with ideas regarding the 'situatedness' of interaction in time and space initially developed through the efforts of time-geographers, has considerably expanded the concern for systems in structuration theory. Ramifications of his concern for the spatio-temporal patterning of systems are evident as well in his more recent writings on the constitution of socio-political forms of control and power relations in social life.

These are but a few of the topics which will be addressed in due course during later chapters of this book. My purpose in this opening chapter will be to establish two themes which provide crucial bearings for all subsequent discussions, and which I believe, in a very broad sense, lend consistency to all concepts in structuration theory. The first theme represents my own interpretation of the meta-theoretical status of structuration theory. This is not a book on the philosophical aspects of meta-theory, and for this reason my discussion will be brief (see also Cohen, 1986). My basic proposal will be that structuration theory maintains the status of what I term an *ontology of potentials*. This proposal is presented with reference to basic ideas advanced by modern, post-positivist philosophers of science.

The second theme, which will absorb most of the remainder of this chapter, addresses what I take to be the most fundamental concept in structuration theory *per se*, the concept of social *praxis*. Discussion proceeds in three stages. In the first stage the significance of *praxis* is established by means of a contrast with an ontological principle presupposed in positivist methods of theory construction: the principle of the uniformity of nature. The second stage establishes how structuration theory conceives regularities of *praxis*. The exposition of this point occurs against the backdrop of focused critiques of the neglect of regularities of *praxis* by four leading students of the production of social activity and interaction: Herbert Blumer, Harold Garfinkel, Peter Winch, and Randall Collins. The third stage also is concerned with regularities of *praxis*, but the focus now turns to how such regularities are reproduced. Here we arrive at Giddens's conception of the duality of structure. Although, as I have said, the duality of structure should not be regarded as providing the key to all of Giddens's efforts to reconcile conceptions of action with conceptions of collectivities, the concept remains indispensable to these efforts, and it must be clearly understood. (The duality of structure also figures prominently in Chapter 6.) It will be evident during the course of this chapter that structuration theory's emphasis upon *praxis* involves a 'decentering' of the subject in favour of a concern for the nature and consequences of the activities in which social actors engage during their participation in day-to-day life. But this 'decentering' of the subject in no way denies the need for an account of the actor *per se*. Giddens's theory of the acting subject therefore is a crucial adjunct to his account of social *praxis*, and the chapter will close with a discussion of the elements of this theory.

To conclude these preliminary remarks I want to clarify, in brief, how the centrality of social *praxis* to structuration theory should be understood. *Praxis* initially may appear to denote instances of conduct and interaction produced by social agents. But as I shall employ the term its primary definition is considerably broader than this denotation would suggest. *Praxis* should be regarded as synonymous with the *constitution of social life*, i.e. the manner in which all aspects, elements, and dimensions of social life, from instances of conduct in themselves to the most complicated and extensive types of collectivities, are generated in and through the performance of social conduct, the consequences which ensue, and the social relations which are thereby established and maintained. To speak of *praxis* as the constitution of social life entails a concern not only for the manner in which conduct, consequences, and relations are generated but also for the conditions which shape and facilitate these processes and outcomes, conditions which are essential to the production of social life, but which also are sustained only in so far as the production of social life continues to occur. This view of *praxis* is equally relevant to the constitution of action and the constitution of collectivities, because both aspects of social life are generated and reproduced or altered in and through social *praxis* itself.

Like all summary statements, the foregoing remarks conceal the complexities of the issues involved. It is one thing to acknowledge the centrality of *praxis* as a matter of principle, and quite another to expand this basic insight into a fully elaborated account. The objective of structuration theory is to provide such an account. The present chapter deals with the status of this account, and the view it incorporates of the production and reproduction of social conduct.

An ontology of potentials: the post-positivist status of structuration theory

Although there presently is no canonical doctrine known as positivism, the term continues to make sense in so far as it refers to principles that assume or assert that methods which couple nomic propositions with empirical observations comprise means which are suitable for the formation of knowledge across all domains of scientific inquiry. Given the extent to which positivism as so defined has influenced the course of development in modern social theory – an influence which extends beyond the development of positivistic theories to theories that presuppose objections to positivistic doctrine – it may seen curious that Giddens has not launched structuration theory through a critical encounter with positivistic principles. His writings establish beyond any doubt that he is quite familiar with these principles and the full array of criticisms that have been lodged against them both in the philosophy of science as well as in social theory *per se* (see *NRSM*, ch. 4; *SSPT*, ch. 1; *CPST*, pp. 242–4). However, rather than emerging from a confrontation with positivism and positivistic social theory, Giddens has chosen to develop the insights which are fundamental to structuration theory in response to theories and schools of thought that already stand at some remove from positivistic points of view. Proceeding in this way has enabled him to avoid diversion into the thicket of issues in which those who debate the merits and liabilities of positivistic social science remain entangled. But a more fundamental reason why positivism does not provide a suitable backdrop for his work is that the issues in which structuration theory originates are of a different order from those which absorb the attention of positivistic social theorists.

The invocation of positivistic principles in the development of social theory is the most obvious expression of an enduring concern throughout the field for preferred forms of knowledge and epistemological legitimacy. While Giddens has a number of important proposals regarding the nature and critical intent of social scientific knowledge (see *CS*, ch. 6; *CPST*, ch. 7; *NRSM*, ch. 4; also Cohen, 1984), he is unwilling to shape his inquiries to conform to a predetermined set of epistemological principles. Instead, he takes his bearings from central problems in the subject-matter to which social scientific knowledge ultimately refers. To concentrate upon epistemological issues, he argues:

> draws attention away from the more 'ontological' concerns of social theory and it is these upon which structuration theory primarily concentrates. Rather than becoming pre-occupied with epistemological disputes and with the question of whether or not anything like 'epistemology' in its time-honoured sense can be formulated at all, those working in social theory, I suggest, should be concerned first and foremost with reworking conceptions of human being and human doing, social reproduction and social transformation. (*CS*, p. xx)

Social theorists grown weary with the seemingly endless round of debates regarding appropriate forms of knowledge may welcome Giddens's decision to initiate structuration theory along ontological lines. While subject-matter and epistemological principles inevitably stand in a reciprocal relationship, neither domain can be reduced to the other without residuum, and each must be granted a degree of autonomy if imagination and insight are to thrive. But, despite this autonomy, the objectives Giddens pursues in the formation of an ontological theory of the constitution of social life do not stand apart from the concerns of social science at large. To the contrary, the main purpose of social theory from this point of view is to inform theories of substantive structures and social processes, and to subserve the prosecution of empirical research (*CS*, pp. xvii–xviii).

By casting his conceptions of social phenomena in ontological terms, Giddens obviously contravenes positivistic injunctions against metaphysical postulates. The revocation of these injunctions is one of the liberating consequences of the post-positivist revolution in the philosophy of science. But some caution is in order. In the first place, if positivism is in decline in the philosophy of science, it remains an influential doctrine in social scientific circles, particularly in the United States (representative scholars include: Peter Blau, Hubert Blalock, Ronald Burt, James Coleman, George Homans, Jonathan Turner, Walter Wallace, and Harrison White). In the second place, the post-positivist revolution does not invalidate some of the most prominent concerns that lead positivists to be wary of metaphysical insights.

One of the principal objectives pursued by the progenitors of positivist social science was to expunge from social thought all theories and methods that ascribe effective agency or consequence in the determination of the course or character of social life to abstract forces or qualities conceived exclusively in metaphysical terms. These hypostatised modes of theorising exemplified in many social contract theories and carried to an extreme in the works of Hegel, convey edifying insights that continue to inspire valuable lines of thought in ethical and political philosophy. But conceptions of social phenomena developed in this way generally involve deductions of the necessity or inevitability of historical circumstances and events from the metaphysical mechanisms which are purported to regulate social life at large. In one of the earliest condemnations of this strategy, Auguste Comte – who by no means was innocent of the faults he identified in the works of others – characterised the speculative spirit of metaphysical theories as 'at once ideal in its course, absolute in its conception, and arbitrary in its application' (Comte, 1893, vol. 2, p. 57). Over a century later, Comte's reaction reverberates in the works of his successors. Thus, Robert Merton seeks to dampen an enthusiasm for master conceptual schemes from which to derive all subsidiary theories by suggesting that they verge toward the large philosophical systems of the past, which despite their varied suggestiveness remain scientifically sterile (Merton, 1968, p. 51; Merton implicitly alludes to the works of Parsons in these remarks).

There is wisdom in these objections which should not be dismissed no matter how much one may disagree with positivistic social theorists on other grounds. To attribute agency or consequence to hypostatised metaphysical forces or qualities is to distort the formation of substantive theories as well as empirical investigation of concrete social processes. The diversity that is evident across different societies and civilisations must be trimmed and shaped to preserve the fundamental metaphysical insights. For the same reason, historical discontinuities that are inconsistent with these insights must be set aside or suppressed. While few modern social theorists recommend such procedures, they remain evident in many theories of social evolution, as well as theories that postulate fundamental 'needs', or the priority of material or ideal factors as ubiquitous characteristics of all collectivities. Restrictions of this kind not only disturb positivistic social theorists, but all social scientists who refuse to subordinate their inquiries in deference to canonical doctrines and systems of thought.

Post-positivist philosophers of science certainly do not sustain hypostatised modes of metaphysical theorising. But they do claim that metaphysical or ontological conceptions of the subject-matter to be investigated in any given scientific domain are required to fill the void created by the underdetermination of theories by fact. Without entering into the details of the complex arguments that have been advanced in this regard, it is useful to make mention of the views of some of the leading figures in post-empiricist philosophy.

The turn to metaphysics already is evident in the early works of Karl Popper. The disengagement of scientific discovery from empirical inquiry, which is fundamental to Popper's thought, leads him to acknowledge that the process of discovery is impossible without faith in certain metaphysical ideas which are unwarranted from an empirical point of view (Popper, 1968, p. 38). Several decades later, Thomas Kuhn expands upon a similar point in an introductory passage to *The Structure of Scientific Revolutions*:

> Effective research scarcely begins before a scientific community thinks it has acquired firm answers to questions like the following: What are the fundamental entities of which the universe is composed? How do these interact with each other and with the senses? What questions may legitimately be asked about such entities and what techniques employed in seeking solutions? (Kuhn, 1970, pp. 4–5)

While Kuhn summarises what unmistakably are metaphysical questions regarding the constitution of the subject-matter investigated by members of a scientific community, his main concerns revolve around the socio-historical dimensions of scientific practice. However, his views are ratified by post-positivist scholars who take a more methodological slant. According to Imre Lakatos, at the centre of a scientific 'research programme' there is a 'hard core' as well as a 'positive heuristic', both of which can be formulated in metaphysical terms (Lakatos, 1978, vol. 1, pp. 47–52, 110–11, 115). The success of a 'research programme' as evaluated by Lakatos depends upon the capacity of its metaphysical elements to inspire satisfactory explanations of empirical research (Lakatos, 1978, vol. 1, pp. 48–52). Although Larry Laudan differs from Lakatos on a number of central issues, he proposes a similar view of the place of metaphysical commitments as an ontology that specifies in a general way the types of fundamental entities in a given domain and the modes in which these entities interact. Specific theories explain empirical problems in terms reducible to this ontology (Laudan, 1977, p. 79 *passim*). Roy Bhaskar offers an account of the significance of ontological entities in a realist theory of science that is far more robust than the accounts proposed by Kuhn, Lakatos, and Laudan. Adopting a transcendental perspective, Bhaskar argues that beneath empirically demonstrable patterns of events there must be mechanisms conceivable in ontological terms that operate in conjunction with one another to constitute the actual states and happenings of the world. In his view, such mechanisms are the 'intransitive objects' of scientific theory (Bhaskar, 1978, pp. 45–56 *passim*).

To advance further into issues regarding the status of ontological assumptions would be an epistemological digression of the sort Giddens suggests social theorists would do well to avoid. However, it is immediately evident that unlike metaphysical modes of theorising, the post-positivist accounts cited above discourage the hypostatisation of abstract forces or qualities. The principal means to this end is the distinction drawn between ontological conceptualisations of fundamental entities or mechanisms on the one hand, and substantive theory and empirical research on the other. The ontological element of scientific theory can be understood as a series of internally consistent insights into the trans-historical *potentials* of the phenomena that constitute a domain of inquiry: i.e. fundamental processes and properties that may be activated or realised in various ways in diverse circumstances and on different occasions. These potentials are irrefutable on empirical grounds because they are formulated without regard to their manifestations in the empirical flux of events. But for the same reason, the development of substantive theories is required to determine how these processes and properties operate and appear in any given context, and these theories are subject to empirical refutation. A primary consideration in the formulation of ontological concepts of this kind obviously must be to allow the widest possible latitude for the diversity and contingencies that may occur in different settings. Therefore, hypostatised accounts of the trans-historical determination of circumstances or the universal trajectories of events are neither necessary nor desirable. To the contrary, an acceptable ontology of potentials should be sufficiently flexible to allow for the development of a variety of different substantive theories addressed to the same subject-matter.

Structuration theory is thoroughly consistent with this post-positivist view of the nature and objectives of ontological insights. *The structurationist ontology is addressed exclusively to the constitutive potentials of social life: the generic human capacities and fundamental conditions through which the course and outcomes of social processes and events are generated and shaped in the manifold ways in which this can occur.* The absence of hypostatisation in structuration theory is evident in the extent to which

Giddens refrains from imposing any substantive restrictions on his ontological concepts. These concepts do not attribute trans-historical priority to specific practices or processes of social production and reproduction; no universal 'needs' are proposed either for collectivities or social actors; and Giddens vigorously insists that all modes of theory that postulate or imply any functional teleology or universal trajectory of social evolution are misleading and incorrect.

The ontological flexibility of structuration theory will be made clear, both in the present chapter and those to follow. However, there is one general point that deserves special mention here. Commentators who quarrel with the absence of systematically related propositions in Giddens's writings on structuration theory (see Archer, 1982; McLennan, 1984, see also 1988) overlook the hypostatisation of social life that would result were he to proceed in this way. Because structuration theory concentrates upon the generation of all aspects of social life as it occurs in social *praxis*, a systematisation of ontological propositions would entail some degree of systematisation in the processes and outcomes of social *praxis* as well. But the absence of systematic propositions is not simply a matter of methodological prudence. It is evident through-out Giddens's writings that he has a deep respect for the protean capacities of social agents to reproduce and transform their own historical circumstances. Social agents, not social theorists, pro-duce, sustain, and alter whatever degree of 'systemness' exists in social life. Hence, to the degree that sets of systematically related propositions are in order, this is a matter for substantive theories addressed to specific types of socio-historical circumstances. This point of view, of course, is directly opposed to the pervasive reliance on systemic modes of analysis in Talcott Parsons's 'grand theory'.

From the principle of uniformity to the production of social life

Since the various interpretations of positivist doctrine involve philosophical reconstructions of methods for the development and acceptance of theory and evidence drawn from diverse case studies in the natural sciences, positivist social scientists generally have not adopted these doctrines on ontological grounds. If positivist procedures actually implied nothing regarding the constitution of the subject-matter in any given domain of inquiry, then it might be possible to formulate structuration theory in accord with these methods. But, as theorists of action such as Alfred Schutz and Aaron Cicourel have demonstrated, positivist doctrines do intrude on how social scientists conceive of the constitution of social life (see Schutz, 1962, pp. 3–45; Cicourel, 1964). Their arguments indicate that positivist strategies of observation and measurement neglect and distort the complex cognitive rationalities and strategies that comprise fundamental aspects of human social *praxis*. Structuration theory concurs with these criticisms of positivist strategies of research (for example, *NRSM*, pp. 131–5; *CPST*, pp. 248–53, ch. 7 *passim*). But to dwell upon these strategies is to overlook a reason for structuration theory's departure from positivism that strikes at a primordial ontological assumption implicated in positivist theory rather than positivist research.

There are certain respects in which my development of this issue intersects Roy Bhaskar's critique of positivist epistemology, but I shall proceed independently, for two reasons. The first is that Bhaskar's critique presupposes the transcendental strategy he incorporates in his realist theory of science. While other elements of Bhaskar's philosophy of science might be reconciled with structuration theory, it remains unclear whether it is either necessary or useful to accept the burdens involved in the defence of Bhaskar's transcendental reasoning. The second reason for not following Bhaskar's lead is that he is intent on preserving continuities between the constitution of natural domains and the domains of social life, with the important proviso that social structures – which he takes as the mechanism that generates social life – are produced through social *praxis*, and hence may be only relatively enduring (see Bhaskar, 1979, pp. 47–9). By contrast, my discussion of the discrepancy between positivism and structuration theory accentuates a fundamental discontinuity between nature and society, one that turns directly on the characteristics of social *praxis per se*.

Robert Merton articulates the wisdom conventional among positivist social scientists when he asserts that a knowledge of the logic or methodology of scientific procedure does not contain or imply the particular content of sociological theory (Merton, 1968, pp. 140–1). The sheer variety of the conceptions of social phenomena that have been developed in conformity with positivist principles would seem to suggest that Merton is correct. Individualist theories of social behaviour and exchange, as well as holistic theories of social structure incorporating varying degrees of emphasis upon idealist or materialist factors, are all represented within the positivist tradition. Yet Merton himself, in an early essay on the sociology of science, presents a lucid account of an ontological assumption that contradicts his assertion of the thematic neutrality of the logic of science:

> The *basic* assumption in modern science 'is a widespread, instinctive conviction in the existence of an *Order of Things*, and in particular an Order of Nature'. This belief, this faith, for at least since Hume it must be recognized such, is simply 'impervious to the demand for a consistent rationality'. In the system of scientific thought of Galileo, Newton, and of their successors, the testimony of experiment is the ultimate criterion of truth, but the very notion of experiment is ruled out without the prior assumption that Nature constitutes an intelligible order, so that when appropriate questions are asked, she will answer, so to speak. Hence this assumption is final and absolute. (Merton, 1968, pp. 635–6)

In proposing this view, Merton quotes from commentary by A. N. Whitehead. According to Whitehead, the belief in the order of nature presumes that all phenomena are the result of recurrences in nature, exemplifications of general principles which reign throughout the natural order. This belief did not originate in scientific method; it arose well before the advent of modern science (Whitehead, 1925, pp. 3ff). Stephen Toulmin provides a summary statement of what this belief involves. The typical scientist, he suggests, 'begins with the conviction that things are not just happening (not even just-happening-regularly) but rather that some fixed set of laws or patterns or mechanisms accounts for Nature's following the course it does, and that his understanding of these should guide his expectations' (Toulmin, 1961, p. 45). Karl Popper fixes the status of this principle of the uniformity of nature when he notes that 'it expresses the metaphysical faith in the existence of regularities in our world' (Popper, 1968, p. 252; see also p. 278).

It is important to recognise that the principle of uniformity does not provide a comprehensive set of insights regarding the subject-matter at issue in any given theory. In the first place, this principle clearly is insufficient in itself to establish anything regarding specific kinds of patterns or mechanisms. In the second place, no specific account of causation or teleology is implied. Finally, the principle of uniformity by no means requires that empirical circumstances and events must occur in the same way under all conditions; determinate conjunctions of uniformities may result in rare or unprecedented outcomes in any given instance. The only point upon which the principle of uniformity insists is that a trans-historical order of forces or relationships between entities exist in the world to which scientific inquiry is addressed.

The principle of uniformity often is used as a warrant for inductive methods of theory construction, and a uniformitarian 'extensionalist argument' has been shown by Thomas Wilson to be embedded in the philosophical foundations of mathematical methods as well (see Hanson, 1969, chs 21, 25; Willer and Willer, 1973, pp. 35–6; Wilson, 1984). But since belief in the uniform order of nature originates prior to modern science, the principle of uniformity cannot be treated simply as a methodological artifact. To the contrary, unless positivist science is to be seen as a quixotic enterprise, methodological directives to develop and employ propositions that take the form of statements addressed to universal regularities – whether or not these are rigorously nomological – must presume the existence of uniformities in the subject-matter at hand.

The majority of positivist social theorists appear to have adopted the principle of uniformity via their acceptance of methodological directives of this kind. But a few theorists have implied or proposed an awareness of this ontological implication of positivist methods. Thus, Walter Wallace, whose recent work marks him as one of the most sophisticated positivist theorists in the present era, invokes Popper's contention that the principle of uniformity is a metaphysical belief, and then declares:

> [just] as astrophysicists assume that the same processes (whether these processes are known or not) that prevail now and here on Earth prevail across the cosmos and throughout all past and future time, . . . similarly sociologists assume that the same

processes (again whether known or not) prevail across all societies, past, present, and future. (Wallace, 1983, p. 461)

Social theorists who propose or accept a positivist strategy for theory construction imply a commitment to the principle of uniformity on methodological grounds. But a uniformitarian outlook is characteristic of many other theories as well. Those functionalist theories that can be reconstructed in the nomothetic manner proposed by Carl Hempel (1965) and Ernest Nagel (1967) certainly can be included in this group. Harold Bershady (1973; see also, Camic, 1987) has indicated that a drive to establish universal laws is embedded in the works of Talcott Parsons. Merton's well-known proposal for the development of theories of the middle-range may seem to steer clear of the principle of uniformity. But this would be true only if his conception of these theories limited their scope to historically bounded collectivities and processes. As it is, Merton denies the historical specificity of middle-range theories and holds only that they are limited to a determinate range of conceptual issues. The ultimate goal remains to consolidate these theories into a progressively more general conceptual scheme (Merton, 1968, pp. 45, 51).

Whether or not the principle of uniformity is ever contradicted in nature, common experience suggests that a multitude of natural regularities operate in similar ways under the same conditions, whenever and wherever they occur. Presuming this point, a question arises that is much older than social theory in the modern era: is social life continuous with nature, or can it be distinguished from nature on determinate grounds? Giddens establishes his position on this issue in the opening pages of his first book on structuration theory:

The difference between society and nature is that nature is . . . not produced by man . . . While not made by any single person, society is created and recreated afresh, if not *ex nihilo*, by the participants in every social encounter. *The production of society is a skilled performance, sustained and 'made to happen' by human beings. (NRSM, p. 15)*

While Giddens establishes an unequivocal distinction between nature and society, it is not immediately evident where he stands on the principle of uniformity. That he resists a uniformitarian outlook is made abundantly clear in his objections to all forms of universal generalisations (*NRSM*, pp. 153–4; *CPST*, pp. 242–4; *CS*, pp. xviii–xix, 343–8). But the issue to be considered here is why Giddens is unwilling to accept the existence of uniformities. In dealing with this issue, I shall concentrate on elements of Giddens's account of the constitution of social agency and social practices. To this end I shall bracket, for the time being, issues regarding social reproduction and the reconciliation of structure and action.

Before turning to the anti-uniformitarian implications of the concepts of agency and practices, it may be helpful to situate Giddens's view in this regard *vis-à-vis* other non-positivist theories of social action. Although currently in decline, a line of thought promulgated in Max Weber's methodological writings holds that social action is inherently identifiable with reference to the subjective orientations which individual actors assume toward their acts. Against this position, it must be emphasised that structuration theory does not adopt a methodological, or ontological, individualist stance. Giddens does acknowledge that individuals remain the only 'moving objects' in social relations, and activities of all kinds (see *CS*, p. 181); a view which entails that the subjectivity of actors – i.e. agents (the terms are interchangeable) – cannot be left out of account, and that agents' motives and wants must be involved in disposing or impelling them to engage in social conduct. Nevertheless, in structuration theory it is the performance of conduct *per se* which stands out at the centre of concern. Although Giddens explicitly warns against a 'deconstruction' of the agent, he makes it quite clear that structuration theory presupposes a 'de-centering' of the agent (*CPST*, pp. 44–5; *CS*, p. xxii). *Praxis*, as I indicated above, stands at the centre of concern in the structurationist ontology. (For arguments against methodological individualism, see *CPST*, pp. 94–5; *CS*, pp. 213–21.)

Over the past several decades individualist accounts of action have been supplanted by schools of thought concerned with the production of social conduct. These schools have contributed a great deal to the development of Giddens's thought. However, there is one tendency among many studies in this area from which structuration theory departs. In most studies of the negotiation of meaning in symbolic interactionism an intrinsic association is presumed between social action and communication. The same tendency is present, albeit to a lesser extent, in ethnomethodological studies which concentrate upon conversational procedures while dealing far less extensively with the non-discursive aspects of the production of social activities.

While Giddens accepts that conversation and the negotiation of meaning are prominent characteristics of social practices, his conception of human agency shifts attention to a more basic aspect of all human conduct: the power to intervene in a course of events or state of affairs (*CS*, pp. 14–16; *CPST*, p. 88; *NRSM*, pp. 110–11). This connection between agency and power logically precedes and informs Giddens's account of social practices. Indeed, power in this generic sense is logically prior to all matters regarding subjectivity or the reflexive monitoring of conduct (*CPST*, p. 92; *CS*, p. 15). This is because social agency depends solely upon the capability actors maintain and exercise to 'make a difference' in the production of definite outcomes, regardless of whether or not they intend (or are aware) that these outcomes occur. Since 'to make a difference' is to transform some aspect of a process or event, agency in structuration theory is equated with transformative capacity.

As matters stand, there is nothing in this account of agency to deny the existence of social uniformities. If social agency results in determinate outcomes, then the same can be said for billiard balls which collide in illustrations of Newtonian mechanics, cells that divide during mitosis, and so forth. But from the uniformitarian standpoint, the production of natural outcomes is not under the control of the entities involved. With a limited allowance for higher species in the animal kingdom, the operations and interactions among elements and objects in nature are said to result from the interplay between their indigenous properties and exogenous circumstances. A distinguishing feature of the exercise of social agency, on the other hand, is that the interventions undertaken by social agents, to some greater or lesser extent, always are under their own control. As Giddens insists, at any phase in any given sequence of conduct any given agent could have acted in a manner somewhat different than she did (*CS*, p. 9; *CCHM*, p. 53; *CPST*, pp. 92, 267, n. 15). To the extent that this point is granted, it becomes difficult to presume that social activity will be produced everywhere and always in a manner that corresponds to the order of nature. In principle, any given pattern of social conduct may be altered by the actors who are engaged in its production. This is not to deny that much of social life is comprised of regularities in conduct, but it does prohibit conceiving these regularities as elements of a trans-historical order of uniformities.

It has been argued that Giddens's contention that agents 'could have acted otherwise' implies that all actors exploit a generous degree of freedom in their conduct (Archer, 1982, pp. 459–60; Carlstein, 1981, pp. 52–3). As Giddens now has indicated at length, structuration theory directs a great deal of attention to both social and material constraints that any individual agent may be unable to change. The topic of constraint will be discussed at length in Chapter 6. But at this point it is germane to draw implications from the structurationist conception of agency with regard to determinism and freedom (note, not free will, since agency stands prior to subjectivity).

In addressing this issue, it is important to bear in mind what has been said regarding the substantial leeway that ontological theories should allow for the diversity of situations and events to which they can be applied. Adopting a fixed position on the degree of freedom or constraint in the exercise of agency prior to the development of substantive theory and empirical research would be to restrict the scope of structuration theory. Giddens's contention that enablements and constraints in the exercise of agency will vary considerably in different historical circumstances (*CS*, p. 179) signifies an unwillingness to establish an *a priori* position on questions of freedom or determinism. Considered in this light, the proviso that, in principle, agents are always capable of 'acting otherwise' represents only a denial of a throughgoing determinism of agency by forces to which the agent must respond automatically. But if structuration theory denies a thoroughgoing determinism it stands equally opposed to unqualified freedom. There are two ways in which to establish this point. First, Giddens argues that in every social relationship there is a dialectic of control involving the asymmetrical access to and manipulation of the resources through which agents influence one another's behaviour. It is central to this concept that no agent engaged in interaction ever is completely autonomous (see Chapter 5). Second, to make a point that anticipates subsequent discussion on the production and reproduction of social activity, the latitude of freedom of agency crucially depends upon the range of practices that an agent is competent to perform. However great this range may be, unqualified freedom is denied because no agent is sufficiently skilled to perform every type of practice that her fellow actors have mastered. Thus, the conception of agency in structuration theory resists the polarities of both a thoroughgoing determinism and unqualified freedom, while preserving all possibilities between these polar extremes.

The historical diversity of social practices

While the structurationist conception of social agency provides fundamental grounds to deny the transposition of the principle of uniformity from nature to social life, this point can be elaborated by turning to Giddens's account of social practices. The capability of intervention is activated in these practices, and such practices 'make a difference' to the course and outcome of social activities that may involve the sequential and interactive generation of numerous practices undertaken by others.

A prominent aspect of Giddens's distinction between nature and society is that the production of social life is a *skilled* performance. Social practices can be understood as skilful procedures, methods, or techniques, appropriately performed by social agents. This definition suggests a correspondence with the concerns of ethnomethodologists. However, as previously noted, while Giddens considers Garfinkel's investigations of the rational accountability of action to be highly significant to an understanding of social conduct, he does not limit his account of practices to discursive accounting procedures *per se* (for pertinent remarks, see *CS*, pp. 78–83). There are a variety of practices that may be conducted in the absence of others: for example, attending to matters of personal cleanliness and appearance, voting by secret ballot. Moreover, as Erving Goffman has demonstrated in exquisite detail, many subtle but consequential modes of physical gestures and bodily postures resist reduction to conversational procedures.

If social life is distinguished from nature by the exercise of agency in social practices, then the basis for this distinction consists in the skills and resources required for any given practice to be performed. It is in addressing the constitution of praxiological skills that human consciousness first arises as a major theme in structuration theory. However, the specific mode of consciousness, i.e. *practical consciousness* of social skills, must be distinguished from *discursive consciousness*, i.e. the level of awareness determined by the ability to put things into words (*CS*, pp. 4–7; see also, *CPST*, pp. 57, 73). The distinctive quality of practical consciousness is that agents need be only tacitly aware of the skills they have mastered, although it generally is possible to concentrate discursive attention on these skills when the occasion arises. It is noteworthy that by stressing actors' tacit awareness of skills and procedures, Giddens is able to propose that *practices can be performed without being directly motivated*; indeed he claims that much day-to-day conduct occurs in this manner (*CS*, p. 6; *CPST*, pp. 59, 218; see also below on the theory of the acting subject).

The awareness of procedures of action can be conceived as a form of knowledge; i.e. a knowledge of 'how to do something', or 'how to go on'. Clarifying Alfred Schutz's conception of 'stocks of knowledge', Giddens refers to *mutual knowledge*: a knowledge that is shared by all who are competent to engage in or recognise the appropriate performance of a social practice or range of practices (*CS*, p. 4; *CPST*, pp. 73, 84, 251–3; *NRSM*, pp. 88–9, 107). Both social practices and mutual knowledge are initially conceived in unitary terms. However, for analytic purposes they may be dealt with as a series of rules. Since these rules refer to tacitly understood procedures, they are to be distinguished from legal codes, bureaucratic regulations, and other rules that are discursively formulated. Two aspects of rules can be identified in analytical terms, although both always are intricately interwoven in knowledge and practice. The semantic aspect of rules refers to the qualitative and procedural meaning of practices, the locales associated with their performance, and some (not all) of their likely outcomes. The normative aspect of rules refer to the same practices, locales, and outcomes from the standpoint of rights and obligations that establish their legitimate or illegitimate nature as well as the appropriate and inappropriate ways in which practices may be carried out. (For a more extensive discussion of rules, see Chapter 7.)

Since social agency involves interventions that alter or transform social events, i.e. that contribute to their production, there must be an aspect of social practices that refers to how this influence is exercised. Giddens introduces the notion of resources to serve this end. Resources refer to the facilities or bases of power to which the agent has access, and which she manipulates to influence the course of interactions with others. It should be understood that the manipulation of resources does not occur in discrete practices. Their mobilisation always involves both semantic and normative aspects of mutual knowledge. Conversely, resources provide the means whereby these semantic and normative rules are actualised. Two categories of resources, which, again, are interwoven in concrete practices, may be distinguished in analytical terms. Authoritative resources are capabilities that generate command over persons (life-chances, spatio-temporal positioning, organisation and relations between human beings). Allocative resources are capabilities that generate command over material objects (raw materials, means of production, produced goods). (For a more extensive discussion of resources, see Chapter 5.)

Unlike social agency, there is nothing in the structurationist conception or social practices that logically entails a rejection of the principle of uniformity. Nevertheless, the burden that a uniformitarian theory of social practices must assume would tax the limits of the most resolute and ingenious positivist. To transpose the principle of uniformity from nature to social practices would require postulates to the effect that: social actors in all historical epochs and across all civilisations are knowledgeable regarding similar procedures of action; that they construe and apply the semantic and normative aspects of these procedures in the same way; and that they have access to the same kinds of resources. These are daunting propositions to uphold. They imply far more than the claim that human beings everywhere have similar needs. Needs (e.g. food, shelter, sex, nurture of the young) can be fulfilled through a variety of different practices, and there may be considerable variation in the degree and kind of satisfaction that results when these practices are carried out. What these uniformitarian postulates actually imply is nothing less than the reduction of historical diversity to fundamental forms of social conduct in the production of social life.

I know of no positivist theorist who has succeeded in identifying trans-historical uniformities in social *praxis*. Even George Homans, whose positivist credentials are beyond question, suggests that the 'historicity' of human behaviour and institution poses difficulties for the type of scientific explanation to which he is committed (Homans, 1974, p. 41). Homans, of course, confines his theoretical propositions to the reinforcement or suppression of social behaviour based upon the rewards and punishment received by social actors. This behaviourist theory is controversial in itself, and it most certainly runs counter to the tenets of structuration theory. But for present purposes it is sufficient to note that Homans, in effect, sidesteps the problem of 'historicity' at the start of his work by bracketing the content of behavioral norms, and *ipso facto* the historical diversity of conduct (Homans, 1974, p. 2).

Giddens refuses to deny historical diversity as a fundamental characteristic of social practices. Human beings, he observes, are unlike animals because they are not biologically programmed to produce social life; although, obviously, some allowances must be made for the universal qualities of the human organisms (*NRSM*, p. 160; but see also *CPST*, p. 244; *CS*, pp. 47, 216–17, 174). In the absence of any instinctive forms of activity it is difficult to imagine any alternative mechanism that would provide for trans-historical regularities of conduct. Moreover, unlike natural processes, it is not intuitively obvious that many uniformities of practice actually exist. Indeed, on the basis of immediate appearances, the variability of practices between geographically and historically remote civilisations and societies seems far more significant than do their broad similarities.

The polymorphic diversity of human practices is one important reason why Giddens holds that the concept of agency cannot be fully elucidated apart from historically specific modes of activity (*CPST*, p. 56). In structuration theory the types of resources to which agents have access, the knowledgeable skills involved in the practices they perform, as well as their discursive knowledge of broader social conditions, always exist within determinate historical and spatial bounds. It may seem paradoxical to affirm the variability of social practices in ontological terms. Ontology, after all, refers only to those aspects of a subject-matter that exist wherever it is found. But here again it must be understood that structuration theory provides an *ontology of potentials*. Proceeding on this basis it is consistent to maintain that one potential possessed by all social agents is the ability to produce historical variations in their own forms of conduct. Because this ability is presented as a potential, it is equally consistent to hold that it is not always exercised.

The obligation incurred in adopting this position is that no aspect of social *praxis* conceived in ontological terms can refer to historically determinate processes or events. This is exactly how Giddens develops his account of social practices in structuration theory. Consider, for example, his analytic distinction between rules and resources as characteristic features of all social practices. Neither of these concepts logically entails any historical content. Moreover, while allocative resources involve the control of material items, and rules are inherently idealist in nature, Giddens makes no claim that either factor must figure more prominently than the other in the production of historical activities and events. Finally, unlike Talcott Parsons, Giddens does not propose any necessary systemic configuration of rules and resources that must be employed in the analysis of historical instances of social conduct. By refraining from stipulations regarding the content, priority, and systematic relationship between rules and resources, Giddens preserves the greatest possible latitude for historical variation. Investigators who draw upon the structurationist ontology therefore are free to address these issues in different ways, depending on the specific forms of practices carried out in any given historical domain, and the theoretical issues they wish to pursue in their works. The only substantive postulate of structuration theory they must honour is that all historical practices and circumstances are subject to change.

Regularities of *praxis*

In many quarters of modern social science a denial of positivist methods, and the uniformitarian outlook they entail, is associated with a suppression of interest in social regularities. This is especially the case for theories and research devoted to the production of social action. While the existence of regularities of *praxis* is acknowledged in virtually all of the numerous programmes in this field, beginning with Weber's idiographically oriented definition of social action there has been a pronounced tendency to focus upon the generation and meaning of instances or forms of activity within the boundaries of the settings within which these activities occur. As I will indicate below, even scholars such as Peter Winch and Randall Collins, who have attempted to address regularities of conduct, ultimately remain wedded to a view of social action *in situ*, and for this reason they fail to provide adequate accounts of how regularities are produced.

While structuration theory requires a rejection of the principle of uniformity, it is equally opposed to the insufficiencies of latter-day theories of action as regards the nature and reproduction of regularities of *praxis*. Giddens, as I have said, absorbs many insights from these theorists. But unlike them, he emphasises that generalisations ultimately based upon the reproduction and consequences of historically bounded forms of conduct are very much in order in social analysis (*CS*, pp. 343–7; *CPST*, pp. 242–4). However, Giddens's critiques of theories of action have not accentuated the problem of regularities, although a critique of this problem is implied in his remarks on the closely connected issue of the neglect by theorists of action of the structural properties of collectivities. The connection between these points can be summarised in terms of the reconciliation of structure and action provided in the duality of structure. Simply put: to neglect the reproduction of regularities in practice makes it impossible to determine how enduring structural properties are generated and sustained; conversely, to neglect structural properties makes it impossible to determine the conditions agents require to reproduce such regularities.

There are advantages to be gained by elaborating Giddens's account of the reproduction of regularities in the duality of structure against the backdrop of the problem of regularities in theories of action. In the first place, it affords the opportunity to clarify the nature and significance of these regularities in structuration theory. In the second place, it is possible to discuss how Giddens takes account of some of the legitimate concerns that have made theorists of action hesitant to deal with the reproduction of regularities. I shall begin by presenting a brief, highly selective, consideration of the problem of regularities in the works of four of the most innovative students of social action: Herbert Blumer, Harold Garfinkel, Peter Winch, and Randall Collins. (The omission of individualist theorists such as Alfred Schutz from this discussion is in keeping with the 'de-centering' of the subject in structuration theory.)

The problem of regularities in theories of action

While George Herbert Mead inspired the development of symbolic interactionism, Herbert Blumer must be acknowledged as the founder of the Chicago School which comprises the dominant trend within this tradition. The Chicago School's neglect of structural issues has been dealt with by both exponents and critics (for summaries, see Meltzer, Petras and Reynolds, 1975, ch. 3; Maines, 1977). Here I shall summarise only those aspects of Blumer's thought that relate directly to issues regarding the problem of regularities.

What often goes unnoticed in Blumer's work is that he does make some allowance for stable and repetitive sequences of interaction (Blumer, 1969, p. 17). Most situations people encounter, he suggests, are associated with, or 'structured' by (Blumer, 1969, p. 86), definitions and interpretations they have previously acquired. Serious consideration to what this contention implies might have led Blumer to conceive of trans-situational properties of interaction from a collective point of view. However, in his most well-known essays Blumer does not follow this route. Instead, his remarks on regularised situations and encounters appear as points of departure from which he launches into issues regarding the significance of 'undefined' situations and novel forms of interaction alignments (Blumer, 1969, pp. 17ff, 86).

It is fundamental to Blumer's perspective on interaction that social acts are generated through symbolically-mediated behaviour between actors. In an essay specifically addressed to the relevance of his perspective to structural issues, Blumer asserts that it is quite common in modern societies for situations to occur in which the actions of participants are not regularised and in which the interpretations of symbols shift and vary. Such actions depart or surpass the structural dimensions of the social organisations in which they occur. In another essay Blumer holds open the possibility of situational novelty in universal, and hence ontological, terms (Blumer, 1969, pp. 18, 88–9). But whatever the status of this point, Blumer's persistent sensitivity to the possibility of novelty in situated conduct corresponds with his methodological proposal for investigators to consider the distinctive, unique, and particular characteristics of every 'object of inquiry' before inferring what it shares in common with other 'objects' in conceptual terms (Blumer, 1969, pp. 148–9). His emphasis upon 'undefined' situations coupled with this methodological proposal effectively enjoin a reduction of the purview of symbolic interactionism to situated instances of social conduct.

Blumer's regard for innovations in interaction should not be dismissed. If agents were unable to originate new forms of activity then it would be impossible to account for the extraordinary variation in social conduct that has been exhibited in the course of human history. But even members of the Chicago School have become dissatisfied with the impediments to the study of regularities and collective aspects of social life that necessarily result from Blumer's reductive point of view. Proposals now exist to merge symbolic interactionism with the trans-situational concerns of semiotics (see MacCannell, 1976; Perinbanayagam, 1985). Until now there has been little dialogue between symbolic interactionism and structuration theory. While semiotically informed symbolic interactionism probably would continue to differ from structuration theory on a number of salient points, it would create openings for fruitful exchanges in the future.

As in Blumer's works, there is a strand of thought in Harold Garfinkel's original formulation of the ethnomethodological research programme that might lead to an interest in the reproduction of regularities of social practices. This strand of thought is made evident when Garfinkel suggests that members of a society maintain standardised expectations regarding the character and consequences of social action. But by the same token 'members' cannot be regarded as 'judgemental dopes' who merely conform to existent standards. To the contrary, Garfinkel insists that standardised actions are discovered, created, and sustained by social actors during the course of these actions themselves (Garfinkel, 1967, pp. 66–7). It is consistent with this point for Garfinkel (with Harvey Sacks) to propose that everyday activities exhibit a formal structure independent of any given cohort of actors, but produced and recognised as the practical, situated accomplishment of the members of a particular cohort (Garfinkel and Sacks, 1970, p. 346). This proposal suggests two lines of inquiry that may be pursued: (i) the practices and procedures by which the standardised features of forms of activity are produced may be thematised; or (ii) attention may be confined to the production and recognition of these forms in particular situations (Garfinkel, 1967, p. 10). While ethnomethodologists engaged in conversation analysis have advanced along the first of these lines, Garfinkel and others have pursued the second, more situated and specific approach.

This reversion to the situation stems from the way in which Garfinkel conceives the production of accounts and contexts summarised in the notions 'indexicality' and 'reflexivity'. Indexicality means that all items raised for discussion are inherently equivocal apart from accounting procedures through which they are assembled as particular features of an ethnographic context. This context is composed of items indexed during the previous course of discussion. Hence the accounts produced by 'members' are reflexively tied to the socially organised occasion where they are generated. Whatever is typical or potentially repetitive does not depend upon any 'context-in-general' but rather upon the reflexive indexicality of the accounts generated through the use of methods in situated instances of conduct (Garfinkel, 1967, pp. 4–10).

As John Heritage recently has demonstrated, Garfinkel's emphasis upon the production of indexical accounts in situated contexts is coextensive with a finitist perspective in which every use of concepts, rules, typifications, etc., must ultimately be referred to specific, local, contingent determinants (Heritage, 1984, pp. 120–9). Since Garfinkel (1967, p. 10) acknowledges an 'enormous standardisation' in how organised interaction is accomplished and recognised, this finitism does not imply Blumer's caution regarding the contingent possibility of novelty in forms of conduct. It stems instead from an insistence upon rigorous attention to nuance and detail that is a hallmark of ethnomethodological research in the works of Garfinkel as well as those whom he has influenced.

Garfinkel's finitist deference to the complexity of social procedures is expressed in a series of methodological policies he recommends: policies that effectively foreclose an interest in social reproduction. These proposals, in brief, stipulate that: every feature of any case of inquiry be addressed as a particular, located,·

organisation of practices; that such practices be viewed as contingent accomplishments; and that every setting be viewed as self-organising with respect to its intelligibility and representation of social order (Garfinkel, 1967, pp. 32–4). The effect of these policies is to place methodological brackets around questions regarding both the reproducibility of social practices as well as the intrusion of enduring properties of collectivities into locally organised methods and procedures. Garfinkel's well-known policy of 'ethnomethodological indifference' also brackets the consequences of social conduct (Garfinkel and Sacks, 1970, p. 345). Hence, while Garfinkel may acknowledge an 'enormous standardisation' in how activities are organised, at the same time he also recommends that instances of common activities be recognised for purposes of inquiry as 'another first time' (Garfinkel, 1967, p. 10; for developments in ethnomethodology that converge with structuration theory, see Maynard and Wilson, 1980; Wilson and Zimmerman, 1979–80).

A shift of concern from the generation of specific instances of situated conduct to reproduced forms of conduct is evident in the work of Peter Winch. Winch's post-Wittgensteinian conception of the objectives of social science underscores the point that when participation in a general kind of activity occurs, the participants rely upon rules which specify what is to count as 'doing the same kind of thing' in relation to that activity. All participants have learned of these activities in similar ways, and the rules on which they draw can thus be said to rest upon a context of common activity within a social group (Winch, 1958, pp. 83–7).

To put matters in this way suggests that Winch concentrates upon how established regularities of conduct are reproduced through a reliance upon commonly shared rules. But the objectives Winch upholds for social science actually move in an entirely different direction. Instead of entertaining questions regarding social *praxis* as a process of social reproduction, Winch proposes to accept 'forms of life' as they stand. Social scientists, Winch believes, should study modes of conduct in order to understand them: i.e. in order to give accounts of the nature of social phenomena. Shared rules of conduct become sociologically relevant as criteria to identify and elucidate these kinds of activity (Winch, 1958, pp. 40ff, 86–7). This standpoint, it should be added, in very general respects draws Winch toward the position of continental philosophers of hermeneutics such as Hans-Georg Gadamer.

That empirical inquiry in the social sciences must rely upon interpretative accounts justified by criteria participants use to recognise their own activities is accepted as a methodological necessity in structuration theory (see Cohen, 1984; *CS*, pp. 339ff). But social scientists cannot rest content with issues regarding the elucidation of recurrent forms of conduct. They also must be concerned with procedures of reproduction and social transformation, as well as with the consequences that ensue from general kinds of activities. Therefore, while Winch's notion of rules verges on becoming a concept that can be dealt with from a trans-situational point of view, because he overlooks these topics established rules which provide for the reproduction of regularities merely form the boundary of his approach (*NRSM*, p. 51).

Randall Collins's works on the 'micro-foundations' of 'macro-sociology' offer a useful counterpoint to Winch's approach. Like Winch, Collins accepts the iterative nature of social activities. But unlike Winch, Collins retains a central interest in the processes through which forms of conduct are reproduced by absorbing analytical insights from Erving Goffman as well as from several leading ethnomethodologists. But the most pronounced point of contrast between Collins and Winch is that Collins denies that trans-situational rules of conduct contribute to the constitution of persistent modes of social activity.

One of Collins's central contentions is that all varieties of 'macro-structure' can be translated and reduced to quantitative aggregations, distributions, and configurations of 'micro-events'. Collins is led to this position by the ethnomethodological strategy of ultra-detailed empirical research. Transposing this strategy into a theoretical key, Collins suggests that while individuals within 'micro-situations' may harbour 'macro-views' and make 'macro-references' in their conversations, such views and references are merely aggregates of their moment-by-moment sensory and subjective experiences, glossed or reified in thought and discourse. Since all social reality is 'micro-experience', Collins denies that social rules, norms, and values are appropriately conceived on a 'macro-situational' basis (Collins, 1981a, pp. 991, 995; 1981b, p. 105).

A problem Collins now must resolve is: in the absence of trans-situational rules or norms, how can an account of reproduction of regularities be adduced from situated instances of repetitive conduct? Although he acknowledges that cultural resources and emotional dispositions enter into the reproduction of or change in patterns of interpersonal relations, he does not propose either phenomenon as the bedrock for an account of social reproduction. Cultural resources are topics of conversation invoking a common cognitive reality among participants in interaction. But this must be balanced against one of Collins's crucial claims, which is that human beings operate within a very limited range of cognitive capacities (Collins, 1981a, p. 995; 1981b, p. 103). Extrapolating from Collins's arguments, it also appears that while emotions provide propensities (e.g. confidence, warmth, enthusiasm) to act in certain ways, such propensities cannot account for the specific kinds of activity reproduced in any given situation. Ultimately, Collins provides a basis for reproduction by introducing a surprising materialist twist into conventional ethnomethodological views of the contextuality of social activities. 'The micro-reality of any "social structure"', he contends, 'is some patterns of repetitive associations among people in relation to some physical object or place . . . because human cognitive capacities do not allow people to organize in any other way' (Collins, 1981a, p. 996). 'The repetitive behaviours . . . are primarily based upon the *physical* plane' (Collins, 1981b, p. 103).

Giddens has lodged a number of objections to Collins's approach, but he has not dealt with this materialist account of social reproduction (*CS*, pp. 140–2). To anticipate later discussion it should be noted that the physical aspects of social locales play a prominent role in social reproduction from the standpoint of structuration theory. But Collins's reduction of the reproduction of conduct to repeated instances of activity in the same physical circumstances overlooks the following point: while material objects and the physical capacities and appearances of the human body may constrain certain modes of conduct and facilitate others, these material circumstances in and of themselves do not provide social actors with the competence to reproduce forms of social conduct time after time in the same type of setting. Indeed, in many physical settings the same actors may undertake different activities on different occasions (e.g. in family kitchens, on city streets). Moreover, the material requisites for at least some modes of conduct may not be terribly restrictive in nature. Given face-to-face propinquity, actors may converse, hold meetings, and so forth, in a wide (but not unlimited) range of settings. Given modern means of communication and transportation even bodily co-presence is unnecessary for many significant forms of interaction to be carried out (see below). But in all cases, unless actors sustain a knowledge of how standardised aspects of conduct are appropriately performed in suitable locales they will be unable to reproduce these activities as a matter of course in their day-to-day lives. Acknowledgement that social agents sustain an ongoing awareness of social skills and procedures requires a greater respect for human cognitive capacities than Collins allows. It equally suggests that an adequate approach to social reproduction cannot avoid some reference to trans-situational rules implicated in these skills and procedures.

Social institutions: practices and context

Summarising the items mentioned in the foregoing perspective yields a series of issues that are addressed in Giddens's account of the reproduction of regularities of *praxis*. As opposed to Blumer and Garfinkel, Giddens places emphasis upon persistently-repeated forms of conduct; as opposed to Winch, Giddens concentrates directly upon how forms of conduct are reproduced; finally, as opposed to Collins, Giddens ascribes great importance to the trans-situational nature of human social skills. But these scholars also raise points with which Giddens must contend. The account of reproduced forms of conduct he presents in structuration theory sustains Garfinkel's concern for the reflexive elaboration of context and action while incorporating a respect for the physical settings of conduct that absorbs points raised by Collins. In the duality of structure Giddens establishes how social practices are reproduced but also preserves Blumer's insistence upon opportunities for innovation.

The absence of an adequate conception of reproduced forms of conduct in many theories of social action stands behind Giddens's call for an *institutional theory of everyday life* ('AI', pp. 164–5; *CPST*, p. 81). The term 'institutional' is not used here in an off-hand manner but rather has a programmatic intent. The concept of *social institutions* in structuration theory specifically refers to routinised practices that are carried out or recognised by the majority of members of a collectivity (*CS*, p. 17; 'AI', p. 164; *CPST*, p. 80). Institutions in this processual sense should not be confused with references to institutions which denote forms of social organisation. Giddens, incidentally, is on solid philological ground in his use of this term. According to Raymond Williams (1983, pp. 168–9), references to institutions as established practices entered common English parlance well before alternative references to institutions as organisations were widely employed.

Most social scientists acknowledge pervasive and enduring repetition of customary practices in tribal societies and other small-scale groups. But the extraordinary diversity of social practices in modern Western civilization obscures the extent to which institutionalised routines are constitutive of the daily transaction of events. Some mundane but nevertheless highly consequential modes of conduct are reproduced throughout Western civilisation and beyond: e.g. the payment of taxes on income and profits to support state activities, the establishment of labour contracts between workers and employers, the use of the automobile. Other routines such as formal political procedures, culinary conventions, etc. are essential to the course and cycle of social events in specific societies or a small group of societies. Less extensive domains in which institutionalised forms of conduct are reproduced include particular social classes as well as age-specific, gender-specific, ethnic and regional groups.

An emphasis upon reflexive contextuality as an integral element of social encounters is sustained in Giddens's account of social institutions; although he departs from Garfinkel by absorbing Goffman's insights into the many aspects of contextuality that are established in non-verbal gestures. However, unlike either scholar, Giddens underscores the point that agents can constitute the meaningful context and content of social conduct in an institutionalised manner (*CPST*, pp. 83–4; *CS*, p. 119). To accept that context and conduct may be reproduced, necessarily entails a rejection of the finitist methodological policy that Garfinkel recommends, but it does not deny the utility of adopting a finitist perspective for certain purposes. In the first place, while reproduced practices exhibit a certain degree of consistency that allows them to be conceived as institutionalised regularities, many of the more subtle aspects involved in how they are reproduced may remain unknown: for example, matters of sequencing and timing of conversational procedures. The finitist concentration upon the empirical investigation of individual instances of the production of such practices continues to be the most appropriate way in which these subtle, yet often highly significant, aspects of *praxis* can be discovered and analysed. The results of such studies ultimately deepen our understanding of how regularities of *praxis* are reproduced. In the second place, every instance in which the reproduction of practices and context occurs manifests certain idiosyncracies such as differences in personal mannerisms, as well as local references to determinate circumstances and affairs. Whenever these or other particulars of specific situations are at issue, finitist inquiries are in order.

The physical aspects of social settings play a prominent part in the provision of conditions for the reproduction of institutional activities. Giddens accepts that the nature and contours of physical objects, material boundaries, and the corporeal characteristics of the human body, shape and facilitate the reproduction of both context and conduct. But unlike Collins, Giddens proposes that physical circumstances always interweave with social routines in reproduced practices. The crucial point is that the physical aspects of settings do not simply impinge upon social conduct. Instead, they are mobilised and categorised during the course of social action and interaction (*CPST*, pp. 206–7; *NRSM*, pp. 106–7).

What is implied here is a synthesis of idealist and materialist factors in social reproduction. The reflexive attention to the context of social encounters (which Giddens considers to be an active process of perceptual organisation: *CS*, pp. 46–7) coupled with conversational procedures, may be conceived in idealist terms. Modern means of communication permit a limited degree of contextuality to be generated by agents who are not physically co-present. But the most well-developed modes of contextuality are generated by agents who are in close proximity to one another. Here agents are in position to perceive the doings of others, and to perceive that others are perceiving them as well. Diffuse forms of contextuality that may be sustained on this basis can be distinguished from the more intensive forms of context reciprocally generated by conversational and non-verbal procedures in face-to-face encounters (*CS*, pp. 67–73).

The concept of *locale* in structuration theory joins perceptual and conversational procedures to the material circumstances of social conduct. Locales may be designated by physical circumstances and human artifacts associated with institutionalised activities, but the concept of locale specifically refers to how these material aspects of social settings are used during the course of social routines (*CS*, pp. 118–19; *CCHM*, pp. 39, 161; *CPST*, pp. 206–7; *NRSM*, pp. 106–7). Putting matters in this way departs from Collins by suggesting the possibility of variation in the degree to which material circumstances influence the transaction of conduct. While many practices inherently involve the use of items in specific settings (e.g. agricultural and industrial production), other practices may involve the use of items that are not fixed to one spatial location. However, even in the latter case determinate material boundaries generally are required so that agents may establish a reflexive awareness and engage in discourse. For example, academics find it difficult to create the context for their lectures before large classes being held out of doors.

The reproduction of action and structure in the duality of structure

Giddens's account of the reproduction of institutional practices in the duality of structure provides a basis for his reconciliation of action and structure. It thus represents a dramatic departure not only from prevailing theories of action but also from theories that concentrate upon the properties of social collectivities. Although contrasts between this account and theories of action will be discussed here, it is important to mention an item in Giddens's conceptualisation of collectivities that will be elaborated in subsequent chapters. In structuration theory the patterning of relations in collectivities is constituted by interrelated (but politically asymmetrical) practices reproduced across time and space in various locales. (The term 'structuration' refers to the reproduction of social relations across time and space as transacted in the duality of structure.) Consistent with the ontological flexibility of structuration theory at large, Giddens holds open for substantive inquiry all questions regarding specific systemic patterns as well as the degree to which systems are stable, organised, and permeable. However, he does draw a basic distinction between two modes of integration. *Social integration* concerns reciprocities of practices on the level of face-to-face interaction. *System integration* refers to reciprocal relations between those who are physically absent. For the time being I shall address the reproduction of practices in the duality of structure without taking this distinction into account. To do so I shall concentrate upon the reproduction of individual practices carried out in a system of indeterminate dimensions.

According to Giddens, the duality of structure refers to:

> the essential recursiveness of social life as constituted in social practices: structure is both medium and outcome of the reproduction of practices. Structure enters simultaneously into the constitution of . . . social practices, and 'exists' in the generating moments of this constitution. (*CPST*, p. 5)

It should be evident that none of the theorists of action discussed in this chapter are in position to propose a similar point of view. What is more noteworthy, however, is that during the course of other abbreviated remarks on the conditions associated with regularities of conduct, each of these theorists, with the exception of Collins, mentions an insight that figures prominently in Giddens's conception of the duality of structure. Both Blumer and Garfinkel acknowledge in passing that understandings or expectations are drawn upon and made manifest in and through the procedures whereby 'structured' modes of conduct are repeatedly undertaken during the routine course of day-to-day life. Winch makes a similar point when he suggests that established forms of activity are undertaken by agents on the basis of rules they have learned in the past. In the duality of structure Giddens expands upon his own conception of how rules are implicated in the performance of social practices (see below). Rules now appear as generalisable aspects of procedures that are drawn upon in the reproduction of regularities of *praxis*, a process of reproduction that serves to regenerate these rules as established features of historically-bounded social domains.

Considered against the backdrop of the pre-eminent concern of theorists of action with situated instances and forms of social conduct, Giddens's most significant contribution in the duality of structure is to treat rules regarding aspects of institutionalised conduct as structural properties of social collectivities. Because of the prominent role that this insight plays in the overall development of structuration theory it deserves to be clarified with the greatest possible precision. Since rules are made manifest only when institutionalised practices are reproduced (see below), they cannot be conceived exclusively in holistic terms. Nevertheless, if rules are to be identified in collective terms they must be irreducible without remainder to individual situations where specific instances of conduct are carried out. (This is a modification of the criterion of irreducibility developed in Mandelbaum, 1955.) Irreducibility here implies that rules of conduct are trans-situational, in the sense that they are involved in forms of conduct that are (i) reproduced and recognised many times over during the routine activities undertaken by members of a collectivity, and (ii) reproduced and recognised for a considerable period in the history of that group. Where these criteria apply, rules of conduct may be conceived as trans-situational properties of a collectivity that enter into the reproduction of institutionalised conduct.

Giddens's conception of rules of conduct can be shown to conform to both of these criteria. To elaborate this point it is useful to return to the notion of mutual knowledge, which, as has been indicated in the previous discussion, subsumes the semantic and normative aspects of rules regarding the appropriate performance of social practices. Consider now the characteristics of mutual knowledge pertaining to institutionalised practices reproduced on numerous occasions by numerous agents in daily life. It should be evident that this knowledge cannot be thoroughly reduced to any specific situation of conduct. Indeed, at the same moment numerous agents in many different settings may draw upon the same form of mutual knowledge to reproduce the same general kind of activity.

The case studies of deviant practices that have been instrumental in the early development of symbolic interactionalism and ethnomethodology are somewhat misleading in this regard. From a structural point of view the most prominent rules of conduct are those which are most commonly instituted in mundane practices. A useful thought experiment to determine the structural significance of rules is to imagine what difference it would make to the routine transaction of social events if agents ceased to perform the procedures associated with a determinate category of mutual knowledge. Thus, to take a Durkheimian example, if it is correct to ascribe a great structural significance in Western civilisation to rules regarding the rights and duties of individuals, then the removal of practices in which these rules are in play would make it difficult to sustain the routine course of social events. Such practices might range from subtle procedures of self-assertion and tactful respect for the doings of anonymous persons, to more obvious ways in which the civic rights and obligations of individuals are exercised and fulfilled.

Mutual knowledge of rules of social *praxis* also conform to the criterion of historical persistence. A prerequisite here is that this knowledgeability must be associated with practices carried out in a collectivity beyond the lifetime of any agent or any cohort of agents. A second prerequisite is the designation of means whereby mutual knowledge is preserved and transported across time and space between situations where such practices are reproduced. Giddens's insight here considerably extends the incidental references by Blumer and Garfinkel to the common understandings agents bring to 'structured' forms of conduct. 'Memory traces' regarding how things are done, he suggests, provide a basic means by which mutual knowledge is 'stored' by social agents (*CPST*, p. 64; *CCHM*, p. 35). The type of memory at issue here should not be confused with self-reflective recall of past experiences and events. Memory in the latter sense can be verbally expressed and therefore corresponds to what Giddens terms discursive consciousness. Mutual knowledge fundamentally is sustained and recalled in a tacit manner on the level of practical consciousness.

Theorists of action have provided few insights into the exercise of power. However, it is important to note that resources as well as rules are considered by Giddens to be structural properties of collectivities. In Chapter 5 it will be necessary to consider the significance Giddens ascribes to the storage of authoritative and allocative resources as well as issues regarding the dialectic of control. For present purposes, however, it is sufficient to mention that resources conceived as properties of collectivities do not exert an independent influence upon the reproduction of practices in the duality of structure. Instead, the meshing of rules and resources in institutionalised conduct results in strategies of control: i.e. ways in which agents apply knowledge regarding the manipulations of the resources to which they have access in order to reproduce their strategic autonomy over the actions of others. While resources may be conceptualised as structural properties of collectivities for analytic purposes, strategies of control represent aspects of *praxis* that are reproduced in the duality of structure.

To say that social routines are reproduced in the duality of structure is not to claim that the routinisation of social life is inevitable. Social practices do not reproduce themselves, social agents do, and it must be borne in mind that from the standpoint of structuration theory social agents always are seen to retain the capability to act otherwise than they do. Giddens preserves this crucial qualification when he notes: 'all action exists in continuity with the past, which supplies *the means of its initiation*' (my italics, *CPST*, p. 70). Mutual knowledge and resources conceived in structural terms establish the continuity with the past to which Giddens refers, but they serve only as the media for the reproduction of institutionalised practices and contexts. *There is no guarantee that agents will reproduce regularities of conduct as they previously have done.* For this reason Giddens makes it a matter of principle that: 'the concept of social reproduction ... is not explanatory: all reproduction is contingent and historical' (*CCHM*, p. 27; see also *CPST*, p. 113).

The contingencies of reproduction to which Giddens refers incorporate Blumer's concern for the possibility of innovation in social conduct. But this is only one of several ways in which agents may depart from established routines. First, agents may make mistakes which constitute situational improprieties or cultural lapses. However, the frequency of these errors necessarily is limited. As Giddens notes, if there is any continuity to social life, actors must be right most of the time (*CS*, p. 90). Second, actors who retain the competence and capacity to reproduce routine practices may refrain from doing so. In certain respects this forbearance itself may comprise a skilful course of conduct (e.g. strikes, tactful neglect of situational improprieties). But the alteration of established modes of conduct, the possibility of novelty from Blumer's point of view, undoubtedly represents the most significant contingency of social reproduction. The generation of unprecedented forms of conduct provides the praxiological basis for social transformation. It therefore is extremely important to note that Giddens conceives the possibility for change as inherent in every act of social reproduction (*NRSM*, p. 102). But it is equally significant that continuities of conduct always accompany and facilitate the generation of discontinuities in social *praxis*. Indeed, many institutionalised routines continue to be reproduced even during the most radical episodes of social change (*CS*, pp. 26, 87; *CPST*, pp. 216–17).

It is fundamental to the duality of structure that the structural properties of collectivities (rules and resources) not only serve as the media of social reproduction but also are reproduced as an *outcome* of this process. None of the theorists of action discussed in this essay exhibit a concern for the outcome of social activity. (On the other hand, collectivist theorists such as Durkheim, who underscore structural properties that 'emerge' from social conduct fail to supply an adequate account of social *praxis*.) But the claim that structural properties are reproduced in routine practices requires precise clarification.

As is indicated in Giddens's summary definition of the duality of structure quoted above, structure 'exists' in a manifest form only when it is instantiated in social practices. It otherwise persists between instances of social reproduction only as 'memory-traces' sustained by knowledgeable social agents. To say that structure is reproduced in the duality of structure means that structure is *reconstituted* in each instance where a pervasive and enduring procedure is reproduced. This reconstitution of structure 're-grooves' agents' familiarity with established cognitive outlooks (*CS*, p. 104). That is to say, it reinforces the mutual knowledge of rules and the strategies of control of resources associated with these practices, both for those who actually participate in them as well as for those who recognise that these practices are being performed. This point equally applies to the reproduction of context. In every instance where agents reflexively monitor physical, social, and temporal elements of their circumstances in a routine manner, they reflexively regenerate the contextual relevance of these elements (*CPST*, pp. 83–4). Of course no single act of social reproduction is sufficient in itself to reconstitute structural properties. But the continual repetition and recognition of familiar modes of conduct by numerous members of a social collectivity or group embeds an awareness of these practices deep within their tacit memory of the familiar features of social *praxis* in the circumstances of their daily lives. Conversely, when certain forms of conduct cease or are transformed, the mutual knowledge of the specific configuration of rules and resources associated with these practices begins to lapse and fade. Gradually, through the passing of the generations, the only way to retrieve knowledge of the structuration of these practices is through whatever historical documentation may have been preserved.

The theory of the acting subject

The centrality of *praxis* in structuration theory is nowhere more evident than in the 'decentering' of the subject mentioned earlier in this chapter. Simply put, in structuration theory it is the 'making' of history and the production of social life, rather than the 'makers' or producers of social circumstances and events, to which ontological priority is ascribed. But to 'decenter' the agent is by no means to eliminate a concern for the agent. The practices and interactions through which social life is constituted are the ongoing accomplishment of human beings who retain the capabilities to generate these modes of conduct, and the disposition to activate these capabilities at appropriate moments in social life. Giddens's theory of the acting subject presents a conceptual account of the agent which stands in a complementary relation to issues regarding *praxis* which have been previously introduced. Indeed, certain concepts relevant to the theory of the acting subject already appear in the account of social *praxis*. These include: the distinction between discursive and practical consciousness; the notion that many practices may be carried out without being directly motivated; and the priority of agency *vis-à-vis* subjectivity in social *praxis*.

The term '*acting* subject' signifies Giddens's objective to link concepts relevant to the agent to the exercise of agency in social *praxis*. At the same time it also connotes significant departures from how the agent is conceived in collectivist and what might be termed hermeneutic voluntarist traditions of thought (see *CS*, pp. 1–2). Collectivist theorists, from Comte and Durkheim to modern functionalists, morphologists, and structuralists, treat agents as malleable or manipulable constituents of social life, who are guided or directed in their social conduct by supra-individual forces or circumstances over which they have no control. Hermeneutic voluntarist theories, whose roots run at least as far back as the writings of Wilhelm Dilthey, treat agents as acting subjects, but this action primarily involves the meanings they individually ascribe to historical events, cultural items, and social acts. Structuration theory's account of the acting subject departs from both points of view by conceiving the agent, in the first instance, as a human being who engages in processes through which social life is constituted. In so far as the agent engages in institutionalised procedures, the structural conditions of social life – as they have been defined in this chapter – have a direct bearing on the individual's activities. Moreover, if the description of meaning to conduct is broadly defined to include tacit as well as discursive interpretations, then it too must be taken into account. But the accent still falls on the actor as agent, i.e. as one who 'makes' or produces social activities and events.

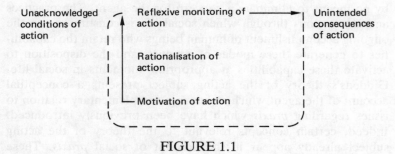

FIGURE 1.1

Figure 1.1 presents the core of Giddens's theory of the acting subject, the stratification model of the agent (*CPST*, p. 56; *CS*, p. 5). At the centre of this model one finds the reflexive monitoring of action, the rationalisation of action, and the motivation of action. All three terms refer to aspects of the agents's subjectivity. But it should be noted that these are not *states* of mind, but rather subjective *processes* which are sustained by the agent on an ongoing basis. These processes must be understood in relation to action, relations indicated by the connections in the model from action to the generation of unintended consequences, and from unintended consequences back to the unacknowledged conditions of action. I shall defer consideration of these connections until after the subjective processes have been discussed.

The reflexive monitoring and rationalisation of action

The reflexive monitoring of action refers to the processes through which agents attend to the ongoing flow of social life. These monitoring processes are reflexive in several analytically disting-uishable, but concretely interrelated ways. On the one hand, agents attend to their own conduct, a form of monitoring which is grounded in the rationalisation of action (see below). But as part of the same monitoring procedures, agents attend to the doing of others as well as to the socially constituted significance of material and temporal aspects of the settings where it is appropriate for specific modes of conduct to be performed. Each monitoring process is highly complex in itself, but there also is an inherently reflexive connection between them in so far as the monitoring of social contexts and events as they occur influences the agent's monitoring of her conduct, while that conduct 'makes a difference' to the doing of others, and the collaborative generation of contexts.

Given the limited capacity of agents to maintain a discursive awareness of the multitude of diverse aspects of their own conduct as well as the conduct of others, much reflexive monitoring occurs tacitly on the level of practical consciousness. This should be evident from earlier remarks. But it also should be noted that the reflexive monitoring of conduct most often occurs as a continuous flow rather than as a punctuated series of moments of attention. This is because the activity being monitored is an ongoing process in itself (*NRSM*, pp. 74–5; *CPST*, p. 55; *CS*, p. 5). It is an immediate implication of this point that a distinction must be drawn between social activity as it is tacitly monitored, and the discursive identification of acts, characterised and interpreted by an agent, or by agents in interaction, through the use of available frames of meaning (*NRSM*, pp. 78–9). The distinction here is that the identification of acts breaks into the ongoing flow of tacitly monitored conduct by way of a pause during which actors discur-sively attend to what has been done in the recent or more distant past, and/or what may be planned for the future. Giddens under-scores the significance of agents' tacit monitoring by noting that discursive moments of attention generally occur only when queries are made to clarify the meaning (both semantic and normative) of events and/or circumstances which are not well understood (see *NRSM*, pp. 80–1; *CPST*, p. 55).

The rationalisation of action, the second subjective process in Figure 1.1, should not be equated with the agent's giving of reasons to others, or even the capability to supply reasons upon request. Both are associated with the rationalisation of action on the level of discursive consciousness. However, the process of rationalisation at issue here primarily occurs on the level of practical consciousness, where the agent grounds her monitoring of her own conduct in her intentions. Intentionality also has a conceptual definition which must be clearly understood (for an extended discussion, see *CS*, pp. 8–14; see also below, Chapter 4). The type of tacit intentionality agents instil in their conduct may be conceived as referring to the subject's purposive application of mutual knowledge. In more detail, intentionality refers to the subject's knowledge or belief that specific kinds of practices will have a particular quality or outcome, and to the subject's use of this knowledge to achieve the quality or outcome involved (*CS*, p. 10; *NRSM*, pp. 76–7). The rationalisation of action thus occurs as a process in which agents maintain a tacit understanding of what their actions accomplish in social life. *It is of the utmost importance to recognise here that neither the concept of intentions nor that of the rationalisation of action in any way implies that agents are, or in principle can be, aware – tacitly or discursively – of all of the consequences of their activities.* Unintended consequences are not only possible, but are recurrent features of social life in the ontology of structuration theory (see below).

Prosaic examples of the nature of and connection between the acting subject's reflexive monitoring and rationalisation of action are very much in order, because these processes occur continuously during the agent's participation in institutionalised routines. Consider, then, an agent involved in a most prosaic form of conduct in modern social life – the exchange of currency for consumer goods. Where the price is fixed and the procedural interaction with the shop clerk is routine, the agent's conduct may seem casual and relaxed. But the agent tacitly is engaged in a complex procedure. In the first place, the monitoring of price, the selection of currency in appropriate amounts, and the transfer of possession of the goods requires a disciplined attention to detail. This attention, in turn, is grounded in the agent's knowledge that a cash transaction results in the purchase and ownership of the item with all of the rights, opportunities, and responsibilities that purchase and ownership entail. From the vantage point of the monitoring and rationalisation of action, the acting subject appears as a disciplined, skilful, and purposive agent even when engaged in routine activities which she has performed many, many times before.

Precisely because of the routine nature of so many social practices, agents often have no need to discursively explain to others their intentions as they go about their day-to-day affairs. However, circumstances may arise when an agent's conduct puzzles others, and prompts them to ask the agent for a reason for what she is doing (*CS*, p. 6; *NRSM*, p. 76). Here a distinction must be drawn between the rationalisation of action and the discursive accounts of reasons that agents provide. This is because the accounts of reasons offered in discourse may diverge from the rationalisation of conduct in a variety of ways, including the rendering of incomplete accounts, dissimulation, etc. However, having made this point clear, it also should be noted that the reasons agents offer comprise the principal basis on which others evaluate their social competence (*CS*, p. 4).

The motivation of action and ontological security

The motivation of action is less directly implicated in the flow of social conduct than are the monitoring and rationalisation of action. This point is consistent with Giddens's observation that many social practices in day-to-day life are performed without being directly motivated. In mentioning this point in the discussion of social *praxis* it was sufficient to note that practices which do not involve an obvious motive occur when agents draw upon tacitly understood forms of knowledge. This insight must be considerably expanded so that a distinction may be made between the monitoring and rationalisation of action on the one hand, and the motivation of action on the other. According to Giddens:

> If reasons refer to the grounds of action, motives refer to the wants which prompt it. However, motivation is not as directly bound up with the continuity of action as are its reflexive

monitoring or rationalisation. Motivation refers to potential for action rather than the mode in which action is chronically carried on by the agent. Motives tend to have a direct purchase on action only in relatively unusual circumstances, situations which in some way break with routines. For the most part motives supply overall plans or programmes – 'projects' in Schutz's term – within which a range of conduct is enacted. Much of our day-to-day conduct is not directly motivated. (*CS*, p. 6; see also *NRSM*, pp. 85–6)

While the distinction between the monitoring and rationalisation of action *versus* the motivation of action set forth in this passage requires no explication, a fundamental question remains to be addressed: if so many practices in day-to-day life are not directly motivated, why then do agents continue to chronically engage in the performance of so many routines. To answer this question requires a concern for *unconscious* motives which *indirectly* dispose agents to undertake institutionalised forms of conduct.

In Giddens's theory of the acting subject, the unconscious comprises a third level of subjectivity sharply separated from both discursive and practical consciousness by virtue of mechanisms of repression and distortion which interfere with agents' recall of unconscious cognitions and dispositions. This view of the unconscious differs from Freudian accounts because, according to Giddens (*CS*, pp. 4–5, 49–50, 93–104; *CPST*, pp. 58–9), the unconscious rarely impinges upon the monitoring and rationalisation of action. Yet the unconscious nevertheless may have an indirect purchase on action. In order to make this point clear, Giddens selectively absorbs insights developed by ego-psychologists (e.g. Erik Erikson, Harry Stack Sullivan, Abram Kardiner) who propose that at the origin of the unconscious lies a basic orientation to the avoidance of anxiety, and the preservation of self-esteem. This orientation initially develops during the primary socialisation process where a 'basic security system' is formed by the infant in interaction with a mothering agent. The 'basic security system' consists of a set of unconscious mechanisms to guard against anxiety-provoking stimuli including mistrust, shame or doubt, and guilt. The mechanisms are unconscious, in part, because they are formed prior to the infant's full acquisition of language (*CS*, p. 57; see also pp. 51–60 *passim*).

The 'basic security system' connects to the unconscious motivation which disposes adults to engage in routines because, according to Giddens (*CS*, pp. 54–5), in adults as in infants the control of diffuse anxiety is the most generalised motivational origin of human conduct. As the infant matures, unconscious motives associated with the avoidance of anxiety shift from the predictable, caring routines established by parental figures to the predictable routine modes of conduct in less circumscribed realms of day-to-day life. The subjective state of mind which is protected by the predictability of routines (as well as by procedures of trust and tact in interaction) is termed by Giddens, following R. D. Laing, a sense of 'ontological security' (*CPST*, p. 219; *CS*, p. 50). Now the experience of, and motivating orientation toward, ontological security may be constituted on an unconscious level of subjectivity, but the maintenance of ontological security is very much an ongoing accomplishment of the acting subject which occurs in and through her participation in routines (*NRSM*, p. 117). The performance of routines, therefore, not only is essential to the reproduction of social *praxis*, and hence to the constitution of institutionalised forms of social life, it also plays a prominent part in the constitution of the mechanics of the personality of the agent (*CS*, p. 60).

As evidence for the contribution of routine modes of conduct to the personality of agents, Giddens cites observation by Bruno Bettleheim into the consequences of the calculated deroutinisation of life imposed upon inmates in Nazi concentration camps (*CS*, pp. 61–4). In 'critical situations' such as these, agents no longer experience any certitude in the predictability of routines, and therefore lose their sense of ontological security. The changes which ensue are profound. Agents no longer have a sense of any autonomy of action, even though some limited degree of autonomy may remain open to them. At the extreme, agents lose even the most basic sense of control of their own physical movements as embodied agents. Based upon these observations and insights Giddens concludes:

> Ordinary day-to-day social life . . . to a greater or lesser extent, according to context and the vagaries of individual personality – involves an ontological security founded on an autonomy of bodily control within predictable routines and encounters . . . In

ordinary social life actors have a motivated interest in sustaining the forms of tact and 'repair' which Goffman analyzes so acutely. However, this is not because social life is a kind of mutually protective contract into which individuals enter, as Goffman on occasion suggests. Tact is a mechanism whereby agents are able to reproduce the conditions of 'trust' or ontological security within which more primal tensions can be canalized and managed. This is why one can say that many of the specific features of day-to-day encounter(s) are not directly motivated. Rather, there is a generalized motivational commitment to the integration of habitual practices across time and space. (*CS*, p. 64; on the contrasting views of Goffman, see Rawls, 1987; Schudson, 1984)

Unacknowledged conditions and unintended consequences

The stratification model of the agent in Figure 1.1 indicates that the subjective processes of monitoring, rationalisation, and motivation at issue in the foregoing discussion are connected to the generation of unintended consequences which recursively reappear as unacknowledged conditions of action. One unacknowledged condition, the maintenance of a sense of ontological security (*CPST*, p. 59), has already been taken into account. A second issue here, however, is the link between unintended consequences and unacknowledged conditions which occurs in virtue of the duality of structure.

The point at issue here can be grasped by posing the question of whether agents must intend to reproduce the structural properties of institutionalised conduct in order for that reproduction to occur. For example, when purchasing goods, must agents intend, even on a tacit basis, to reproduce the properties of currency as an institutionalised resource?; when speaking, must agents intend to reproduce the rules of linguistic practice?, etc. It should be evident that such is not the case. Indeed, lay agents, unlike social scientists, may have no conception whatsoever that their participation in social routines contributes to social reproduction in the duality of structure by re-enforcing their awareness, and the awareness of others, that this is how social life in given circumstances is actually carried out. The realisation by Molière's Monsieur Jourdain that he had been speaking prose for forty years comically illustrates how the unintended reproduction of structures may occur.

Just as the structural properties of conduct may be unintentionally reproduced, so they also may remain unacknowledged conditions of action. That is to say, agents may employ a variety of skills without in any way being aware that these skills are conditions for their participation in social life. Considered from this point of view, the duality of structure may involve the unintentional reproduction of unacknowledged structural conditions. However, there is a most significant qualification to be made. It is entirely consistent with the status of structuration theory as an ontology of potentials that what may be for agents unintended consequences and unacknowledged conditions of action over a given historical period, may thereafter become discursively acknowledged by agents as ongoing outcomes of and conditions for their own social conduct. This potential is linked directly to possibilities for social change, in so far as agents who come to realise that their activities contribute to the maintenance of an oppressive or otherwise undesirable set of social institutions may thereafter begin to initiate measures to alter their previous forms of conduct, depending upon available opportunities *in situ*.

The significance of unintended consequences to the duality of structure is one highly important reason why Giddens positions the power to 'make a difference' in social life prior to any regard for the subjectivity of the agent (see above, p. 24). However, it should be emphasized here that the reproduction of structure is only one type of consequence which may be generated by agents on an unintended basis (see *CS*, pp. 12–14). Another highly relevant form of unintended consequences occurs in the reproduction of the articulated relations which comprise social systems. An account of the role of both unintended and intended consequences considered with reference to the reproduction and organisation of systems appears in Chapter 4. However, before issues in this regard can be considered, structuration theory's innovative account of the patterning of social systems across time and space must be well understood. This account will be developed in Chapters 2 and 3.

2

Latter-Day Morphology and Social Praxis: A Critique

Although critiques of alternative theoretical traditions appear as backdrops elsewhere in this book, this is the only chapter devoted entirely to an exposition and critique of views that fall outside the ambit of structuration theory. The chapter is designed to fill a prominent gap in Giddens's writings with regard to the development of his thought on the articulation and patterning of social systems in time and space, a topic which will be covered in detail in Chapter 3. As will be evident in that chapter, I stress the conceptualisation and analysis of systemic patterns to a somewhat greater extent than is the case in Giddens's writings. But the gap to be filled in the present chapter occurs because of the relatively limited extent to which Giddens has developed his concepts in this thematic domain through critical encounters with previous scholarship devoted to the analysis of patterns of conduct in social life. With the exception of a commentary on the works of Peter Blau (*CS*, pp. 207–13), virtually all of Giddens's criticisms of established views in this regard have been directed against the Mertonian variant of functional analysis (*SSPT*, pp. 112–14; *CPST*, pp. 59–63; 'AI', pp. 168–9). These passages are brief relative to the scope of Giddens's writings in their entirety, but that is not the main problem. Rather, as Giddens (*SSPT*, p. 113) clearly recognises, the functionalist conception of structure – which for Mertonians refers to enduring patterns of behaviour – does not stand at the centre of their theoretical concerns. Lacking a well-defined point of reference, the critical reasoning that stands behind the conceptualisation of systems patterns therefore remains underdeveloped in structuration theory.

The present chapter is intended to provide a more thoroughgoing rationale for structuration theory's approach to system patterns than presently appears in Giddens's writings. Dispensing with all references to functionalism, I shall attend to problems arising in the works of contemporary scholars who have concentrated their efforts, in depth and detail, on the establishment of theories and methodologies pertaining to the morphology of patterns and distributions of social relationships. Representative scholars here include S. F. Nadel, Harrison White, Ronald Burt, and Peter Blau. It must be acknowledged from the start that the scholars to be discussed disagree with one another on many basic issues. Nevertheless, there also exist sufficient continuities in their conceptual and methodological images of social patterns to make a critique of their commonly shared views worthwhile. Because most of these scholars employ the term 'structure' to refer to relational patterns (see Nadel, 1957; Mullins, 1973, ch. 10; Blau, 1974, 1977a, 1977b; Mayhew, 1980, 1981; Burt, 1982), it has become conventional to subsume their works under the general rubric of structuralism, or structural sociology. However, not only does Giddens provide a very different definition for the term, but many other definitions exist as well (see Udy, 1968; Boudon, 1971; Blau, 1975, 1982). To avoid confusion, in the present work I have chosen to refer to the orientation shared by these scholars as social morphology (Giddens's distinction between structure and systemic patterns articulated across time and space will be discussed at the beginning of Chapter 3).

Predecessors of latter-day morphology

Virtually all of the classical founders of sociology refer to articulated patterns of positions and relations in their works, but they differ in the extent to which they accentuate the significance of the forms of such patterns. Indeed, Tocqueville, Marx, Weber, and Mead, head a list of classical theorists who express little concern for explicitly morphological issues. Spencer, Durkheim, and Simmel head the list of classical scholars who propose images of differentiated positions and relational networks. Each of them has influenced latter-day morphologists in a variety of ways. Yet none of these classical morphologists established a viable precedent for the domain of morphological inquiry that has been developed in recent years.

Both Spencer (1873, p. 58) and Durkheim (1982, pp. 57, 111, 135, 203–4, 241–2) issue programmatic suggestions for the creation of a field of morphological studies, but unlike latter-day morphologists neither of them elevate formal patterns of positions and relations to a pre-eminent position in their views on the constitution of social life. A telling contrast serves to underscore this point. Whereas latter-day morphologists claim that social life is rooted in social structure *per se*, Spencer and Durkheim anchor their views of social life in theories of social evolution. For both, structural differentiation, or the advance of the organised structure of the division of labour comprises a fundamental datum, but this datum does not stand alone. The natural complement of morphological evolution consists in the evolution of means which serves to integrate these patterns. Indeed, Spencer (1905, p. 471) treats differentiation as a secondary trait, while integration is the primary trait of social evolution. For Durkheim too (1984, p. 217ff), the division of labour exists in a society where individuals already are solidly linked, and the division does not constitute in and of itself the basic fact of social life. This way of putting matters leads Durkheim to address themes such as the causes of integration and the functional explanation of integration in terms of cultural sentiments, and Spencer to accentuate the integrative significance of material resources, political activity, and cultural symbols, none of which figure prominently under the assumption of the basic importance of articulated patterns that informs inquiries undertaken by latter-day morphologists.

A quite different and, in certain respects, stronger classical precedent for latter-day morphology appears in the works of Georg Simmel. Developing a limited analogy between sociology and geometry, Simmel (1959, pp. 319–23) proposes that one way to study forms of sociation (interaction) is to abstract such forms from their content so that they may be examined on an independent basis. The laws that might be found to inhere in these abstract objects of inquiry, he suggests, must be sharply distinguished from any spatio-temporal realisation; they would be valid regardless of the complications introduced under materially dissimilar circumstances. This proposal certainly seems in keeping with latter-day morphological perspectives, but it cannot be said that Simmel otherwise established a secure foundation from which to proceed. The persuasive force of his insights is vitiated on the one hand by the fragmentary character of his inquiries, and on the other by his neo-Kantian formulation of the distinction between form and content. The former distracts attention from generic morphological issues by moving without systematic organisation between formal aspects of a heterogeneous array of social phenomena (see Levine, 1981, p. 67). The latter raises more problems than it solves, owing to a number of basic inconsistencies in Simmel's methodological insights (see Oakes, 1980). Nevertheless, Simmel did contribute to the later development of social morphology, notably through his influence on Jacob Moreno (see Levine *et al.*, 1976, pp. 838–9). The sociometric research techniques devised by Moreno and his colleagues specifically deal with formal patterns of association among members of small groups.

If Moreno preserved a Simmelian interest in morphological themes, a Spencerian/Durkheimian inclination toward the study of morphological patterns is sustained in the works of British social anthropologists, particularly among those influenced by A. R. Radcliffe-Brown. But while these social anthropologists produced valuable empirical studies, consistent with their classical predecessors, they generally combined a concern for patterns of kinship, political organisation and so forth with an equal interest in issues of functional integration. Thus, structural-functionalism rather than social morphology became a hallmark of work done by Radcliffe-Brown and his followers.

But if Radcliffe-Brown did not directly inspire the development of latter-day morphology, his efforts and those of his colleagues to determine an appropriate definition of morphological structure inspired the British social anthropologist S. F. Nadel to write the work most responsible for the subsequent creation of the field. In *The Theory of Social Structure* Nadel took his lead from the absence of a well-wrought conception of social structure in the anthropological literature. Acknowledging earlier efforts by Radcliffe-Brown and his colleagues, as well as works by Spencer, Durkheim, and Simmel, Nadel (1957, p. 4) observed that little progress had been made in developing a precise meaning for social structure beyond the broad sense in which the term refers to the interrelation or arrangement of 'parts' in some social entity. To rectify the matter, he proposed to treat social structure as a novel and specialised conceptual tool. As opposed to previous anthropological works, as well as to the works of Spencer and Durkheim, Nadel concentrated his efforts upon establishing conceptual and methodological means to apprehend the formal characteristics of structure, carefully distinguishing a concern for structure from a concern for functional effectiveness, as well as from the content, material or qualitative character of the phenomena incorporated in structural patterns. Although Nadel's subject-matter seems in line with a Simmelian approach, he adhered to a positivist rather than a neo-Kantian methodology. The articulation and arrangement of structures discussed in his works are properties of empirical data, something that objects, events, or series of events exhibit or prove to possess through observation or analysis (Nadel, 1957, p. 7).

Much of Nadel's book is devoted to an extensive consideration of the assumptions entailed and the limitations encountered in the conceptualisation of morphological patterns. The arguments he presents are sophisticated and thorough. Despite the many works along morphological lines that have been launched in the thirty-odd years since his book was first published, it remains the best exposition of the suppositions required in order to abstract formal patterns from the more substantive aspects of social life. But this is not to say that Nadel subscribes to the central contention that social life is rooted in positional and relational structures. To the contrary, as his inquiry proceeds a tension appears between his painstaking exposition of each step in the abstraction of schematic morphological images, and his forthright recognition that in more concrete terms structure consists in the general ways people engage in relationships which are carried out in the enactment of rule-guided roles. Structure is abstracted from the pattern of these orderly arrangements (a basis for this point appears very early in his work; see Nadel, 1957, pp. 8–12). As he grapples with specific problems generated by the tension between abstracted images and more concrete patterns, he notes or implies pitfalls that many recent studies have not managed to avoid. As I shall indicate below, one of the most important cautions concerns the attribution of causal powers to morphological structures. Considered in this light, if Nadel provides the best exposition of the abstraction of morphological images, he also provides a valuable source of criticism for how these images have been construed in subsequent works. Both aspects of his thought will be invoked as the discussion proceeds.

Latter-day morphology

Nadel's efforts did not immediately inspire many analytic developments. In social anthropology the more substantive studies of tribal kinship structures that proliferated under the influence of Radcliffe-Brown continued as a major topic of interest for many years thereafter. Studies informed by sociometric methods continued in sociology, and morphological studies of complex organisations, political elites, and urban communities became a staple of social theory and research. Only in the last decades have scholars, most notably American sociologists, created theories and research strategies that make it credible to speak of latter-day morphology as a distinctive analytic domain. Many of them acknowledge affinities and debts to Nadel's pioneering work (e.g. White, Boorman and Breiger, 1976, p. 733; Blau, 1977a, p. 3; Burt, 1982, p. 346), and they generally share Nadel's respect for positivist methodological principles. However, they disregard Nadel's cautious recognition of the abstracted character of morphological images, and they differ and disgree upon the nature of structural configurations, as well as how they should be analysed. Nadel (1957, pp. 14–19) anticipated the most fundamental conceptual division in their works at an early stage in his book. On the one hand he identifies network configurations abstracted from interactions, and on the other he identifies patterns abstracted from distributions of relevant social phenomena (e.g. roles, relationships, sub-groups) which are classified on the basis of their similarity and dissimilarity. It is worthwhile to summarise recent developments in latter-day morphology in terms of the study of each type of configuration.

Network analysis remains far and away the most prevalent variant of latter-day morphology. From this point of view, structures are perceived as patterns of relationships directly or indirectly linking social positions (Laumann, 1973, pp. 2–4), or more narrowly as ties linking nodes in a social system (Wellman, 1983,

p. 157). Major developments in network analysis have combined an interest in formal network structures with the development and application of methods of research specifically designed for the apprehension of networks from this formal point of view. However, not all of these studies concentrate upon relations between social actors. In two of the most frequently cited works on formal network analysis, Harrison White and his associates (White, Boorman and Breiger, 1976; Boorman and White, 1976) propose methods to decompose concrete relationships between actors into analytically distinct contacts or aspects of relations which subsequently are re-aggregated and analysed as 'blockmodels'. Moving in the opposite direction, Edward Laumann (1979) expands the ambit of network analysis to include supra-individual organisations and aggregate groups.

One of the virtues of network analysis is that, unlike Durkheim's programmatic morphology, it does not insist that societies at large must be seen as well-integrated totalities. As Laumann (1979, p. 385) puts it: 'there exists a multiplicity of social relationships linking social positions to one another'. Hence one may study networks within networks, cross-cutting networks, and even contradictory associations between networks. But other than licensing the study of networks on different levels of empirical inquiry, the advantages of this flexibility can be realised only if networks are interpreted in theoretical terms. Unfortunately, with a few prominent exceptions (especially Burt, 1982), little headway has been made in the development of a theory of networks.

Driven by research methods more than theoretical argument, network analysis has rapidly become a highly specialised field of inquiry. Since the basic network image is neutral regarding the constitution of nodes and ties, analysts have been free to develop techniques based upon graph theory, matrix-algebra and narrowly focused modes of survey research and statistical sampling. The diversity of models that has been proposed along these lines has reached a point where merely to classify them requires a considerable effort (see Burt, 1980). But more importantly, the assumptions and definitions advanced with regard to ties and nodes are designed to conform to the particular techniques of research employed, as are the data from which images and models of networks are derived (see Burt, 1980, pp. 131–4). While network analysts adhere to the view that networks have behavioural consequences resulting from structural constraints (Burt, 1982, pp. 9–10; Wellman, 1983, pp. 163–4), their methods do not often provide means to address these issues (see Granovetter, 1979, pp. 504–7). Instead they most often yield only non-generalised descriptive representations of specific networks drawn from equally specific sets of 'network data' (Burt, 1980, pp. 132–3).

Yet for all its limitations, interest in network analysis continues to grow. Monographs, collections of essays, and journal articles addressed to formal properties of social networks have become a fixture on the American sociological scene. At least one major American sociologist, Randall Collins (1986, p. 1351), considers network analysis to hold the potential for revolutionary developments in the formulation of theoretical problems. Reminiscent of claims made on behalf of functionalism in an earlier era, extreme proponents of the 'structural' perspective, which I term latter-day morphology, have begun to suggest that the nature and consequences of social networks comprise the basic subject-matter to which sociology is addressed (Mayhew, 1980, p. 338; for a contrasting opinion, see Blau, 1982, p. 273).

Nadel (1957, pp. 15–16) was more favourably disposed toward a network conception of social structure than towards the alternative view in which morphological patterns are perceived through the distribution of similarities and dissimilarities in roles or relationships. Such patterns, he suggests, provide only elementary descriptions that play a preliminary role in the development of network images. It is, then, somewhat ironic that Peter Blau's recent works (1974, 1977a and b) present the most well-developed theory in the literature of latter-day social morphology. Whereas the empiricist and methodological inclination among network analysts disposes them to an inductive approach to social science, Blau's theory is constructed in a highly disciplined nomothetic-deductive format replete with precisely defined concepts, which are incorporated in systematically organised axioms, provisional assumptions and theorems. The entire theory is meant to pertain to large-scale collectivities.

Apart from a subsidiary concern with territorial distribution (i.e. ecological structure) which will be discussed below, Blau's theory (1977a, pp. 6–8; 1977b, pp. 28–33) is based upon the distribution of people among social positions. Positions are derived from the criteria implicit in the social distinctions people make among themselves in their associations with one another, including natural and acquired attributes such as gender, ethnicity, occupation, wealth, education, and power. These positions are not social roles or relationships, although they are sociologically relevant in so far as they have a discernible effect upon social association. An empirically variable number of people may hold the same social position at any given time, and conversely any individual may hold several different positions. Thus, differentiations of positions refer neither to social behaviour nor to concrete acts, but rather to analytically defined aspects of actors' social identities.

As is true for most latter-day morphologists, Blau is indifferent to the substantive nature or the specific consequences of particular social identities, but quite concerned with the nature and consequences of formal patterns. The specifically morphological quality of his theory is made evident in his conception of structure. Blau's (1977a, pp. 6–11) master definition of structure refers to a multi-dimensional space of social positions. A structure is delineated by its parameters, and parameters, in turn, are comprised of positions organised by a socially derived criterion. Two categories of parameters appear in Blau's work: nominal parameters refer to membership in groups with no distinct rank order; graduated parameters differentiate people in terms of status–rank–order (Blau, 1977a, p. 7). Hence, in any given structure one may find more or less heterogeneity in terms of nominal parameters, and more or less inequality in terms of graduated parameters.

Structure, thus conceived, is said by Blau to have significant consequences with regard to associations or relationships between actors. For example, one of Blau's basic assumptions is that the greater the differentiation of positions, the more extensive are barriers to social intercourse, although more extensive barriers need not be stronger barriers by virtue of their extension (Blau, 1977a, p. 10). However, in proffering this view Blau does not mean to refer to the characteristic practices in which agents engage during social intercourse. Rather, the consequences of the configuration of specific structural patterns are conceived as rates of intergroup relations.

Because of this emphasis upon rates of association, and because Blau also addresses various aspects of his theory to group size and the distribution of populations within and among parameters and positions, he (1977a, p. 16) characterises his theory as aligned with a quantitative conception of structure that derives from Simmel. This quantitative slant distinguishes his conception of structure from the emphasis upon connections (ties between nodes) in structural images induced by network analysts. Yet Blau (1982) also acknowledges the affinities of his perspective with the works of several prominent network analysts. Clearly, the point of intersection between Blau and the network analysts stems from the latter-day morphological emphasis upon structural forms and the ways they affect social relations.

Latter-day morphology and its discontents

Contemporary approaches to social morphology often appear abstruse and complex. The methods devised by network analysts yield results that often prove difficult to grasp for those unfamiliar with the mathematical logic and symbolic notation employed. Blau's theory appears far less arcane, yet the intricate manner in which he elaborates and cross-references his concepts, axioms, theorems and assumptions yields many subtle and technical insights. But, if theory and research in latter-day morphology make for heavy going, the root images of configurations and distributions employed are relatively easy to understand. Notions of both networks articulated through ties between nodes and patterns of differentiation among social positions can be visualised and described in a very straight-forward manner. The very simplicity of these images has a certain seductive appeal. For one thing, as is especially evident in network analysis, this simplicity makes it easy to develop empirical studies of morphological patterns. For another, as Nadel (1957, p. 8) points out, formal morphological concepts can be readily transposed from one empirical setting to another, thereby facilitating comparative investigations. But a crucial question that must be posed is: are network configurations and patterns of differentiation among positions significant features of social reality?

Latter-day social morphologists most likely would resist the ontological bias of this question. Their positivist scientific principles suggest that a phenomenon is a significant feature of social reality if it can be empirically observed. Bruce Mayhew (1981,

p. 633), for example, insists that no assumption that things are real need be made from this standpoint; rather, analysts themselves define what they are studying. Students of morphological structure thus subscribe to what Mayhew terms, following Konrad Lorenz, a 'hypothetical realism' in which all basic assumptions must be consistently subjected to empirical examination with regard to their adequacy. A digression into the epistemological conundrums that this perspective fails to address is not worthwhile in the present context. Yet, if one thing seems clear in an era when the under-determination of theory by facts should be plainly evident for all to see, it is that empirical evidence in itself does not establish a claim to the significance of the subject-matter at issue.

Doubts regarding whether morphological patterns do capture a significant aspect of social reality begin to arise when one considers how morphologists arrive at their structural units or analysis. In the first place, many influential works in the field are accompanied by a disclaimer of the intention to provide a comprehensive account of social structure. Nadel (1957, p. 7) set a precedent here by discounting all concern with the functionalist efficacy and qualitative characteristics of the elements incorporated in concrete structures. Network analysts such as Harrison White and associates (White *et al.*, 1976, p. 734) follow suit in their explicit disregard for the cultural and social-psychological meaning of their units of analysis. In a comprehensive review of network analysis, Ronald Burt (1980, p. 83) notes that while network relations have a morphological form and an interactional content, generic distinctions among relational contents are not well understood on a conceptual level. Finally, Blau frankly states (1977b, p. 27) that he proposes a very narrow view of social structure, leaving out of account implications regarding institutional systems, value consensus, normative orientations, and functional interdependence. In a more comprehensive discussion of formal structural perspectives as developed in sociological inquiry today, Blau observes:

Social structure may be conceptualized in terms of its formal properties, as Simmel does, or in terms of its substantive content as Weber does. Whereas Simmel examines triads independent of whether they are composed of three persons or three nations and whether they are involved in economic or military contest,

> Weber is concerned with the substantive significance of the Calvinist ethic for social conduct and institutions . . . The formal approach is more abstract and general; concern with content is more historical and empirical . . . Generality is achieved at the cost of specificity. Social forms leave out historical contents. (Blau, 1981, p. 20; see also 1982, p. 276)

In adopting an exclusive interest in formal properties of structural patterns, it seems clear that latter-day morphologists are not engaged simply in bracketing other aspects of social life, aspects which include social *praxis* as well as the substantive themes to which Blau refers. Bracketing procedures simply suspend attention to certain facets of the subject-matter at hand *pro tempore* in order to clarify and analyse a particular aspect or dimension of this subject-matter that is of special interest. The implication of bracketing procedures is that the excluded facets of the subject-matter can, and ultimately should, be taken into consideration. Rather than imposing brackets in this way, morphologists claim to arrive at their formal images of social structure through procedures of abstraction: procedures that simply discount or suppress all but the formal aspects of the situations and relationships from which the structural patterns are derived (see Nadel, 1957, pp. 106, 154). Only in rare instances (see Burt, 1982; Nadel, 1957, pp. 114–24) is explicit provision made for non-formal aspects of social life to be introduced into structural images in a systematic fashion. At the extreme, these procedures of abstraction yield an exceedingly spare 'positional picture', which may take the form of an image of structure as relative positions in relationships emptied of all content (Nadel, 1957, p. 108) or, alternatively, the ordered classification of formal properties of structure (Blau, 1977a, p. 15).

The danger in modes of abstraction employed by latter-day morphologists is that one may be left with nothing more than a schematic trace of pattern or order in life. While it remains possible to entertain propositions regarding such schemata, the schemata themselves do not seem important. Many of Nadel's most serious reservations regarding the formal concept of structure he set out to explore crystallise around this issue. He (1957, pp. 149–50) worried that – in the manner of the very different type of structural analysis proposed by Lévi-Strauss – abstract 'positional pictures' might be taken as mental models rather than aspects of reality. Simultaneously he acknowledged that these 'positional pictures' do have a remoteness stemming precisely from the procedures of abstraction employed. But Nadel, at least, carefully indicated throughout his book how he believed it might be possible to disregard various aspects of social life. His successors have not followed his example. Rather, a basic statement of issues to be set aside appears somewhere toward the beginning of their works. Abstraction by fiat is the order of the day.

This seemingly arbitrary abstraction of formal patterns from the richness and complexity of social life at large undoubtedly stands behind the many critical comments raised, not by outsiders, but by scholars sympathetic to morphological projects, with regard to both the anchorage of morphological images of structure in social reality, and the amount of insight to be gained by attempting to perceive structure in this way. With regard to network analysis, Burt (1980, pp. 132–4) notes that network models appear to have an *ad hoc* quality, and that network data involve arbitrary decisions regarding system boundaries. J. A. Barnes (1979, p. 421) forthrightly declares that 'network analysis has no substantively defined home base'. He expresses an extremely cautious attitude toward the algebraic and topological properties studied in network analysis. 'Hopefully, mathematics will remain the ally, but not become the queen, of the social sciences.' J. Clyde Mitchell (1979, p. 439) appears to concur with Barnes: 'In essence data must be decontextualized to make it amenable to formal analysis. In papers dealing essentially with ways of abstracting the sociological sense out of social networks the *procedure* – in extreme cases the algorithm – appears to be the be-all and end-all of the exercise.' Paul Holland and Samuel Leinhardt (1979, pp. 3–4) add yet another voice to the chorus. They suggest that the processes of abstraction involved in network or graph theoretic concepts may render theory construction and empirical research trivial and irrelevant. Finally, Mark Granovetter adds an unusual twist to the preceding criticism. Network models, he insists (1979, p. 517), only appear to be neutral and innocent of theoretical assumptions. Actually, they harbour underlying notions of structure, but notions which often are sufficiently submerged as to escape the attention and judgement of their authors.

Blau's theory of social structure encounters a similar complaint.

Blau, of course, acknowledges that he employs a very narrow conception of structure. He also notes that there is no general agreement upon how the 'parts' of structure should be conceived (Blau, 1977a, p. 2). Thus, he also is moved to acknowledge that his is but one approach to the abstraction of structure from reality (Blau, 1977a, p. 244). The question again is: has Blau managed to abstract a significant aspect of reality? Jonathan Turner in an otherwise favourable commentary on Blau's theory finds reason to doubt that such is the case:

> [A]n objection to Blau's theory is that it excludes so much. Interaction is conceptualized as a rate rather than a process; roles are relegated to their effects on parameters; values, beliefs, norms, and other idea systems are eliminated or ... [dealt with in passing] and the social-psychological properties of the universe are simply eliminated. Moreover, the theory cannot tell us why a given set of parameters exist in the first place ... Thus, I think that Blau's theory achieves parsimony by eliminating many critical dynamics of the social universe including those responsible for variations in his own theoretical variable (nominal and graduated parameters). (Turner, 1986, p. 434)

Emergence and constraint in social morphology: the neglect of social *praxis*

The foregoing criticisms present a strong bill of indictment against the abstraction of formal patterns and distributions from the reality of social life. The accusation they make is, perhaps, best epitomised by Barnes: latter-day morphology lacks a substantively defined home base. Exactly how that home base should be conceived obviously depends upon which aspects of social life to which morphologists do not attend one considers to be of particular importance. As previously indicated, the morphologists themselves acknowledge their neglect of the cultural content of their units of analysis, and many of their critics express concern for this omission. Indeed, Giddens (*CS*, pp. 211–13) voices a similar criticism in his commentary on the theory developed by Peter Blau. Blau cannot avoid cultural considerations altogether if only because his conceptions of position and parameter involve meanings ascribed by social actors to their own conduct as well as to the conduct of others. Giddens expands upon this limited admission of cultural issues to show that actors actually use these meanings to order and organise their own activities. But the point Giddens makes is not that the home base of morphological patterns is found in cultural traditions *per se*. Rather, in keeping with the praxiological outlook inherent in structuration theory at large, he holds that a 'structural approach' to the social sciences cannot be severed from an examination of the mechanisms of social reproduction.

For the purpose of providing a critical rationale for structuration theory's conception of system patterns, I want to enlarge Giddens's criticism of Blau's neglect of social reproduction to include the works of other latter-day morphologists, and to establish the implications of this criticism from a different point of view. Without in any way denying the manifold problems associated with the morphologists' neglect of the substantive content of social conduct, the absence of a proper regard for the significance of *praxis* also is associated with problems in understanding the status of the morphological structures with which they deal. These problems arise by virtue of assumptions regarding the way patterns are constituted in social life which implicitly or explicitly inform many latter-day morphological theories and methods. These assumptions dispose morphologists to neglect the fact that social patterns ultimately exist only in and through the practices generated by social agents.

There appears to be a certain inconsistency in the assertion by morphologists that their units of analysis are conceptual or empirical abstractions from social life, and the programmatic claims they make on behalf of these units. Consider the following summary of the perspective maintained in network analysis:

Network analysts search for *deep* structures – regular network patterns beneath the often complex surface of social systems. They try to describe these patterns and use their descriptions to learn how network structures constrain social behavior and social change ... This emphasis on studying the structural properties of networks informs the ways in which analysts pose research questions, organize data collection and develop analytic methods. (Wellman, 1983, p. 157)

However much it may be true that in practice network analysts simply describe network patterns, it should be evident that in principle they have larger issues in mind. If they were content to pursue descriptions of network patterns, then it might be appropriate to say that they engage exclusively in procedures of abstraction. But it is another matter entirely to propose that network structure *constrains* behaviour and social change. What in the first instance Nadel calls a 'positional picture', now becomes what Durkheim would call a 'social fact' with the capacity to influence social conduct. A similar inconsistency inheres in Blau's theory of social structure. On the one hand, Blau (1977a, pp. 2, 244) contends that his conception of structure is abstracted from observable social relations. But, on the other hand, he insists (1977a, p. 7) that structural conditions have a deterministic influence on social associations between actors, albeit an influence that can be measured only in rates of intergroup relations between actors. The latter proviso permits Blau to hold that physical, biological, and psychological conditions also may influence rates of social association. Moreover, Blau also holds that processes of association between actors must be studied to account for the original etiology of social groups. But Blau makes it entirely clear that established social structures, far from being simply abstract conceptual representations of social processes, possess properties and powers unto themselves. 'Once distinct social positions have become established they channel further role relations and associations' (Blau, 1977a, p. 4).

To be very clear about this, morphological structure most certainly is represented in an abstract manner. The abstraction involved here is meant to reduce concrete patterns to formal images, or formal concepts (see Nadel, 1957, p. 106; Blau, 1981, p. 15; Burt, 1982, pp. 337–47). Abstractions of this kind might preserve a sense in which patterns revert back to the practices through which social life is produced. But to endow morphological structure with the power to constrain or channel social action or relationships is to suggest that it maintains a status apart from the activities that are subject to its influence. This hypostatisation of morphological structures Nadel (1957, pp. 147–8) terms the 'trap of reification', and he was adamantly opposed to getting caught in the trap. It is invalid to speak of an orderliness abstracted from behaviour as guiding behaviour, exercising pressure, or resisting the impact of change because abstract models of order have no concrete efficacy to produce real consequences in social life.

Nadel believed that many instances of reification result from the use of loose language. But today many morphologists state or imply a warrant for perceiving relational or distributional patterns as objects unto themselves. The contention is that social patterns possess emergent properties. Arguments for emergence are not necessarily spelled out in detail. Laumann (1979, p. 394), for example, implies an emergent account of social networks by suggesting that network analysts explain, at least in part, the behaviour of network elements by appeal to specific features of the interconnections among them. The lattice of interconnections which comprise social networks thus stands above and apart from the processes of social life. White and his colleagues (1976, p..735) suggest, following Durkheim, that a theory of networks should be developed in terms of the overall structure that is the context for particular transactions. So common is the belief that structures possess emergent properties, that Blau proposes that it serves as a common denominator among a host of different views, including virtually all accounts of morphological structure. In summary terms this belief maintains that:

> [S]ocial structure refers to those properties of an aggregate that are emergent and that consequently do not characterize the elements composing it . . . The structure of a group differs from the aggregate of its members . . . by those properties that cannot be used to describe individual members and hence describe the group as a whole. (Blau, 1981, pp. 9–10)

Emergent structural properties, thus defined, are the source of external constraint experienced by individuals:

> The underlying principle is that emergent properties are characteristics of social structures over which individuals have no control even when these characteristics are the aggregate results of their own action, and these conditions of the social environment necessarily restrict what people's free will can realize. (Blau, 1981, p. 16; see further, pp. 15–16)

The problem with such arguments does not lie in their emphasis upon constraint *per se*. Structuration theory, too, makes provision for conditions that affect social conduct in a manner that any given individual may be unable to control (see below, Chapter 3 and Chapter 6). The problem is, rather, that the existence of influential emergent properties is postulated, but no mention is made of the processes through which emergence occurs. This dilemma would not arise if the claim was only that properties of collectivities can only be described from a collective point of view, as when one misses the forest by attending too closely to the trees. The issue here is a matter of perception, the point of view from which patterns in collectivities can best be discerned. But descriptions or perceptions are in the eye of the beholder; emergent properties of morphological patterns with the power to influence conduct necessarily must be constituents of social reality. In so far as such properties are said to exist then it indeed becomes obligatory to show how they originate.

Durkheim's (1982, pp. 39–40) well-known references to synthetic processes, metaphorically resembling chemical reactions, that give rise to emergent 'social facts', may be difficult to accept, but at least he recognises the need to account for how emergence occurs. Morphological views of social patterns generally do not make an allowance of this kind. True, Blau suggests that emergent properties may be the aggregate result of social actions, but then he also distinguishes between an aggregate *per se*, and the emergent properties of the structure of a group (see above; and also Mayhew, 1980, pp. 338–9). This absence of an account of processes, means, or mechanisms through which emergent properties are generated is particularly difficult to accept when the formal images and concepts of social patterns at issue in latter-day social morphology appear to so many commentators to be lacking in sociological significance. If such formal, schematic patterns possess emergent properties that can influence social conduct, then it seems all the more necessary to establish their home base. Yet as matters stand, in most accounts the properties of morphological patterns seem to emerge out of thin air.

Some account of social *praxis*, such as that which structuration theory provides, would seem unavoidable in order to meet this requirement. Certainly no morphologist has denied, or presumably would want to deny, that configurations of social relationships or positions are reproduced during the course of interaction.

Where else but in social *praxis* could one identify the processes that generate and sustain enduring patterns of any kind in social life? Yet social morphologists rarely put matters in this way. The significance of social *praxis* eludes their grasp because in addition to proposing an emergent status for morphological properties of collectivities, they explicitly or implicitly presume a conception of action that, rather than stressing the praxiological dimension of conduct, centres upon the cognitions and motives embedded in the consciousness of social agents. A conceptual hiatus thus may be discerned in most morphological works, between properties of collectivities which, because they possess an emergent status, can be considered objective characteristics of social life, and actors' experience and dispositions which can be understood only with reference to the subjective experience and inclinations of social actors.

Morphological works can be somewhat deceptive in this regard since they sometimes do make allusions to social interaction. Nevertheless, the overriding conception of social processes virtually always concentrates upon dispositions to act. For example, Blau (1977a, p. 140) provides the following definition of exchange processes compatible with his structural theory: 'An individual who supplies rewarding services to another obligates him. To discharge this obligation, the second must furnish benefits to the first in turn.' Whether or not this is a valid proposition is beside the point for the purposes at hand. What should be noted is that Blau indicates reasons for actors to behave in particular ways, but he does not specify the procedures involved. Social practices, practical consciousness, social locales, and contextuality, the cornerstones of *praxis* not only from the standpoint of structuration theory, but also from the point of view of Goffman, Garfinkel, Winch, and many others, are completely absent in Blau's account.

Employing emergent accounts of structural properties and subjective accounts of actors' dispositions creates a gap between diversely constituted entities. The difficulties encountered in closing this gap, and the consequent inability to account for how structural properties emerge, can be observed by turning to Burt's work which is pointed toward the development of a structural theory of action. Burt works with highly formalised network images of structure expressed in abstract symbols and algebraic formulae. But, in a manner reminiscent of Blau, the structural positions in these images ultimately refer to statuses associated with specified role relations. Although these status and role sets might be defined from a praxiological standpoint, an argument for emergence is implied in Burt's account of the relational patterns among these positions:

> Although manifest in the relational patterns among individuals, status defining role-sets are not in general reducible to the relations between actors. Rather they are comprised of relations that occur repeatedly in a system so as to constrain and give opportunity to relations between individual actors. (Burt, 1982, p. 42)

Now if all Burt meant to claim here was that relational patterns are abstract concepts, i.e. conceptual descriptions of repetitive relations, then this would not be an argument for the emergence of relational patterns. But, here again, because Burt ascribes powers of constraint (and provision of opportunities) to the relations comprising the patterns, he must be postulating that they possess properties above and apart from instances of conduct. Hence, he is obligated to show how relational patterns emerge as something other than relations between actors.

To his credit, Burt (1982, p. 10) clearly recognises that an account of how actors could be responsible for the patterns of relations first observed as social structure must be one of the tasks that a structural theory of action must fulfil. As I have indicated above, if Burt is to undertake this task he must work with a praxiological conception of action. It thus would be possible for him to show how status/role-sets are generated and sustained as relational patterns. But instead of *praxis*, Burt falls in line with the prevailing views of action in morphological works by emphasising subjective cognitions and dispositions. Burt centres his concept of action (1982, pp. 1–4) on what he terms 'purposive action'. This concept postulates an individual's right to the product of her private property, and her motivation to use that property in rewarding ways. No mention of the praxiological aspects of social conduct appears in these postulates, nor is there any reference to practices, procedures, or the production of activity in the four elements of action he derives from them. These include: (i) a source of action (persons or groups); (ii) conditions for action (goods and labour); (iii) reasons for action (motives, self-interest); (iv) probabilities of alternative actions being performed (evaluations of the utility of the alternatives). In short, Burt addresses the circumstances, reasons, and evaluations that enter into actors' perceptual experience. He thus is prepared to consider *why* actions are performed, and *which* actions might be preferred, but no provision is made for *how* actions are produced. All of this culminates in a premise that underlies the detailed arguments Burt elaborates during the course of his book: actors are purposive under structural constraint. More specifically this postulate holds that an actors' status/role-set (i.e. structural position) influences her marginal evaluation of the utility of alternative actions, partly in regard to her personal conditions and partly in regard to the conditions of others (Burt, 1982, p. 8).

Unlike many morphologists, Burt at least recognises the need to bridge the gap between structure and action. But by adopting an emergent view of structure and a subjective view of action, he can only bridge the gap in one direction. When status/role-sets influence actors' evaluation of the marginal utility of action the move is made from structure to action. But because Burt lacks a conception of *praxis* he cannot account for how status/role-sets are maintained in social life. Relational patterns thus constrain and create opportunities for action to occur. But how action 'is responsible' for the emergence of relational patterns still remains mysterious and obscure.

It should be evident now that Nadel was not mistaken to refer to the reification of morphological structure as a trap. Simply put, in social morphology social actors appear to be caught up in relational patterns which they do not generate. I have been intent to show that morphologists arrive at this impasse because they neglect to consider how relational patterns are reproduced in social life, a neglect that is sustained in their views on social action. I also have indicated that an emphasis upon social *praxis* provides the only means of escape from this dilemma. These remarks have been offered in anticipation of the alternative account of social patterns which Giddens incorporates in structuration theory. Although discussion of this account must be deferred until another aspect of latter-day social morphology has been critically scrutinised, it should be emphasised that a shift to a praxiological view of the ordering and configuration of social activities entails dispensing with all arguments for the emergence of social patterns. Consider the matter from an ontological perspective on the constitution of social life. From this standpoint it seems undeniable that *configurations of relations between social agents do not emerge from social conduct, but rather remain embedded in the ongoing course of activity. The routine repetitions of institutionalised modes of interaction between agents is not something apart from the patterns they form; it is the very stuff of which these patterns are made.* No matter how appealing morphological conceptions and images of social structures may be, in so far as they deny this fundamental insight they inevitably lack a home base in social life.

The eclipse of time and space in latter-day morphology

If social patterns are embedded in the reality of social activity then a concern for time and space becomes difficult to avoid. Social conduct, after all, is always situated in specific settings, and it takes time to engage even in the most fleeting practices, let alone sustained sequences and series of interactions. While classical writings on social morphology did not adopt a praxiological viewpoint, and while they generally overlooked the significance of time, they did express an interest in the spatial extension of articulated patterns. Durkheim (who drew upon the works of classical geographers such as Ratzel and Vidal de la Blanche) incorporated a geographical perspective into the heart of his programme for social morphology. Spencer (1977, p. 107) drew his idea of society from the notion of a general persistence of arrangements between units *throughout the area occupied.* This perspective was sustained in the subsequent works of social ecologists, but not in the works of most latter-day morphologists (see Haines, 1985 for a relevant critique of social ecology).

Social morphologists today vary in the extent to which time and space are acknowledged in their works. The matrix algebraic or graph-theoretic images of social patterns generated by network analysts dispose them to completely neglect time and space, a neglect that some of them explicitly admit (see White *et al.*, 1976, p. 732; Wellman, 1983, p. 157). Nadel and Blau, who are more theoretically inclined, do not disregard time and space to the same extent. Nadel presents an extensive discussion in which he attempts to surmount difficulties posed by the inherent temporality of social conduct. Blau, on the other hand, actually proposes an account of ecological structure to complement the other structural dimensions incorporated in his theory. However, problems can be identified in each of these accounts when they are considered from a praxiological standpoint. In anticipation of the prominence ascribed to the temporal and spatial constitution of social patterns in Chapter 3, it is instructive to spell out the difficulties with Nadel and Blau's respective accounts.

Nadel's arguments are of particular importance because, despite his commitment to abstract formal images of morphological structure, he clearly recognises that time must be expended in the succession of behavioural sequences that constitute patterns of order in day-to-day life. The problem that disturbed him here was how to reconcile the static discourse regarding morphological structures with the temporality inherent in concrete reality. While the language used to analyse structure suggests static states in which positions are fixed and timeless (e.g. in a kinship pattern, or friendship group), this is only 'as if' language. In reality, structure is comprised of positions defined in terms of time-consuming behaviour sequences, and relationships must be abstracted from a repetitive succession of actions (Nadel, 1957, p. 132). Nevertheless, quasi-static accounts of structure can be adduced in so far as a workable constancy, i.e. a 'stationary' state, can be proposed to exist in the processes underlying structural images. Nadel visualises this workable constancy and suggests means to represent it in the following manner:

> If we . . . [employ] . . . a simile of a network – an 'as-if' network to be sure – we should have to admit that its knots keep on being tied and retied – and that parts of it all the time disappear and reappear: but when the knots are being retied and the strands reappear, this happens as it were at the same old places. The picture as a whole remains more or less the same. In other words we are still able to draw up diagrams and blueprints, though they will have to include symbols indicating 'directed movement' (or 'vectors') as well as positions apparently at rest, and though our 'pathways' or 'orbits' will have to allow for jumps from one to the other. (Nadel, 1957, p. 133)

Nadel incorporates temporality so effectively into his network simile that the simile itself can be used to indicate what is wrong with the symbolic means he proposes to represent the presence of temporality in structure. The problem, in brief, is that while the 'vectors' he proposes represent temporal *movement*, they do not represent temporal *duration*. To grasp the significance of duration in the patterns of interaction to which Nadel's network simile is meant to refer, it is crucial to complement a concern for temporality with a concern for the spatial configuration of interactions. A useful example of the spatial configuration of an interactional pattern is provided in Malinowski's summary of the Kula exchange in the Trobriand Islands:

> The Kula is a form of exchange of extensive intertribal character: it is carried on by communities inhabiting a wide range of islands, which form a closed circuit . . . Along this route, articles of two kinds . . . are constantly traveling in opposite directions . . . Each of these articles, as it travels in its own direction on the closed circuit meets on the way articles of the other class, and is constantly being exchanged for them. Every movement of the articles, every detail of the transaction is fixed and regulated by a set of traditional rules. (Malinowski, 1961, p. 81)

The Kula appears as an articulated network consisting of members of various tribes who travel from one spatial setting to another in order to reproduce Kula exchange. Now if Nadel's allowance for the temporal direction of sequences and series of interactions is coupled with Malinowski's recognition of the spatial dimension of the Kula exchange, then Nadel's network simile encounters a set of complications. The time it takes to 'retie the knots' in the Kula depends upon the rate of speed with which tribal members from any given island in the Kula Ring are able to travel across space to the designated island where the appropriate Kula exchange is to be carried out. The 'length' of this articulating 'link' in the Kula network thus appears as a joint function of time and space: i.e. there is a determinate temporal duration associated with the spatial voyage between islands. Symbolic 'vectors' that refer to 'directed movement' are inadequate to grasp this time–space patterning of social relationships: a central aspect of what Giddens terms the time–space distanciation of social systems.

It may be granted that a time–space perspective adds a new

dimension to morphological images of social patterns. But is it essential to take this dimension into account? An affirmative reply must be made from a praxiological standpoint in so far as social actors consume time in their movements between spatially situated settings of conduct. But the necessity to take a time–space perspective toward social patterns into account also can be demonstrated by considering a comparison that might be made between three hypothetical structures conceived, following Nadel, as operating in a 'stationary state' such that all relationships are infinitely repeated in the proper order. Presume now that in this comparison all structures have the same configuration of relations between positions from Nadel's point of view. Thus, a single formal image incorporating 'vectors' to indicate 'directed movement' can serve to represent the common pattern of articulation they share. Yet what may appear to be identical patterns according to Nadel may be quite dissimilar once the time–space dimension is given its due. To simplify matters let us attend to the 'directed movement' between two 'positions' in each of the three hypothetical structures subsumed by Nadel's single pattern. In the first pattern it might be that the agents who reproduce the 'directed movement' are positioned in adjacent locales. Hence there is a short span in time–space involved in the 'directed movement' between the two 'positions'. However, in the second pattern the agents might be situated at far ends of an urban area. Hence the time required to move from one 'position' to the other correspondingly will increase. In the third pattern the agents may reside still further apart in different towns. The time–space gap between them may be greater than in either of its counterparts. Thus, Nadel's single image masks a substantial difference between the connection among these three sets of positions. It becomes evident how important these differences might be to the study of patterns of interaction at large, when it is realised that social patterns generally incorporate numerous interactions between 'positions' which may or may not share the same time–space extension with corresponding interactions between 'positions' in what Nadel might perceive as identical patterns. To overlook these differences is to obscure a crucial aspect of differences in configurations between social patterns.

Whereas Nadel proposes to minimise the significance of temporality in his conception of morphological structure, Blau attempts to incorporate a spatial dimension into his work. Blau, of course, defines social structure itself as a multi-dimensional 'space' of social positions among which a population is distributed. But space here is used in a figurative sense to refer to a theoretically conceived area in which positions and parameters may assume diverse configurations. The more literal conception of space in Blau's writings occurs in his account of what he terms ecological structure, a term which is meant to evoke an affinity with the works of social ecologists such as Amos Hawley and Otis Dudley Duncan. The latter scholars are important for Blau (1977a, p. 158) in so far as they broadened the scope of social ecology beyond the traditional concern with the spatial zoning of urban areas to include a generic concern for the spatial organisation of social relations. Proceeding along similar lines, Blau's conception of ecological structure (1977a, p. 155) is meant to grasp the influence of the distribution of people in physical space on the structure of differentiated positions and the rates of association that develop among them. Consistent with his theory of social structure at large, Blau proposes that both nominal and graduated parameters may be identified in the spatial distribution of populations. But in both instances the central criterion is territoriality: the physical distance between people identified in terms of their structurally defined social position. While Blau appears to accept societal totalities as his basic territorial units of analysis, his propositions need not remain fixed on this level. His remarks suggest that most of them apply equally well to territorial regions of a smaller scale ranging down to cities, neighbourhoods, etc. Regardless of the unit of analysis in question, a crucial issue is that ecological structure is rooted in features of the physical environment that impede or facilitate opportunities for contact between actors. This issue is summarised in a basic principle responsible for the significance of ecological structure: opportunities for social association depend on physical propinquity (Blau, 1977a, p. 173; see also pp. 90–1).

Blau should be applauded for his effort to establish a spatial dimension for the differentiation of social position and the associations between actors. Indeed, there are certain respects in which his insights correspond to specific points incorporated in Giddens's account of the time–space constitution of social systems. Nevertheless, Blau's insights cannot be accepted as they stand. Consider

Blau's contention that opportunities for social associations depend upon physical propinquity. What this proposition implies is that physical distance serves as a barrier to social interaction. Now there can be no denying that distance does make a difference in the course and conduct of social life. But Blau wishes to set aside the temporal dimension of social activity, and hence fails to observe any conjunction between time and space. While acknowledging that all social relations require the investment of time (and also that all social structures exist for limited historical periods), Blau (1977a, p. 158) sidesteps a concern for temporality by proposing that time simply is too interwoven with various social processes and aspects of social structure to single it out for separate analysis. The problem here is that Blau's definition of propinquity cannot be defined without a temporal reference.

As Blau (1977a, p. 165) clearly recognises, efficient means of transportation reduce the effect of physical propinquity on opportunities for contact between actors. But why is this so? The answer clearly cannot be that physical distance has been shortened: the media of transportation connect communities that remain spatially fixed. Transportation media reduce the effects of physical propinquity because they shorten the *time* actors must spend travelling between locales. Propinquity, then, is not merely a matter of physical distance; it is distance considered as the time it takes to move between spatially distinct social settings. To complement earlier examples it is useful to consider an illustration from modern urban life. Presume that three neighbourhoods respectively labelled A, B, and C exist in a large city. A and B are physically separated by two miles, while C stands five miles apart from either one. A spatial perspective might lead one to believe that actors in neighbourhoods A and B might interact with one another more often, and more intensively, than they would with actors in neighbourhood C. But from a time–space perspective matters might appear in a very different light. This would occur if no rapid means of transportation operated between neighbourhoods A and B, while both were served by highways and subway lines running directly to neighbourhood C. The time–space distance between neighbourhood C on the one hand, and A or B on the other, now might be shorter than the time–space distance between neighbourhood A and B despite the fact that the latter are physically much closer together.

A second weakness in Blau's contention that opportunities for social associations depend upon physical propinquity, is that it underplays the role of communication between those who are physically absent, which has enormously increased since the advent of electronic communication. In fairness, it should be noted that Blau (1977a, p. 159) does acknowledge that modern means of communication, like those of transportation, make it easier for actors to maintain contact despite physical separation. But what is neglected here is that electronic communication opens up an enormous range of possibilities for actors to establish and maintain relations that simply did not exist prior to the advent of modernity. Blau's theory conceives social structure in terms of distributions of populations distinguished by their social positions. If the distance between positions is construed from a time–space perspective, then electronic communication media literally change the map. Frequent relations between those who maintain given positions now may extend across entire societies, or even around the world, in the time it takes to transact a telephone call.

This concludes my critique of latter-day morphology. In this critique I have sought to indicate that a concern for social patterns cannot be divorced from a concern for social *praxis*, and that once attention is directed to the reproduction of patterns as it occurs through social *praxis*, a concern for the spatio-temporal dimension of social patterns cannot be left out of account. Structuration theory's account of social patterning gives sustained attention to both of these points. This aspect of the ontology of structuration theory is elaborated in Chapter 3.

3

The Patterning and Articulation of Systems Across Time and Space

Systems and structure in structuration theory

Subject to the charge of excessive formalism, lacking a basis in social *praxis*, neglectful of the time–space constitution of social patterns; all of these problems damage the credibility of latter-day social morphology. Yet the importance of the subject-matter to which morphologists attend cannot be denied. Issues central to their work, such as the articulation and configuration of patterns in the relations between actors, have figured prominently in the social sciences since the dawn of the discipline, and no doubt they will remain on the agenda for generations yet to come. Although it would be unwise to equate social morphology, with its formalist connotations, with the account of social patterning Giddens develops in structuration theory, the set of concepts he provides preserves the morphological concern with social patterns while providing a home base for these patterns in modes of interaction reproduced across time and space. As I have mentioned above, a shift to a praxiological outlook does away with the problematic claim that collective patterns possess emergent properties, as well as the concomitant distinction between hypostatised patterns and the consciousness of individuals. In structuration theory, agents, with a practical consciousness regarding appropriate procedures, maintain these patterns during the course of their active participation in social routines. In anticipation of subsequent remarks (see below, and Chapter 6) it should be stressed that to deny emergent status to social patterns entails no disregard of social constraints. However, the kinds of constraints at issue appear very different from those proposed by latter-day morphologists in so far as they affect the ability of social agents to engage in sequences and interconnected series of interactions.

It should be emphasised here that Giddens's thought on the time–space constitution of social patterns has matured considerably during the course of his writings. Issues of temporality and spatiality play little part in *New Rules of Sociological Method* and the articles pertaining to structuration theory published in *Studies in Social and Political Theory*, although Giddens does suggest that functionalist theories neglect time in their conceptions of structure (see *NRSM*, p. 120). The first sustained discussions of the significance of time and space appear in *Central Problems in Social Theory* (pp. 3–4, 53–65; ch. 6). However, many concepts are introduced here only in a programmatic fashion. *A Contemporary Critique of Historical Materialism* is the first work where time and space begin to move to the centre of Giddens's thought. But here many issues of importance to structuration theory at large are developed in keeping with his more substantive and historical themes. Theoretical issues are better developed in *The Constitution of Society* where, informed by insights derived from recent works in time-geography, Giddens (*CS*, p. 110) proposes that issues regarding the time–space constitution of social systems stand at the very heart of social theory. He proceeds to make good on this claim by expanding upon concepts introduced in previous works and by proposing many new concepts as well. It is in the nature of the structurationist ontology that no set of issues regarding the constitution of social life stands apart from the rest. The delayed development of Giddens's account of the temporal and spatial dimensions of social patterns makes it particularly important to grasp how issues in this regard are woven into other elements of structuration theory.

As I have argued above, many of the problems with latter-day morphological images of networks and positional patterns originate from their failure to consider how the order of relationships they are meant to represent is maintained in the course of social life. Although there are reasons indigenous to morphological perspectives that account for this state of affairs, Talcott Parsons's formulation of the problem of order may be responsible for the fact that the question of how order is maintained simply does not arise in most morphological works (Ronald Burt is an exception here). This contention may seem far-fetched at first glance. But it becomes more plausible once the realisation sets in that Parsons's definition of the problem of order has stood without challenge throughout the development of latter-day morphology.

The difficulty with Parsons's problem of order is that it does not directly apply to the subject-matter at issue in social morphology. That is, it does not centre on enduring patterns in social relationships. Rather, as Giddens has observed on numerous occasions (e.g. *NRSM*, p. 98; *CPST*, pp. 101–2, 217–18; *CCHM*, pp. 29–30; *PCST*, pp. 54–5) Parsons counterposes order to disintegration, thereby implying that order may be equated with the means of integration, regulation, or social control. Deriving inspiration from his interpretation of Hobbes, Parsons (1961, p. 96) suggests a problem of order concerned with the conditions on which order depends. Because Parsons accepts that order is most securely established if social processes take place in conformity with paths laid down by a system of norms, he appends the term 'normative' to his formulation of the problem of order (Parsons, 1968, pp. 91–4). Yet in the midst of this discussion Parsons also recognises that order can be conceived from a different point of view, one that appears far more in keeping with a straightforward concern with the configuration of patterns. This he terms 'factual order'. What distinguishes factual order from its normative counterpart is that its antithesis is not disintegration, but randomness or chance. In certain respects factual order seems more deeply embedded in social life than normative order. Given the breakdown of normative order, Parsons holds that order in the factual sense still may be found. That is, uniformities of process may continue to exist. As Giddens observes (*PCST*, p. 54), this is an extremely general view of order. But if such is the case, it at least hints at the possibility that a problem of order might be defined in terms of the patterning of processes rather than regulation through norms.

Although Giddens does not propose anything like a morphological definition of the problem of order, he does provide a formulation of this problem that picks up the significance of patterns of social activities. As opposed to Parsons's concern for the normative conditions through which social integration may be regulated, according to Giddens:

The problem of order is how *form* occurs in social relations, or (put in another fashion) how social systems 'bind' time and space. All social activity is formed in three conjoined moments of difference: temporally, structurally . . . and spatially; the conjunction of these express the *situated* character of social practices. (*CCHM*, p. 30; see also *CS*, pp. 35, 181; *CPST*, pp. 216–17; *NRSM*, p. 98)

Unlike Parsons, Giddens does not elaborate structuration theory as a systematic response to the problem of order he perceives in social life. Nevertheless, by interpreting the problem of order in the manner indicated above, he directs attention to the praxiological constitution of patterns. The central theme of this problem of order is not simply that form exists, but rather how form is generated in the reproduction of patterns of interaction. Order consists in the *forming of form* chronically repeated in routine cycles of social conduct.

Giddens's reference in the foregoing passage to 'three moments of difference' involves a vital conceptual distinction between social systems and social structure. In structuration theory, systems comprise concrete patterns of interaction; patterns, that is, which extend across time and space (this absorbs two of the three 'moments of difference'). Structure (the third 'moment of difference') refers to normative and semantic rules (or mutual knowledge) as well as authoritative and allocative resources that enter into the procedural skills that agents maintain, and which enable them to reproduce practices they recognise as appropriate for the routine situations they encounter in day-to-day life. Through the duality of structure each instance in which the reproduction of given practices, or set of practices, is reproduced serves to draw rules and resources into a new temporal moment. As practices are reproduced many times over in different settings, structure not only is drawn through time but through space as well.

How then does structure 'bind' time and space in social systems? The answer to this question hinges on perceiving a system as an interconnected or articulated series of institutionalised modes of interaction reproduced in spatially distinct social settings over a determinate period of history. Deferring the question of how the articulation of interactions occurs in social *praxis*, it can be said that structure 'binds' these interactions by enabling agents to

reproduce the reciprocal practices through which they are constituted in a manner such that interactions across time and space (or
time–space) in different settings comprise a reproduced ordering
of social relationships. Notice that the ordering of social relationships continually is in the process of being reproduced. To
borrow Nadel's network simile, 'knots' (interactions) repeatedly
are tied and retied so that as some disappear others reappear.
Thus, because systems always are in the process of being reproduced, they cannot be abstracted from time and space (cf. *CPST*,
pp. 61–2, 201–2), nor can they be conceived as an emergent
'object'.

Since systems have a concrete existence in articulated series of
interactions reproduced across time and space, their patterns may
be discerned in the ongoing course of social events. But structure
cannot be apprehended from a concrete point of view. Specific sets
of rules and resources exist only in the moment when the
reproduction of specific practices, or reciprocal practices comprising a mode of interaction, are carried out. While structural rules
and resources are no less 'real' as a result, to conceive structural
patterns requires a bracketing of procedures of social conduct so
that inferences can be drawn regarding how rules and resources
mesh together. A crucial point here is that since the course and
conduct of social activity is set aside in order to analyse structure,
structures are not conceived to extend across time and space (see
Chapter 6). Lacking any temporality or spatiality, structure involves what Giddens terms 'a virtual order of differences'.

Considered from a somewhat different angle, concrete systems
are not structures in themselves. Rather, upon examination,
systems exhibit structural properties in the procedures whereby
they are reproduced (*CS*, p. 17; 'AI', p. 169; *CPST*, pp. 64–6;
SSPT, pp. 117–18). The term 'structuration', from which structuration theory takes its name, grasps the simultaneous reproduction of structure and systemic relations which occurs as patterns of
interaction are reproduced in and through the duality of structure
(*CS*, p. 25, see also p. 17; *CPST*, p. 66; *NRSM*, p. 121).

While further consideration of the analysis of structure is
reserved for Chapter 7, it must be reiterated that structure provides for the cultural and political content of social systems.
Failure to bear this crucial point in mind in the following discussion may lead to the premature conclusion that structuration

theory primarily is concerned with patterns no less formal than those at issue in latter-day social morphology. Such, definitely, is not the case.

Having underscored this point with what I trust is sufficient emphasis, a few words are in order on the methodological status of social systems. In some respects social systems appear to fall through the slats in a bilateral set of brackets Giddens provides for methodological purposes in structuration theory (see *CPST*, p. 80; *CS*, pp. 30, 285, 288). On the one hand there is *the analysis of strategic conduct*. Attention here focuses upon the procedures through which social activities are generated and reproduced; a subject which includes the practical and strategic consciousness of agents and the strategies of control they exercise within contextually demarcated boundaries of activity. On the other hand there is *institutional analysis*. The focus here is on structural properties as chronically reproduced properties of systems. The brackets involved in this distinction hinge upon the temporary suspension of an interest in the structural properties of systems in the analysis of strategic conduct, or the temporary suspension of interest in the performance of social practices in institutional analysis. As thus defined this distinction appears well-suited to facilitate theory and research with regard to the procedural content of practices versus the structural properties of collectivities. But no provision is made for consideration of the time–space configuration of system patterns. To conceive the time–space patterning of interactions from the standpoint of the analysis of strategic conduct would entail the introduction of so many details of social *praxis* that the patterning itself would almost certainly fade from view. Institutional analysis, on the other hand, is intended to facilitate the apprehension of the interwoven rules and resources that 'bind' social systems.

Giddens, I believe, must be faulted for not giving serious consideration to the methodological brackets required in order to analyse the time–space patterning of social systems. To fill this gap in structuration theory I propose the need for a third mode of bracketing corresponding to institutional analysis but intended to facilitate the apprehension of system patterns. In what I term *systems analysis*, temporary brackets screen off both the structural properties of social systems and the contingencies of interactions that depart from institutionalised routines. What remains in view is the ordering and the articulations between interactions in time and space. It cannot be too strongly emphasised that these brackets are entirely provisional. The only way to gain a comprehensive account of the constitution of collectivities is to combine the study of system patterns with the study of structural patterns. Moreover, for many purposes it may be absolutely necessary to refrain from both system analysis and institutional analysis. This is particularly important in the empirical study of critical episodes of historical transformation. Here only full-fledged empirical accounts of social circumstances and events can account for how both structural and systemic patterns are redirected, reconfigured, or replaced.

System patterns and time-geography

In formulating concepts regarding the time–space constitution of system patterns, Giddens has been strongly influenced by insights originating in the works of time-geographers such as Thorsten Hägerstrand, Alan Pred, and Tommy Carlstein. The following passage summarises aspects of the time-geographic approach that Giddens considers of particular importance:

> The interconnection of time and space can be explored in terms of the participation of social actors in cycles of social activity as well as at the levels of the transformation of society itself. Time-geography deals with the time–space 'choreography' of individuals' existence over given time-periods: the day, the week, year, or the whole life-time. A person's daily routine of activities, for example, can be charted as a path through time–space. Thus the social transition involved in leaving home to go to work is also movement through space. Social interaction from this point of view can be understood as the 'coupling' of paths in social encounters. (*CPST*, p. 205)

Presuming that the notion of time–space is familiar from the last chapter, it can easily be seen that time-geography shares with structuration theory a non-emergent view of social patterns; in this case the patterns individuals follow, and thereby reproduce as they move across time–space during the routine course of their social activities.

But while time-geography provides Giddens with many novel and important insights into the interconnection between time and space in social interaction, he has repaid this debt by carrying the time-geographic perspective in new directions, thereby expanding the domain of issue to which it is addressed. Thus, whereas many time-geographers initially neglected the structural content of both actions and contexts of interaction, Giddens (*CS*, pp. 116–17) insists that these matters must be taken into account. Time-geographers have responded to this argument with criticism as well as favour (for example Carlstein, 1981; Thrift, 1985; and various essays in Gregory and Urry, 1985). But the significance of this move is that it forestalls the possibility that time-geography might end up exclusively devoted to topographic models; i.e. it might neglect procedural aspects of conduct to the point where, in the manner of social morphologists, patterns traced out in time–space comprise their only topic of interest. A crucial point to bear in mind, as Giddens observes (*CS*, p. 363), is that human beings 'make their own geography', as much as they 'make their own history'.

Having said this, the time-geographic approach does open up opportunities for structuration theory to construe the patterning of activities and interactions in social life from a point of view unanticipated in social morphology. But, here again, an expansion of the time-geographic perspective can be discerned. As Giddens indicates in the summary of the time-geographic approach I have excerpted in the foregoing remarks, many works in time-geography concentrate upon the time–space paths followed by individuals during the course of a given time period. There is undeniable value in viewing matters in this way, not only because individuals are the agents of social reproduction, but also because, as corporeal beings, individuals undertake movements across time–space. For these reasons, as will be indicated below, attention must be directed to the material circumstances of corporeality and social locales that shape and constrain opportunities for interaction. But from the praxiological standpoint of structuration theory attention need not focus exclusively on the doings of specific individuals. Rather, one may concentrate on the reproduction of system patterns across time and space for periods of history extending beyond the lifetime of any given individual. Although social *praxis* figures in both of these perspectives, it is construed on two different levels of temporality. Giddens (*CPST*, p. 96; *CCHM*, pp. 19–20; *CS*, p. 35) proposes the following set of categories:

Levels of temporality

durée of day-to-day experience: 'reversible time'

lifespan of the individual: 'irreversible time'

longue durée of institutions: 'reversible time'

The concepts of 'reversible' and 'irreversible' time which Giddens absorbs from Lévi-Strauss (1963, p. 301) may seem obscure at first glance, but they should not be overlooked since they provide the underpinnings for the approach to system patterns incorporated in structuration theory. Irreversible time signifies a non-repetitive temporal span of events, exemplified and made manifest in the life-cycle of human beings. Reversible time refers to cycles of activities that are chronically repeated. Now an emphasis upon the reversible time of day-to-day experience has a variety of applications in social theory and research. But attending to cycles of activity from this point of view makes it difficult to discern reproduced patterns of interaction. While Giddens does not put matters in quite this way, one basic problem here is that during the individual's reversible cycle of activities and interactions she may engage in various interactions that figure in a number of different system patterns. This, of course, is a purely analytical distinction since individuals are agents who reproduce institutionalised system patterns. Nevertheless, this distinction is a familiar feature of social life. In the modern era we speak of taking a job, or going to school, or coming home to our families, to indicate that our paths of activity as individuals intersect various ongoing systems or patterns of interaction. Even in peasant villages and tribal societies one may find that the patterning of interactions in kinship systems is distinguished in some way from the patterning of activities in the production of goods or artifacts.

The ordering of interactions in system patterns – an ordering that extends across time and space in ways that remain to be discussed – is best conceived as occurring on the level of the reversible time of the *longue durée*. *Institutionalised interactions, rather than individuals, appear as the constituent elements of social systems.* Thus it becomes possible to perceive patterns as involving only some of the encounters any individual maintains with others on a repetitive basis. In addition, one may discuss changes in the individuals who participate in these encounters. This may involve a rotation of individuals, as some agents halt their systematically relevant activities while others join in. The social mobility of agents who suspend their participation in certain types of interactions in the system so as to engage in others may be grasped in a similar way. However, it should be emphasised that statistical representations of rotation and mobility must be augmented by accounts of the kinds of practices involved in making these moves. As Giddens (*CS*, pp. 304–10) points out, quantified studies of mobility often obscure both the structuration of social practices and agents' motives and reasons for following certain options rather than others.

The articulation of system patterns: social integration and system integration

Since structuration theory postulates no emergent properties for patterns of interaction, the way in which various types of interaction are linked or articulated across space and time in diverse locales takes on considerable importance. Articulation, it must be clearly understood, cannot be conceived exclusively as the interconnections between interactions. Structural sets of rules and resources play an essential part in 'binding' the interactions through which the institutional articulation of system occurs (see *CS*, p. 185). However, the topic at hand will be confined to two generic categories of *praxis* through which diverse interactions are joined in the time–space constitution of social systems. These categories are *social integration* and *system integration*.

The term 'integration' must be clarified from the start. Giddens (*SSPT*, pp. 124–5; *CPST*, pp. 76–7, 270, n. 57) derives the terminology of social and system integration from David Lockwood's critique of Parsonian normative functionalism. However, while Lockwood's critique is sound in many respects, he retains a sense of integration which distinguishes between order versus

conflict (see Lockwood, 1964, pp. 245, 250). Although Lockwood's terminology departs from Parsons's, the conceptual connection between order and integration in his work has a limited
affinity with Parsons's formulation of the problem of order. Given
Giddens's alternative proposal regarding the problem of order it
would be inconsistent to define integration in this way. In structuration theory, *integration* refers to regularised ties or interchanges sustained through reciprocities of practice (*CPST*, p. 76;
SSPT, p. 124). In terms I earlier employed in discussing Giddens's
problem of order, integration refers to the forming of form in
system patterns. Hence the counterpoint to integration in structuration theory is neither conflict nor the absence of regulation.
Rather it is the absence of a stable ordering of reciprocal practices:
i.e. a breakdown of social reproduction.

Because integration refers to ties or interchanges it has an
obvious bearing on the articulation of system patterns. But the
concepts of social integration and system integration grasp different types of ties. Some caution must be exercised in marking this
distinction. In Giddens's writings prior to *The Constitution of
Society* (*SSPT*, p. 124; *CPST*, p. 77; *CCHM*, p. 29), social integration referred to reciprocities of practice between agents,
while system integration referred to reciprocities between groups
of collectivities. This line of demarcation obscured the fact that in
structuration theory collectivities or groups are not agents in
themselves. While shorthand descriptions of the activities of
corporate collectivities may be proposed, the exercise of agency
takes place only in the practice and interactions carried out by
social actors (*CS*, pp. 220–1). By leaving open the possibility for
systems to engage in reciprocal practices with one another, the
distinction Giddens initially drew between social integration and
system integration implied the possibility of a cleavage between
'micro' and 'macro' levels of analysis. Were this possibility to be
realised it would run directly counter to his objective to reconcile
concepts regarding collectivities with those regarding action (see
Dickie-Clark, 1984, p. 108).

Although Giddens has not discussed this problem at length, he
now has remedied matters by providing a new conception of
system integration (*CS*, p. 39, n. 32). More important for the
present discussion, this new conception expresses the appreciation
for the time–spacing patterning of interactions exhibited in his

more recent works. *Social integration* still refers to reciprocities of practice between actors. But a stronger emphasis now is placed on the fact that the reciprocities are transacted in circumstances of co-presence. *System integration*, by contrast, now refers to reciprocities between actors or collectivities across extended time–space; i.e. connections between those who are physically absent (*CS*, p. 28). It is not entirely clear why Giddens inserts an unqualified reference to reciprocities between collectivities here. Presumably, he means to allow for shorthand summaries of interactions between agents across spatially and temporally separated locales that serve to establish connecting relations between diverse systems. Diplomatic relations between states in an interstate system, for example, often are carried out through interactions between designated agents who may be situated so as to be absent from one another.

Before entering further into how reciprocities between actors (in both senses of the term) contribute to the articulation of system patterns, two points must be made about system patterns at large. First, while Giddens does provide a concept of a societal totality, societal systems figure less prominently in structuration theory than is true in many schools of thought. Moving outward, societies appear within intersocial systems. Moving laterally, certain systems (which conceivably might range from trans-national enterprises to extended families) may cross-cut societal boundaries. Moving inward, societies both are social systems, and are constituted by the intersection of multiple social systems. There will be more to say on societies in Chapter 7. The second point to be made about systems at large is that they may vary in the degree to which they cohere as patterns. This logically follows from the fact that diverse kinds of reciprocities of practice establish diverse forms of relations between agents (see *CS*, p. 27). Since systems differ in the strength of their 'ties', they also differ in the degree to which they exhibit well-defined boundaries (cf. *CS*, p. 165). Both of the preceding points provide appropriate means to understand why Giddens (*CS*, p. 210) looks with favour on Blau's recognition that societies are not all of a piece. This, in fact, is one of the few issues on which structuration theory and latter-day social morphology fully agree.

Social integration and material constraints

All social systems, including those which extend across the broadest spans of space and time, involve articulation sustained through various modes of interaction in circumstances of co-presence (*CS*, pp. 36, 64). However, in order to clarify the role played by social integration in the articulation of system patterns, it will be helpful initially to confine discussion to small-scale systems where the transaction of most social relations occurs on a face-to-face basis: e.g. families, neighbourhoods, factory and office work-units, peasant villages and tribal societies. While Giddens (*CS*, pp. 70ff) provides a typology that distinguishes various modes of interaction, the guiding thread in these cycles of activity are focused encounters between two or more agents. During the course of such encounters agents establish intimate contexts and engage in absorbing activities through the mutual coordination of talk, as well as the reflexive monitoring of facial expressions and bodily posture. Because focused encounters involve so many reciprocal practices between agents, when they become a matter of routine they often serve to establish well-defined social relationships.

How then do considerations regarding time and space enter into the articulation of system patterns reproduced in and through face-to-face encounters? A basic point here is that in systems of this kind encounters are ordered as a series or cycle so that certain interactions occur prior to others. Seriality thus implies temporal ordering. But a temporal ordering must be combined with a spatial ordering in so far as face-to-face reciprocities are reproduced in diverse settings. The time–space articulation of systems reproduced exclusively through social integration thus refers to the manner in which serially ordered modes of interaction are interconnected or linked to one another across time and space. To establish how this occurs, some thought must be given to conditions that shape the opportunities for face-to-face interaction in time and space.

What initially lends a time–space dimension to all face-to-face encounters is the need for agents to establish what Giddens (*CS*, p. 118; *CCHM*, p. 39; *CPST*, pp. 103, 206–7) terms their *presence-availability*. A necessary condition for presence-availability is that agents must gather at the same time in a common locale. But presence-availability does not refer solely to the time–space proximity of agents. The point is, rather, that they must be situated so that they may mutually monitor and align their conduct with one another. Hence, agents situated several feet apart in a vacant room may share a higher degree of presence-availability than when they appear in the same proximity but are seated in different aisles of a crowded theatre. Therefore, in addition to the time–space proximity of agents, the concept of presence-availability incorporates a concern for the conjunction of material circumstances and social procedures that is involved in the constitution of social locales (on locales, see above, p. 41).

Presence-availability appears to be a matter of no great consequence from the standpoint of morphological studies that emphasise emergent properties of social patterns above and apart from social *praxis*. Yet beneath the deceptively prosaic observation that agents must gather simultaneously in appropriate locales so that they may generate and reproduce modes of interaction, lies a new approach to a topic that morphologists consider to be of great importance: constraints that affect the course and conduct of social activity. By establishing constraints associated with presence-availability not only does structuration theory avoid ascribing effective power to emergent properties, but this strategy also provides structuration theory with insights into factors that figure prominently in the articulation of face-to-face relations.

Since this marks the first discussion of how structuration theory deals with matters of constraint, a number of points of clarification are in order. First, consistent with the emphasis upon social *praxis* in structuration theory, the locus of constraint always involves circumstances that enter into the performance of conduct. Second, while the topic at hand refers to constraints associated with presence-availability, Giddens also establishes concepts pertaining to structural constraints and sanctioning procedures (these are extensively discussed in Chapter 6). Third, within the circumstances of conduct the concept of constraint in structuration theory incorporates a concern for the motives and wants that impel or dispose actors to prefer modes of conduct and interaction that they may or may not be able to pursue (see Chapter 6). Finally, to make an extremely important point, all references to circumstances of constraint simultaneously refer to circumstances of enablement. The complimentary connection between enablement and constraint by no means is a contradiction in terms. It logically follows from the fundamental insight that all social agents retain a capacity to 'make a difference' in the ongoing course of social events. Because the exercise of agency serves as a necessary condition for the production of social conduct, circumstances that restrict or deny certain types of activity also enable other modes of conduct to be performed (*CS*, pp. 173–4). All of the preceding points are reflected in the following synopsis:

> All action occurs in contexts that, for any given single actor, include many elements which that actor neither helped to bring into being nor has any significant control over. Such enabling and constraining features of contexts of action include both material and social phenomenon. (*CS*, p. 346)

The constraints that influence presence-availability are material in nature. They refer to the ways in which both the human body as well as relevant features of the physical milieu of interaction serve to limit opportunities for social agents to engage in face-to-face interaction with one another (*CS*, pp. 174–5). Drawing upon concepts devised by several time-geographers, and in particular Thorsten Hägerstrand, Giddens categorises these constraints under two headings: coupling constraints and capability constraints. In addition he adopts concepts referring to the 'packing' of activities and items in space and time from work done by the time-geographer, Tommy Carlstein (*CS*, pp. 113–16; see also, Hägerstrand, 1970, 1975; Parkes and Thrift, 1980, pp. 22, 272; Carlstein, 1980). While these concepts refer to a highly complex set of issues in time-geography, they can be briefly summarised as follows.

Coupling constraints refer to biologically established conditions of human corporeality that influence activities agents undertake jointly with others. These conditions fundamentally involve the sensory and communicative faculties of the human body (*CS*, pp. 76–7). Thus, the limited range of human visual and auditory perceptual organs and vocal mechanisms circumscribe the effective perimeter in which full presence-availability may be maintained. Sensory and communicative faculties also influence the course of conduct when agents come together. Visual, auditory, and linguistic aspects of face-to-face interaction generally are limited by these faculties so that at any given time only a small number of agents may mutually align and coordinate their reciprocal practices. Moreover, these same faculties generally impose the requirement for a sequencing of practices, as exhibited in turn-taking procedures and other procedures to organize the flow of conversation and activity. It should be emphasised that while coupling constraints establish limits to interaction, they do not *determine* how face-to-face reciprocities are transacted in detail. As demonstrated in ethnomethodological research (see Heritage, 1984, ch. 8 *passim*), socially established rules regarding turn-taking and reciprocal monitoring vary between cultures and among different groups.

Capability constraints refer to a variety of corporeal and physical conditions that shape opportunities for agents to come together in a given social locale. One such condition, the finitude of the agent, will be set aside for the purposes at hand. Those capability constraints that directly influence presence-availability in day-to-day life stem from the indivisibility of both the human body and many of the physical objects and artifacts that constitute material aspects of locales where interaction is carried out. These conditions influence the spatial and temporal co-presence of actors in very obvious ways. First, the indivisibility of the human body ordains that given agents may meet and mingle in only one locale during any given period of time. Second, the indivisibility of material features of locales (e.g. the architectural contours of rooms, houses, office buildings, factories, etc.) restricts the number of agents who may gather and interact. Carlstein proposes a spatial mode of 'packing' to grasp this point. Third, to introduce a point of great importance for subsequent remarks: given the indivisibility of the body and the limits on 'packing' in any given locale, if agents are to interact with numerous others during the course of their social routines, at least some of them must move from one locale to another, a move that extends across time–space. Fourth, all human agents experience the recurrent need for food and sleep, activities they must interpolate within the temporal order of their daily routines. According to Carlstein, only a limited number of time-consuming activities can be 'packed' into a given temporal period.

In the preceding summary coupling and capability constraints have been presented from the standpoint of the individual. By virtue of the limits imposed upon the possibility for any given agent to establish presence-availability with others, the *durée* of her daily experience assumes a temporal sequencing of interactions that becomes a sequencing in time–space in so far as she does not remain situated in a single locale. Thus, coupling and capability constraints to some extent serve to limit the time–space paths agents follow and reproduce in their daily routines. Yet despite the manifest importance of these constraints for the time–space patterning of day-to-day life, agents generally remain only tacitly aware that they exist, save those occasions when daily routines are broken. This circumstance offers a choice bit of evidence in support of Giddens's high regard for practical consciousness.

Shifting now from the patterning of activities from the standpoint of the actor, to the patterning of systems, it can be seen that coupling and capability constraints shape and channel the seriality of institutionalised face-to-face encounters through which the articulation of small-scale systems occurs. In order to pursue this point it must be understood that most collectivities have defined locales of operation associated with routine forms of social encounters (*CCHM*, p. 39). The means by which encounters in one locale are joined or articulated with encounters carried out later on in the same setting, or subsequently transacted in different locales, are provided by the presence-availability of appropriate actors (cf. *CCHM*, p. 39; *CPST*, pp. 206–7). The human body, in effect, serves as the vehicle that connects one set of face-to-face encounters with others during the course of system reproduction.

Since individuals must reproduce the institutionalised encounters which comprise small-scale systems, it follows that the serial ordering of such encounters will be subject to the same capability and coupling constraints that influence the agent's cycle of activities. In order to establish their presence-availability in one locale agents must defer other opportunities for conduct. At the close of any given encounter relevant to system reproduction they are able to engage in further sequences of interaction which may, or may not, be germane to the system. Where the former holds true, they may remain in the original locale so as to engage in interaction with new agents who converge on the scene. Alternatively, they may disperse to other locales in order to establish the presence-availability required for the reproduction of other modes of interaction incorporated in the system. As the serial ordering of encounters proceeds, a pattern is marked out that represents the articulation of the system extending across time and space.

System integration

Coupling and capability constraints obviously restrict the time–space extension of systems articulated exclusively through face-to-face encounters. Since embodied agents serve as the means through which the articulation of encounters is reproduced, the locales of operation in the system generally must be situated in close proximity to one another. More far-flung patterns are possible, of course, as is exemplified by the Kula exchange. But, as Giddens observes, before the advent of modern capitalism there was no large-scale society in which the village community-grouping – which hinges upon the presence-availability of agents who reside in close proximity – did not remain a basic unit. Even in the case of the Roman *latifundae*, where agents of the empire established political and economic relations between local activities and the imperial administration, the small-scale community with its kinship system and traditional ways of life continued to serve as the basic mode of social order (*CCHM*, pp. 102ff; for other examples, see *CS*, pp. 165–8).

A profound alteration in the configuration and articulation of system patterns has been part and parcel of the radical transformation of social life brought about in the era subsequent to the proliferation and institutionalisation of practices associated with capitalism and the concomitant development of the modern state. To be sure, social integration through interaction in circumstances of co-presence continues to sustain many contemporary groupings. Nuclear families and bureaucratic offices, urban neighbourhoods and rural communities, as well as factory work units and local schools, all remain patterned through the serial reproduction of face-to-face encounters. But these modes of social integration now are enmeshed in systems of far greater time–space extension. To use the terminology of structuration theory (*CS*, pp, 171, 181; *CCHM*, pp. 4–5, 91–7), such systems exhibit a far greater degree of *time–space distantiation*. Examples in abundance appear throughout modern social life, ranging from inter-social systems and societal totalities to capitalist enterprises, the modern state and other types of complex organisations.

The expansive time–space distanciation apparent in modern social systems has been stimulated by, and in turn has facilitated, a massive centralisation of authoritative and allocative resources. Although we take this centralisation for granted today, it did not exist to anything approaching the present extent even as recently as a century ago. While I shall allude to certain points in this regard that have a particular bearing on the configuration and articulation of system patterns in subsequent remarks, a more thorough discussion of the political organisation of administrative systems will be presented in Chapter 5. The topic at hand is system integration: reciprocities between absent agents.

Means to engage in interaction between those who are absent from one another have existed in various forms at least since the advent of literacy and writing. However, the time–space distanciation of communication still depended upon the physical movement of embodied agents. The cycle of correspondence was governed by the time required to travel across the territory separating the locales in which agents resided (*CPST*, p. 204). The advent of rapid and efficient means of transportation and shipping coupled with the development of electronic media for the transmission of communication between agents, share direct responsibility for changing this state of affairs. Giddens places an extraordinary emphasis on the transformation of social relations they have combined to produce:

> Communities of high presence-availability in *all* cultures prior to only some hundred years ago, were groupings of individuals in close physical proximity to one another. The corporeality of the agent, the limitations upon the mobility of the body in the trajectories of the *durée* of daily activity, together with the physical properties of space, ensured that this was so. The media of communication were always identical to those of transportation. Even with the use of fast horses, ships, forced marches, etc., long distance in space meant long distance in time. The mechanization of transport has been the major factor leading to dramatic forms of time–space convergence . . . But the most radical disjuncture of relevance in modern history (whose implications today are very far from being exhausted) is the separation of media of communication, by the development of

electronic signalling from the media of transportation: the latter always having involved by some means or other, the mobility of the human body. Morse's invention of the electromagnetic telegraph marks as distinctive a transition in human cultural development as the wheel or any other technological innovation ever did. (*CS*, p. 123)

The electronic-communications media figure so prominently in these remarks because for the first time in history the embodied agent need not serve as the only means whereby reciprocities of practice are conveyed across time and space. This does not dissolve all coupling and capability constraints: turn-taking, for example, is quite pronounced in electronic communication. But coupling and capability constraints associated with the establishment of face-to-face co-presence no longer need apply. The intrinsic relationship between time and space is radically altered as a result. Because electronic media almost instantaneously shuttle communication across a potentially unlimited territorial expanse, the distance in time between agents shrinks to the point of insignificance. (The brief delay between transmission of messages from the moon and their reception on earth seems far more exceptional than the fact that these messages moved from the 'base station' to points around the world in five to ten seconds.) But as the temporal gap between agents contracts, the spatial extension expands so that no locale supplied with devices in proper working order is too remote to be reached (cf. *CCHM*, p. 40).

The expanded range of contact between agents is not entirely without cost. Certain intimacies of face-to-face interaction are lost as a result. The telephone, for example, while it preserves the inflections of vocal discourse, fails to transmit the physical gestures, facial expressions, and postural alignments that comprise routine means of conveying tacit information and emotional cues in full-fledged social encounters. In some instances this attenuation of interaction may be exacerbated since electronic communication creates possibilities for impersonal forms of contact between agents who not only may be unacquainted with each other, but who even may be unacquainted with any other agents in their respective locales. However, modern means of transportation can mitigate this contingency. Where presence-availability is called for or desired in order to augment communication between agents, journeys to distant locales often are possible without placing undue burdens on agents' time or energy. Modern means of transportation, of course, also connect distant locales by providing for the rapid and dependable trans-shipment of raw materials, goods and commodities throughout most populated quarters of the globe.

While changes brought about by the ongoing revolution in communication and transportation generate many consequences that social scientists have yet to explore, the point to be underscored here is the role they play in the articulation of social systems. For illustrative purposes consider a local factory as it might have existed early in the nineteenth century versus how it might appear today. In the earlier instance, the local factory, situated close to a port or a direct source of raw materials, most likely would be an autonomous enterprise, a social system that from the standpoint of production and administrative control might be conceived to stand as an independent organisation. (Matters would appear otherwise from a market-oriented point of view.) The dominant mode of articulation of the social relations in the factory would be face-to-face encounters among and between workers, managers, and quite often owners who returned to the factory on a day-to-day basis. Today many factories, while they still involve face-to-face interactions among and between workers and lower-level managers, are incorporated in large-scale enterprise with locales of operation in a variety of spatially distant settings. Upper-level managers or owners, as the case may be, often remain in a locale removed from all factory sites where industrial production occurs. While upper-level managers also engage in routine face-to-face encounters with one another in order to formulate and execute corporate policies and strategies, they gather information from factories and issue orders and directives to them via the electronic transmission of oral and written communication.

As this example suggests, the electronic media provide for an expansion in the scale of operations of social systems by establishing new modes of articulation in the reciprocities between absent agents. While face-to-face encounters continue to establish many articulating links in these systems, the multiple locales incorporated in large-scale systems are tied together through contacts between agents that flow across electronic cables as well as channels of mechanised transportation that span the air, land, and sea. Having made this point clear, a question arises as to whether or not these altered conditions of system articulation retain a serial ordering of interactions corresponding to that in small-scale systems.

Seriality, of course, enters into those interactions joined together in the system that require the presence-availability of agents at appropriate locales. However, in so far as the ordering of activities across different locales is at issue – i.e. the forming of form in large-scale system patterns – the coupling and capability constraints impinging upon face-to-face encounters no longer mandates seriality. Nevertheless a very rigid seriality of activities often is evident in large-scale systems. Trans-national capitalist enterprises, state bureaucracies with offices in different locales, urban school systems, etc. each exhibit an institutionalised and repetitive cycle of activities. But instead of issuing exclusively from coupling and capability constraints, this seriality stems from the control exercised by agents with access to centralised resources who coordinate the processes of system reproduction (see *CS*, pp. 151–4; see also below on administered systems, in Chapter 4, and on administrative power, in Chapter 5).

The serial ordering of practices and interactions in large-scale systems introduces a new time–space dynamic into system reproduction. Activities carried out at a designated time in one locale have a direct bearing on those subsequently transacted in a different setting, which in turn have a direct bearing on further activities in yet another locale. The procedures of articulation between locales may involve electronic communication and/or the shipment of appropriate materials or commodities. Considered at large the entire system thus exhibits an extensive cycle of interconnected modes of conduct patterned in a temporal sequence across spatially separated locales of operation.

An important consequence of time–space seriality in system reproduction is that it penetrates, and to a great extent organises, the time–space paths institutionalised in the daily routines of individual agents. Whereas prior to the advent of large-scale systems (e.g. capitalism and the modern state) the daily routines of the majority of individuals drew upon and reproduced established traditions, today the seriality exhibited in commutation patterns, shopping trips, regularly scheduled meetings and appointments, etc. is geared into the schedules maintained in industrial, administrative, commercial, and educational organisations. While the undermining of tradition and the concomitant rise of impersonal relations and egoistic motives and interests cannot completely be accounted for on this basis, Giddens (*CCHM*, pp. 150–2) considers this 'routinisation of daily life' to be a matter of considerable importance.

System integration and system density

Tracing out the time–space articulation and seriality of system patterns reproduced through diverse modes of social integration and system integration presents opportunities and challenges for theory and research well beyond the narrow compass of latter-day studies in social morphology. Giddens has begun to explore this realm in his substantive works, but it is fair to say that many basic questions remain to be posed and many fundamental insights remain to be developed. Even Giddens's conceptual framework itself should not be considered to be complete as it stands. Here I would like to propose an issue that Giddens appears to have slighted in his primary emphasis upon the time–space distantiation of large-scale systems.

An evident feature of large-scale systems is that by incorporating modes of interactions between agents an increase occurs in what might be called, following Durkheim, the density of the social system: i.e. an increase in the frequency of relations between different actors in the system (cf. Durkheim, 1984, p. 201). With due allowance for the primary focus upon societal totalities in Durkheim's work, the following passages from *The Division of Labour in Society* prefigures the point I wish to make here. Itemising various factors he holds to be involved in the historical development of density, Durkheim (1984, p. 203) suggests, 'Finally, there is the number and speed of the means of communication and transmission. By abolishing or lessening the vacuums separating social segments, these means increase the density of society.'

Now to elaborate this point it can be observed that because electronic communication (media that only recently had been developed in Durkheim's era) frees agents from the need to move bodily through time and space so as to establish presence-availability, they may interact (e.g. by telephone) with a greater number of different actors in a single day than they would ordinarily encounter in face-to-face interaction over the course of a far greater period of time. The addition of electronic communication, mechanical and electronic office machines, also contributes to the increasing volume of interaction by reducing exponentially the time required for the production of written correspondence in large-scale systems among their members, patrons, clients, and so forth. To be sure, non-electronic delivery services for written correspondence inevitably are slower than their electronic counterparts. Nevertheless, typewriters in an earlier era, and word-processors as well as high-speed computers today, have made it possible for a relatively small clerical staff to generate a large volume of letters, memoranda, commercial statements, and recordings of financial transactions, and to store this correspondence and the ensuing replies.

In proposing to complement structuration theory's concern for the time–space distantiation of large-scale systems with a conception of the increasing volume of reciprocities of practice between absent agents, I do not mean to suggest an evolutionary theory of morphological development such as appears in Durkheim's *Division of Labour*, nor a formalistic focus upon frequencies of contact as appears in Blau's latter-day morphological theory. As against an evolutionary perspective it must be stressed that technological devices only create opportunities for the volume of interaction between absent agents to increase; they do not ensure that these opportunities will be realised. The origins of technological means of communication and their applications in large-scale systems can be determined only through historically oriented theory and research focusing upon the growth of capitalism and the bureaucratic organisation of social systems. The emphasis in structuration theory on the modes of *praxis* involved in communication between absent agents already moves beyond Blau's formalistic point of view. But in addition it is absolutely essential to take the *content* of interaction into account. For many purposes this will require structural analysis. However, as I previously have mentioned, interactions between absent agents often are more impersonal than face-to-face encounters. Hence, as the volume of such interactions increases corresponding to the growth of large-scale systems, the sense of impersonality and anonymity so characteristic of modern social life is likely to grow and be amplified, and the articulating links in social systems are likely to become increasingly attenuated.

But if the evolutionary aspects of the classical morphological perspective and the formalism that permeates Blau's latter-day works must be set aside, incorporating a conception of the volume of reciprocities of practice into structuration theory's account of large-scale systems creates openings to several other morphological issues. For one thing, a growth in opportunities for interaction via system integration concomitantly creates opportunities for an increase in the variety of agents who participate in system reproduction. For another, an increasing volume of reciprocities across time and space can enhance the development of specialisation in social practices. Both of these issues, of course, must be construed in a broader historical perspective. In proposing them here all I wish to suggest is that the *classical* (as opposed to the latter-day) morphological agenda can be refashioned so as to yield many important insights through the development of spatio-temporal concepts within structuration theory.

Regionalisation of locales

Beyond their common concern with the configuration of social patterns, for reasons I have set forth throughout this chapter structuration theory does not directly intersect many of the specific issues addressed by *latter-day* social morphologists. However, with due recognition of the manifest differences involved, there is one point of intersection with Blau's account of ecological structure. Blau, it will be recalled, derives his views on ecological patterns from a concern for the distribution of actors across a territorial expanse, and the consequences of territorial propinquity or distance for the frequency of contact between them. By virtue of his concern for social reproduction, Giddens places no great emphasis upon a narrowly defined conception of territorial distribution of populations. However, he does provide an extensive account of the regionalisation of locales: an account that has some affinity with Blau's concerns in so far as it is addressed to the clustering and zoning of contexts in time and space.

It will be recalled that in structuration theory locales are not simply material environments in which conduct occurs, but rather contexts of interaction generated and reproduced as agents engage in practices that draw physical aspects of interactional settings into the course and conduct of social activity. Bearing this point in mind, if agents repeatedly return to the same *milieu* to engage in interaction, as is the case in the reproduction of social systems, the physical properties of locales contributes to the 'fixity' of their institutional practices (*CS*, p. 118; *CCHM*, p. 39). From a systemic standpoint this 'fixity' appears as defined locales of operation. For social agents this 'fixity' consists in tacit forms of mutual knowledge regarding the material settings where, at appropriate time-periods, certain modes of conduct routinely are carried out. Thus, 'fixity' implies a spatial as well as a temporal dimension.

The spatial dimension of fixity can be discerned quite easily in face-to-face encounters. As agents repeatedly move from one setting of interaction to the next they reproduce a spatial differentiation of locales that appears to them as stable characteristics of day-to-day life. A spatial fixity also is involved in many modes of interaction between absent agents. Officials and staff of bureaucracies, for example, typically are assigned to work at specific offices or desks. This facilitates routine communication with absent agents by establishing an address and phone number where they may be contacted by agents at other worksites which may be in the same office building or in settings at more remote bureaucratic locales of operation.

The temporal fixity of locales has not attracted the attention of many social scientists other than those at work in time-geography. It involves the fact that agents very often arrive and depart from institutional locales at recurrent and routine intervals of time. Eviatar Zeruvabel – one of the few contemporary sociologists of time – refers to this phenomenon as the standardisation of temporal locations (Zeruvabel, 1981, pp. 7–9). Zeruvabel observes that the rigid scheduling of activities in modern Western civilisation typically does not occur in non-Western ways of life. But while rigid scheduling most certainly is part of what Weber saw as the formal rationality of modern Western patterns of action, even highly traditional social systems incorporated some degree of temporal ordering of locales. For example, peasants in agricultural villages typically moved back and forth from their evening quarters to the field where they cultivated their crops, in a temporal cycle of activities geared into larger temporal durations associated with the growing season as well as their cultural traditions. Rituals such as Sabbath worship involve a temporal ordering of locales where worship and other ceremonial activities are undertaken as a matter of routine.

If locales are differentiated in space as well as time, they may also be differentiated in a single time–space dimension. Giddens offers an illustration here by expanding upon Erving Goffman's well-known distinction between front and back regions (*CS*, pp. 73–8, 122–30; see also, Goffman, 1959, ch. 3). As Goffman observes, social agents often maintain a spatial zoning between frontal regions where they carry out 'public' modes of conduct, and back regions where modes of conduct which conventionally are suppressed in public come to the fore. Physical barriers often serve to demarcate the boundaries of regions so that surveillance is less obstructed in the front than it is in the back. Where such barriers do not exist, agents may establish symbolic boundary markers. Giddens (*CS*, p. 119) augments Goffman's insights by noting that spatial regionalisation often coincides with a temporal standardisation of locales. As an example he considers the time–space zoning of a modern house as established and reproduced through the practices of its inhabitants. Members of a household may routinely gather in a room set aside for common meals at specific times during the day, in other rooms at other times for work and recreation, while at the end of the day they withdraw to their bedrooms for rest and sleep. Many other examples are commonly found in day-to-day life. Office buildings and schools frequently are zoned so that activities during working hours occur in one set of locales, while lunch-time activities are carried out in a different area; houses of worship separate sanctuaries where services are held at certain hours from meeting rooms and recreation halls where regularly scheduled activities are undertaken at other times during the day or week.

Building upon these examples in close quarters, Giddens (*CS*, pp. 130–2) expands the notion of the regionalisation of locales in time and space to larger collectivities. This involves an expanded definition of social locales:

Locales may range from a room in a house, a street corner, a shop floor of a factory, towns and cities, to the territorially demarcated areas occupied by nation-states. But locales are typically internally *regionalized*, and the regions within them are of critical importance in constituting contexts of interaction. (*CS*, p. 118; see also, *CCHM*, pp. 39–40)

The heterogeneity of the examples of locales Giddens provides in this passage reflects the fact that structuration theory does not insist upon ascribing priority to collectivities of any given scale. Thus social systems articulated and reproduced through face-to-face encounters may be studied in terms of the time–space zoning of locales, or one may focus on the time–space zoning of large-scale systems articulated and reproduced through diverse connections between face-to-face encounters and encounters between absent agents. Giddens provides several different sets of concepts to grasp the regionalisation of locales and the contextuality involved in their constitution through routine social practices. One set (*CS*, p. 124) expands Goffman's front-region/back-region distinction to permit concepts regarding the enclosure and disclosure of activities to vary between them. Another (*CS*, pp. 130–2) reconstructs and interrelates conventional distinctions between established groups and outsiders on the one hand, and central regions/peripheral regions on the other. But the set of concepts that is of most basic importance presents a classification of four analytically distinct but concretely combined *modes of regionalisation*: form, span, duration, and character (*CS*, pp. 121–2).

Form refers to the boundaries separating one region from another. As in the case of small-scale locales, boundaries may be established on the basis of physical features of the architecture or terrain, or – as for example in certain boundaries between states – demarcation may occur on a symbolic basis. An important point here is that the permeability of boundaries may vary to a considerable extent. Boundaries demarcating schools, factories, prisons, and other disciplinary organisations may be specifically designed to cut off possibilities for inter-regional interaction (*CS*, pp. 123–5, 145–7). The Great Wall of China and the Maginot Line exemplify attempts to construct impermeable barriers on a massive scale. Modern means of warfare and air transport, of course, now obviate the effectiveness of projects of this kind.

The *span* of a region refers to the time–space extension of the actions with which it is associated. Prior to the modern era the spatial span of regions generally was circumscribed by slow, inefficient, and unreliable means of transportation. Today, the span of regions may be considerably larger owing to the revolution in means of transportation and communication. The temporal span of a region can refer not only to the time it takes to traverse the distance between intra-regional settings, it also – following Zeruvabel rather than Giddens here – may refer to the zoning of standardised temporal locations of activities. Hence the temporal span of work activities in modern cultures typically extends over five workdays during the week, while the temporal span of family activities absorbs weeknights and weekends.

The *duration* of a region refers to the extent to which it is institutionalised in the *longue durée*. The duration of regions thus is co-extensive with the historical continuity of the practices through which it is reproduced. It can be observed that the duration of regions in modern systems often is shorter than in their traditional counterparts, where clusters of interaction often were regionalised with the same form, span, and character for many hundred of years. The shortened duration of modern regions thus reveals another aspect of the ebbing of tradition from social life (see *CCHM*, pp. 152 *passim*).

Finally, the *character* of a region refers to its time–space ordering within a single region, a region that itself may comprise one of several zones within a larger system. Many complications can be introduced here. It is particularly important to resist the urge to treat regions within regions as if the boundaries of the larger system circumscribe all of the activities in its more localised settings. Large cities, for example, incorporate many 'mixed' regions where activities relevant to diverse commercial, governmental, educational, and industrial systems are carried out virtually side-by-side, demarcated only by symbolic or socially constructed physical barriers. In the same way, regions where activities are ordered in the operation of trans-national enterprises may sit cheek-by-jowl with residential areas incorporated within societal totalities.

Structuration theory, it now should be clear, incorporates a novel approach to the patterning of systems which sets out in a direction unanticipated in the works of latter-day morphologists. But the account of the constitution of social systems is far from complete. Social systems not only are patterned and articulated across time and space, they also are coordinated and controlled, i.e. organised, in and through various forms of social *praxis*. These modes of system organisation will be the subject of discussion in the next two chapters.

4

The Organisation of Social Systems: 'A Non-Functionalist Manifesto'

In the glossary included in *The Constitution of Society* (p. 377) Giddens defines a social system as 'the patterning of social relations across time–space understood as reproduced practices'. This definition correctly establishes the centrality of *praxis* in the constitution of systems, and it also implies a concern for spatio-temporal articulations (via modes of social and system integration) through which the morphological patterns of systems are generated and maintained. But in other respects the definition is incomplete, especially since it makes systems appear as if they just happen to be patterned and reproduced in certain ways. But the patterning of systems is by no means a fortuitous matter. Social systemic patterns not only are reproduced in and through social *praxis*, they also are organised by means of institutionalised forms of conduct. Given that human beings harbour no inborn instincts to organise social systems in determinate ways, capabilities to do so must be regarded as one of the basic human potentials with which structuration theory is concerned; potentials which may be realised in a variety of different ways. The present chapter is devoted to how structuration theory conceives the principal ways in which the organisation of systems is achieved and maintained through the exercise of these potentials in the constitution of social life.

As was the case with regard to system patterns, my discussion of organisational themes in structuration theory will extend somewhat beyond insights available in Giddens's texts. While Giddens

114

is responsible for all of the main concepts to be discussed, and while a concern for the thematic implications of these concepts is evident throughout his works, at no point does he provide a consolidated account of the broad range of issues involved in systems organisation from the standpoint of structuration theory. One basic extension of Giddens's thought in this regard should be noted from the start. Giddens does not use the term 'organisation' in the generic sense which I employ in this chapter. Instead he restricts the term to what I shall refer to as administered systems. Giddens's well-developed and, in several respects, highly original views on administered systems, as well as his generic account of power and domination which informs these views, will be discussed in Chapter 5. For now it is sufficient to make clear that, in my use of the term, systems organisation denotes a concern for the coordination and control of systems at large, including but not limited to the administered mode of system organisation.

Despite the absence of a consolidated discussion of the organisation of systems in Giddens's works, the origins of his insights in this thematic domain are obvious and well-developed in his critical reflections on the functionalist tradition in social theory. Accordingly, this chapter begins with a selective summary of issues involved in this critique.

Functionalism and system organisation

Giddens (*CPST*, p. 7) terms structuration theory a 'non-functionalist manifesto', and he backs this up with numerous critical commentaries most of which are tied in some way to his arguments in 'Functionalism: après la lutte' (*SSPT*, ch. 2; see also *NRSM*, pp. 119–21; *CPST*, pp. 59–60, 111–16, 210–15; *CCHM*, pp. 16–19; 'AI', pp. 165–7; *CS*, pp. 12, 293–7). But as he freely acknowledges, few points remain to be argued in the functionalist debates, and, in the end, the critics of functionalism must be judged to have gained the upper hand (*SSPT*, p. 96). So why then drive redundant nails into a well-sealed coffin? One reason, of course, is that functionalism, like Lazarus, never was buried once and for all. Indeed, since the publication of 'Functionalism: après la lutte', a full-blown revival of functionalism seems well under way (see Cohen, 1979; Alexander, 1985; Faia, 1986; Habermas,

1987). This revival sustains Giddens's judgement that whatever the outcome of the functionalist debates, many basic issues were not adequately resolved. Yet Giddens does not aim to reopen the proceedings in his own critique. Critics of functionalism, he believes, arrived at a dead end, because, from an ontological standpoint, they threw the baby out with the bathwater. This is true in particular for critics – especially those from the methodological individualist camp – who proposed to dispense altogether with issues regarding the overall organisation of systems by reducing the concerns of functionalism to the subjective orientations of actors. By contrast, Giddens argues:

> [W]hatever the limitations of functionalism . . . it always placed in the forefront problems of institutional organization, and was firmly opposed to subjectivism in social theory. I believe this emphasis still to be necessary . . . [But] my aim is not to rescue functionalism from its critics, nor to re-examine the course of the debate as a whole; it is, by identifying certain of the inherent flaws in functionalist thought, to develop the rudiments of a theoretical scheme that can replace it. (*SSPT*, p. 96)

To establish how Giddens's critique of functionalism figures in the development of structuration theory requires a prior sense of what functionalism means. The problem is that the term applies to two partially overlapping, but also partially distinguishable, theoretical strategies. On the one hand an array of theorists (e.g. Durkheim, Malinowski, Parsons, Poulantzas, Wallerstein) overtly or covertly use functionalist models as a resource in the development of analytical accounts of diversely conceived systems. While these theorists disagree on many basic theoretical principles and postulates, they all develop accounts in which the organisation of systems is associated with the satisfaction of substantively conceived functional needs. For a second group of theorists, functionalism is treated as a topic in itself rather than a resource which remains embedded in a larger theoretical account. This line of thought was initiated by Robert Merton, and has been extended in a variety of works all of which address functionalism as an abstract model or method for theory construction.

Giddens's understanding of functionalism tacks between the functionalism-as-resource and the functionalism-as-topic points of

view. While pointed comments in opposition to theories that apply
functionalist postulates appear throughout his works, he reserves
his most well-developed criticisms for views expressed by Merton
and his successors with regard to the methodological relevance of
functional analysis. This strategy has the virtue of parsimony in so
far as it avoids the need to compare and contrast the plethora of
views expressed by theorists who use functionalism as a resource.
In particular, whereas those who might be termed 'grand functionalists' each postulate a different set of functional needs,
Mertonians generally adopt the more catholic position that functional systems must meet an unspecified set of functional needs
that ultimately refer to systemic adaptation or survival. Since the
diverse functional needs postulated by 'grand functionalists' typically also can be defined in terms of system survival, Giddens's
criticisms of Mertonian views implicitly refer to their views as well.
But to accomplish this, as well as to pave the way for the
development of a non-functionalist approach to system organisation, Giddens must interpret Mertonian arguments in ontological
terms. Although Giddens does criticise certain functionalist postulates on methodological grounds, his larger concern is to establish
specific problems in the account of the constitution of social life
which functionalist models and methods imply.

Considered in terms of the development of structuration theory
Giddens's critique of functionalism moves in two different directions, only one of which will be at issue during the course of this
chapter. In some instances his purpose is to establish oversights
and omissions in functionalist models that call for the insertion of
non-functionalist concepts with regard to structure, power, etc.
While these arguments comprise elements without which Giddens's 'non-functionalist manifesto' cannot be regarded as complete, I shall dispense with them here since they do not speak
directly to issues regarding systems organisation. All of these
non-functionalist themes are developed in full elsewhere in this
book. There are other instances, however, when Giddens's purpose is not to identify omissions in functionalist models, but rather
to underscore errors in their theoretical assumptions. I shall
concentrate on these issues below in order to establish the
reasoning that leads to the non-functionalist account of systems
organisation Giddens proposes in structuration theory.

It is impossible to concentrate exclusively on Merton's own

views in discussing the errors of functionalist analysis. Few other works in the history of social theory are as cautious and circumspect as Merton's essay on functionalist analysis. While Merton does propose a paradigm for functionalist analysis, his penchant for raising unsettled issues (e.g. the 'basic queries' in Merton, 1968, pp. 104–8) makes it difficult to identify an unambiguous format for functionalist analysis in his arguments. Functionalist analysis in Merton's account remains a puzzle in which crucial pieces are lacking. Merton's successors (see especially Gouldner, 1959, 1960; Nagel, 1967; Stinchcombe, 1968, pp. 80–101; Faia, 1986) have filled in the puzzle in various ways, and the picture that results does not always correspond to all of the elements of Merton's thought. For example, most of them treat Merton's famous distinction between manifest and latent functions as a peripheral empirical contingency, rather than as a central element of their functionalist formats. Conversely, they generally make much of a central issue that remains murky in Merton's work: namely, the systemic relation that feeds back from a system to those elements that generate consequences which are functionally relevant to systemic needs. Arthur Stinchcombe carries this line of reasoning to a logical extreme, by dispensing with the notion of system in favour of a functionalist image of 'reverse causal logic' between a stabilising homeostatic variable under tension and functional items (behaviours or behavioural arrangements) that contribute to the maintenance of a steady state in the homeostatic variable.

For present purposes these variations on Mertonian themes may be generalised by relying on the acute summary by Walter Wallace (1969, pp. 25–8). The following points included in Wallace's proposal will be taken to comprise essential elements of the functionalist account of systemic organisation. First, all functional needs or imperatives reduce to the imperative or need for systemic persistence. Second, in order to explain the existence of a given social phenomenon, its functional consequences for a larger system of which it is a part must be determined. Third, and most important, the explanation of the existence of phenomena involves the hypothesis that the *system* produces consequences that 'repay' functional phenomena by sustaining them, and 'repay' dysfunctional phenomena by eliminating them.

In the last analysis, then, functionalism does not literally view a social phenomenon's consequences for larger social structures [i.e. systems – IJC] as the most direct explanation of that phenomenon, but rather as intermediate indicators of the true direction of explanation, i.e. as indicators of the larger social structure's consequences for the phenomenon in question. (Wallace, 1969, p. 26)

Finally, Wallace reflects the position of most Mertonians by refraining from making postulates regarding the distinction between latent and manifest functions central to his summary.

Structuration theory may be a 'non-functionalist manifesto', but like all manifestos it shares certain ideas in common with that to which it remains unalterably opposed. With regard to system organisation, structuration theory disengages and preserves the notion of systems comprised of activities interrelated through their consequences from all references to both functional needs and systems *qua* systems as self-maintaining entities. Structuration theory also reinstates the centrality of the distinction between intended and unintended consequences. But in doing so it reformulates and clarifies Merton's definition of intentions, and it also places a more pronounced accent on intended outcomes than is expressed anywhere in Merton's work.

Deferring further consideration of how structuration theory reconstructs those aspects of functionalism which it does not disavow, some words are in order on those aspects it rejects. Giddens's objections to the imputation of functional needs to self-maintaining systems are hardly original: they centre on the problem of illegitimate functionalist teleologies that reappears as the critical undertow to every wave of functionalist theorising. However, Giddens's criticisms on this count stand apart from many others in so far as his programmatic objectives turn upon ontological, rather than methodological, themes. That is to say, he remains primarily concerned with problems regarding the proposition that systems as collectivities are constituted in a manner that permits them to act upon their own needs so as to organise (through systemic processes of re-enforcement or elimination) those of their parts that do or do not generate functional consequences. However, this is not to say that Giddens completely neglects the methodological implications of functionalist analysis. One aspect of his reformulation of functionalist themes involves a methodological proposal regarding counter-factual propositions. This proposal is quite useful in itself, and I believe that it also has methodological implications which extend beyond issues discussed in Giddens's texts. However, since this proposal does not deal with the main ontological thrust of Giddens's criticisms of functionalism I shall withhold further comment on it for an excursus which appears at the close of this chapter.

Giddens (see especially *SSPT*, pp. 109–12) launches a two-pronged assault on functionalist postulates that imply the existence of self-organising collectivities. On the one hand he shows that in many instances the imputation of systemic needs and teleologies involves conceptual redundancies. On the other hand he undermines the non-redundant propositions that remain outstanding in this regard. The arguments for redundancy are particularly important because they foreshadow constructive steps in the development of structuration theory. Consider first a systemic interpretation of Stinchcombe's notion that homeostatic variables select, re-enforce, or eliminate behaviours or behavioural arrangements based upon their stabilising consequences *vis-à-vis* the variable. This notion may be interpreted systemically either by presuming that the homeostatic variable is vital to the stability of a larger system, or by treating the recursive loops between the variable and the activities to which it is related as a small-scale system unto itself (for Giddens's view, see *SSPT*, p. 110). The notion of functional need is redundant here because it is unnecessary to postulate that the system stabilised through the operation of the homeostatic variable has a need of any kind. Nor for that matter must functional needs be imputed to the homeostatic variable itself. This is not to say that needs may not find a place in this scheme. Conceived as intentions, such needs may be ascribed to agents who generate consequences which they anticipate will contribute in some way to the persistence of the system in a steady state. Where systemic participants do not intentionally contribute to homeostatic dynamics, the notion of systemic needs is still redundant, because all that is involved is the institutionalised organisation of a set of interrelated activities and consequences in which changes in one or more activities evoke changes in others, until the cycle of adjustments comes full circle to evoke readjustments in the activities which originally set the cycle in motion. The system harbours no motives or 'reasons' why this cycle occurs, and *ipso facto* neither the system *qua* system, nor any given homeostatic variable can be said to 'pay back' behaviours that generate consequences relevant to that system's needs.

A related way to render the notion of a teleologically self-organising system redundant is to observe that in many systems politically powerful agents maintain and exercise capabilities that serve to coordinate and control systemic activities. A functional notion of systemic needs is superfluous here because whatever needs are involved in systemic organisation are defined – and can be redefined – by those agents in position to control the system. These agents – and not the system *per se* – 'pay back' others whose activities contribute to fulfilling the politically established needs, and these 'pay backs' in themselves may constitute one of the needs that must be fulfilled. There may be a kind of teleology at work here: but it is a teleology established and maintained by participants in the system, rather than a teleology attributable to the system itself. It should be added that only the dominant agents necessarily must be aware of the definition of system needs they establish and pursue. Whether or not other agents act upon or even recognise these needs is a contingent matter (cf. *SSPT*, p. 108).

Another proposal associated with functionalist systems that organise their operations to satisfy their needs involves situations in which enduring systems are said to persist in so far as they have adjusted or adapted so as to meet the prerequisites for system survival. The problem of tautological definitions must be avoided here: i.e. definitions of survival prerequisites defined in terms of the qualities of surviving systems. This can be done by invoking some process of selective adaptation (Turner and Maryanski, 1979, pp. 125–6). But even accepting this move, it remains unnecessary to postulate a functional teleology. Selective adaptation is, rather, an elliptical way of referring to an outcome of a process that the term itself does not define (*CCHM*, p. 21). But the key question is: presuming that such processes have been identified, do they involve any teleological dynamic linked to systemic needs? This certainly is not the case if adaptation means only that homeostatic cycles of activities and consequences result in adjustments that perpetuate the system in the midst of given exigencies that threaten its survival. Indeed, Michael Faia, who has developed one of the most thoroughgoing arguments on behalf of functionalist-homeostatic theories of adaptation, indicates his willingness to dispense with all terms which imply that systems maintain volitions of this kind (see Faia, 1986, pp. 5–6). Similarly, no systemic conception of functional needs or teleology is required where processes of adaptation are set in motion and controlled by politically dominant agents. Whether systems adapt or fail to adapt to a given set of circumstances here depends on the range of facilities dominant agents have at hand, how well they employ these capabilities, and how clearly they define the kinds of adjustments that would bring about an adaptive outcome.

Once these redundant applications of the concept of functional needs are set aside, the only way to connect systemic needs to functional outcomes of any kind must involve the proposal that systems *qua* systems maintain collectivistically conceived capabilities to actively intervene in the operations and relations among its own constituent parts so as to ensure that its systemic needs are met. Few functionalists, regardless of whether they are methodologically or theoretically inclined, care to advance arguments of this kind, and most insert qualifications to forestall such arguments (e.g. Durkheim, 1982, pp. 119–20). Yet echoes and undertones of the organic teleological metaphors that initially inspired functionalist social theory often are amplified into proposals which implicitly reinstate that which is overtly denied. One need look no further than the notion appearing in Mertonian works – but not in the works of Merton himself, who was far too cautious to fall into the trap – that systems 'repay' their functional parts. Despite the presence of the scare quotes indicative of metaphorical terminology, the implication is unavoidable that the *system* controls the payroll, so that it operates, according to its own design, to satisfy its needs. It is this seldom advocated but commonly employed line of functionalist reasoning that Giddens rejects, and sets out to replace.

From collective agency to system reproduction

Giddens's objections to functionalist teleology stem from his denial of any ascription of agency to any constituents of social life other than to agents themselves. In functionalist analysis the notion that systems 'repay' or 'eliminate' their own parts according to the merits of the contributions of those parts to the satisfaction of systemic needs implies that systems *qua* systems are endowed with independent capabilities to intervene in social life. Systems thus appear responsible for organising the activities through which they are reproduced. As opposed to this view, Giddens (*CPST*, p. 112) holds that: 'the notion of system [reproduction] *presupposes* that of social reproduction; reproduction is not a mysterious accomplishment that social systems manage to carry out via the activities of their "members"'. In speaking of social reproduction as the basis for system reproduction, Giddens reserves powers of agency for social agents themselves. But this move should not be understood as a regression to any form of methodological individualism. It should be evident by now that in structuration theory agents can engage in the reproduction of systems only in so far as they undertake institutionalised modes of conduct. These routinised practices effectively serve as the vehicles through which systems are reproduced, vehicles which are activated by agents through their participation in day-to-day life. Hence agents reproduce the organisation of systems, but systems do not reproduce the organisation of agents nor do they activate the practices in which agents engage. Any claims to the contrary hypostatise systems, thereby obscuring many of the most fundamental processes through which systems are coordinated and controlled.

To adopt this position does nothing more than sever the notion of agency from the notion of system. It does not deny that systems may be conceived to possess institutionalised properties that facilitate and channel the practices which agents reproduce. Nor does it deny that these properties can be identified in collective terms. However, it does prohibit the imputation of any collectively defined intentionality or rationality to systems. Agents may or may not intend their activities to contribute to the reproduction of systems, but systems *qua* systems harbour no 'reasons' why this conduct occurs. And if systems harbour no 'reasons' why conduct occurs then they not only lack capabilities of agency, they also lack the prerequisites to actively imbue agents with intentions regarding system needs.

Reproduction circuits and processes of structuration

The notion of system reproduction through social reproduction replaces all references to collective agency in structuration theory, and thus sets the stage for a non-functionalist account of how systems are coordinated and controlled. But before entering into the latter topic the nature of system reproduction itself must be clarified. Two concepts figure prominently in this regard: reproduction circuits and processes of structuration. Giddens introduces the concept of reproduction circuits only in the latter stages of *The Constitution of Society* (pp. 190–2), and even here he does not deal with it in any great detail. However, in my view, reproduction circuits should play a more central role in structuration theory than Giddens's brief remarks would suggest. In defining them here I shall therefore extend the concept beyond Giddens's own definition. According to Giddens (*CS*, p. 192), reproduction circuits may be defined as 'tracks' of processes which feed back to their source. His definition also includes references to the actual conditions of social reproduction as well as the regionalisation of systemic locales across time–space. The point that Giddens fails to explicitly mention here, although it is implied in the notion of 'feedback' (*CS*, p. 14), is that *reproduction circuits involve the interaction of activities through their consequences or outcomes.* Giddens accentuates the significance of unintended consequences in his remarks on 'feedback', but I see no reason why intended consequences should be excluded in this regard. Hence I shall define a *reproduction circuit* as a cycle of routinised activities and consequences which are reproduced across time–space within and between institutionalised locales.

One reason why reproduction circuits are important is that they provide the content which complements the spatio-temporal systemic patterns discussed in Chapter 3. That is, reproduction circuits provide the content for all morphological inquiries conducted within the brackets of systems analysis. Reproduction circuits therefore can be regarded as spatio-temporal patterns conceived in praxiological terms. In this view articulations via modes of *social integration* involve consequences and outcomes generated in circumstances of co-presence so that the activities of agents in a given physical setting are interrelated in various ways. Such interrelations may involve face-to-face interactions and/or small-scale sequences of activity such as occur on assembly lines or other arrangements or divisions of labour. Articulations via modes of *system integration* involve the transmission of outcomes of activity between agents who lack presence-availability.

Several cautionary remarks regarding reproduction circuits must be entered so as to eliminate certain ways in which the concept may be misunderstood. First, the strength of the relations (in morphological terms, the 'ties') between articulated activities and consequences in reproduction circuits is an empirically contingent matter. This is simply a reiteration of the point established in the last chapter that systems may be more or less well-integrated, and hence their boundaries may be more or less porous. Second, reproduction circuits potentially are always subject to alteration, in which case they may be looked upon as circuits of change. Third, reproduction circuits may be conceived in theoretically abstract terms to refer to generalisable characteristics of an indefinite number of empirical instances of a given type of system, or they may be conceived with reference to the concrete character- istics of an historically specific system. Hence, to take a simple example, one might use the concept of reproduction circuits in the formulation of a substantive theory of traditional kinship systems in a given civilisation, or one might use the concept to develop an ethnographically 'thick', detailed account of a specific kinship system that is under investigation.

It may seem at this point that the concept of reproduction circuits is simply a redundant redefinition of the concept of social system which already refers to articulated patterns comprised of institutionalised practices and relations. This conceptual redun- dancy actually occurs in so far as a system is conceived as a single reproduction circuit. However, not all systems are constituted in this way. While it is always possible to conceive a system as a single reproduction circuit, it is also possible to conceive complex systems in two additional ways which, it should be added, are not mutually exclusive. On the one hand, systems may consist of a series of distinct, but *interconnected* reproduction circuits. On the other hand, systems may consist of a set of *overlapping* or *intersecting* reproduction circuits. Interconnections or intersec- tions between reproduction circuits may be represented in terms of their regionalisation across time and space. However, the term 'reproduction circuit' also implies a concern for the constitution of these interconnections and intersections which occurs in social *praxis*. Thus, the concept of reproduction circuits *inter alia* creates opportunities in structuration theory to consider topics such as 'boundary spanning relations' (Lawrence and Lorsch, 1969, pp. 23–30) and 'tight and loose coupling' (Perrow, 1984, pp. 89–94). It should be recognised, however, that reproduction circuits are defined here in ontological terms. Hence in addition to complex organisations, the concept may apply generically to larger collectivities such as societies, empires, and world-systems as well, as well as smaller systems such as families, work-groups, and communities.

The three possible ways in which reproduction circuits may be implicated in social systems can be illustrated in a relatively clear-cut way with reference to the modern nation-state. A specific bureaucratic department of the state may be conceived as a series of interconnected, but spatio-temporally distinct offices each of which comprises a reproduction circuit unto itself, and all of which are connected *via* modes of system integration. Alternatively, the bureaucratic department may be conceived as one reproduction circuit among others bound up in the larger state system, which also includes executives and upper-level executive administrators, parliamentary bodies, and the judiciary. The relations between the various reproduction circuits of the state may be viewed as interconnected with one another in a sequential manner or as overlapping one another, so that certain activities, or analytically isolable aspects of activities may be implicated in two or more reproductions circuits (for example, when a head of state signs a bill into law the consequences of that activity simultaneously represent an outcome of parliamentary proceedings, an order to be implemented by administrative bureaus, and in some instances a legal statute that is applicable to the proceedings of the judicial system). Of course, it also is possible to consider a relatively well-coordinated system such as the nation-state as a large-scale system unto itself, in which case elliptical terms may be used to describe reproduction circuits between its various 'branches' (for example, the system of governmental checks and balances set forth in the US Constitution).

To turn now to the praxiological aspects of reproduction circuits, some consideration must be given to the structuration of systems and reproduction circuits. It is worthwhile to begin by recapitulating how social reproduction occurs via the duality of structure in the case of an individual social practice. Any institutionalised procedure or practice can be reproduced only in so far as the agents who engage in that procedure have mastered and retain pertinent forms of mutual knowledge, and only in so far as they have access to the resources required to implement the procedure. This interwoven constellation of knowledgeability and resources comprises the *conditions* for the reproduction of that practice. In the absence of these conditions an agent cannot reproduce that practice. An elementary kind of *structuration* occurs when an actor does reproduce the practice. In virtue of the duality of structure, the reproduction of the practice regenerates conditions for its reproduction (see above, pp. 41–7). It should be indicated here that the conditions of a given practice serve as *structural constraints*. This topic will be elaborated in Chapter 6.

The structuration of social systems (i.e. one or more circuits of reproduction) differs from the structuration of an individual practice, because systemic practices are interrelated (in interactions or via reciprocities between absent agents) through the *consequences* of activities. (The following discussion expands upon *CPST*, p. 104; *CS*, p. 14). These consequences occur as *transformations* of the empirical content of social events and/or material objects. The concrete transformations of events and circumstances are the outcome of the exercise of human agency; the interventions by agents that 'make a difference' in the course of system reproduction. *Systemic relations are maintained and reproduced as these results of social conduct are transmitted or transported to other agents who may be situated in the same spatio-temporal setting, or who may be situated in the same setting at a later time, or who may be situated in another systemic locale across some interval of time–space.* These agents, in turn, may engage in further transformations of the outcomes of activities which have been transmitted/transported to them. Each transformation in some way changes the content of events and/or material objects.

But for all these transformations in content the procedures involved in system reproduction may be highly institutionalised, and chronically repeated in the same sequences, and in the same spatio-temporal settings for extended periods in the *longue durée*. Indeed, different agents may come and go while the systemic reproduction circuits remain chronically regenerated aspects of social life. To illustrate this point, consider a reproduction circuit that might typify the systemic organisation of a modern bureaucracy. On a day-to-day basis executive committee meetings are held resulting in certain policies which thereafter are implemented, and this implementation is documented in files that ultimately are retrieved and monitored by the executive committee which originated the policy. Each activity in some way involves an intervention that transforms bureaucratic circumstances and events, yet the procedures involved may be subject to a sufficiently small degree of variation that they may be understood by the bureaucratic personnel themselves to maintain a substantial continuity for an extended period of time. During this period the same modes of mutual knowledge and resources serve as structural conditions that facilitate and channel the reproduction of activities as well as the transmission of the outcomes of activities to appropriate agents in designated settings. Indeed, the outcomes themselves may vary from one cycle of the bureaucratic reproduction circuit to the next, while the structural conditions (reproduced via the duality of structure) remain the same.

Although all agents who participate in the reproduction of a given system are likely to have some discursive understanding of its overall articulation and structural configuration, including the systemic distribution of resources, it is quite possible that agents may lack a specific grasp of the structured routines, or the institutionalised transformations of circumstances and events which are transacted beyond the realm of their day-to-day conduct. Systems are comprised of practices interrelated through their consequences, but – leaving out of account agents with access to stored resources of information (see Chapter 5) – the further removed the consequences of an act in time and space from the context in which these consequences originate, the less likely these consequences will be known to their perpetrators. This point has a direct bearing on the discussion of unintended consequences which appears below (see also *CS*, p. 11). It also has a general bearing on the conception of systems in structuration theory: *the fact that systemic relations cannot be reproduced unless agents at least tacitly know what they are doing does not entail that such relations can be conceived solely in terms of individuals* (*CS*, p. 215). *Although systems are not agents they do exhibit structural properties, and one or more reproduction circuits which can be identified in collective terms rather than with reference to individuals or individual practices.*

Modes of system organisation

To this point discussion has focused on system reproduction as the basis for the non-functionalist account of system organisation Giddens incorporates in structuration theory. The notion that system reproduction occurs through processes of structuration in which activities are interrelated through their outcomes or consequences anchors the constitutions of systems in the exercise of agency which occurs in social *praxis*, rather than in the exercise of agency by systems in pursuit of their own functionally defined needs. But if the notion of system reproduction precludes the postulation of teleologically effective functional needs, a prominent gap remains outstanding in this account. In functionalist theories and analytic models social systems do not reproduce themselves: they rather 'repay' or 'eliminate' behavioral items, thereby coordinating and controlling their own processes of reproduction. In structuration theory, three modes of system organisation supplant this functionalist account of coordination and control.

While Giddens provides the concepts for the three modes of system organisation to be discussed in the following pages, he neither uses the term 'mode of system organisation' nor does he specifically distinguish references to coordination and control in this regard. Therefore, several points of clarification must be made at this point. Coordination in modes of system organisation specifically refers to ways in which the articulation of practices and relations across time and space is established and maintained: i.e. the procedures which ensure that the consequences of *praxis* generated in one locale are coordinated with other activities in that locale, and/or activities situated in one or more distant locales. Control in modes of system reproduction refers to ways and means through which activities and outcomes of activities involved in system reproduction are instituted and regulated.

It should be emphasised that the discussion of modes of system organisation here is cast in generic terms which allow clear-cut conceptual distinctions to be made. Since these clear-cut distinctions do not necessarily correspond to the modes of organisation in any empirically given system, two highly important qualifications are required. First, the three modes of system organisation to be discussed are presented as if the coordination and control of systems occurs in a problem-free, routine manner. This, obviously, is seldom the case. Not only is it probable that deviation from the established course of system reproduction will occur, but this viewpoint fails to encompass possibilities for system change. Second, while the three modes of system organisation are conceived and exemplified in the following remarks as if they were mutually exclusive alternatives, *in reality compound or hybrid combinations of these modes are frequently more the rule than the exception.* The purpose of dealing with these modes on an individual basis is only to distinguish them from one another with an appropriate degree of conceptual precision.

In his early writings Giddens develops his thoughts on system organisation through strategic appropriations from the work of Walter Buckley, who applies general systems theory to the development of sociological analysis (*NRSM*, p. 121; *SSPT*, pp. 115–16; *CPST*, pp. 74–5). The move was warranted by the fact that Buckley, like Giddens, explicitly disavows all references to functional teleologies. However, in more recent publications Giddens has dispensed with references to the systems-theory origins of his insights, and I will follow suit with the exception of the following remarks.

While Giddens and Buckley equally adhere to a non-functionalist standpoint, their thought otherwise differs in several important respects. Buckley (1967, pp. 58–9; see also, Archer, 1982) stresses morphogenesis (i.e. the elaboration of systemic forms) at the expense of morphostasis (i.e. the maintenance of these forms). As I have emphasised in Chapter 1, structuration theory, as an ontology of potentials, accepts stasis and change as equivalent possibilities in social life. Buckley, no doubt, would affirm this position. However, his preference for morphogenetic themes leaves the impression that few issues of importance require attention with regard to morphostasis. That such is not the case may be seen by turning to an ontological point where Giddens and Buckley disagree. Buckley (1967, pp. 94–9) adopts a view of social activity derived from George Herbert Mead, which stresses the significance of communicative alignments between agents as the basis for conceiving interaction and joint acts. One result of this move is that the role of agency, considered as active and consequential interventions, recedes, and the processual transaction of communication in social relations comes to the fore. This, in turn, makes it difficult to conceive the ontological recursiveness of structure and action proposed in the duality of structure. In place of this recursiveness, Buckley (1967, p. 78) relies on a concept of emergence which synthesises the consequences (both intended and unintended) of activity into a 'complex emergent product'. However, the notion of emergence is as murky, and as fraught with epistemological and ontological ambiguities here, as it is in latter-day morphology (see Chapter 2). In particular, it remains unclear if agents reproduce the conditions which they rely upon to reproduce their activities in instances where morphostasis occurs. If the use of the term 'emergence' signifies that they do not, then system and agents appear to be ontologically heterogeneous: i.e. systems as emergent entities constrain but do not facilitate agents' conduct, and systems 'emerge' over the heads of agents rather than through their doings. Giddens, of course, sets out to overcome the enormous dilemmas associated with all views of this kind, and for this reason his account of the structuration of systems – including the structuration or morphostatic systems – cannot be reconciled with Buckley's approach.

The manifest differences between Buckley and Giddens are obscured to some extent by the fact that Giddens continues to employ Buckley's terminology. However, instead of relying upon the emergence of modes of system organisation, and at the same time in order to avoid the postulation of any teleologically defined functional needs, Giddens conceives modes of system organisation with reference to whether organisation occurs through the unintended or intended consequences of action. I shall discuss Giddens's original and important clarification of the differences between unintended and intended consequences in the following section. However, it may be useful at this point to provide a synoptic overview of the three modes of system organisation in structuration theory. This can be done, in a manner that extends Giddens's work, by cross-referencing the distinction between unintended and intended consequences with the distinction between coordination and control which I introduced above.

	Coordination	Control
homeostatic system reproduction	U	U
self-regulation through feedback	I	U
reflexive self-regulation (administered systems)	I	I

U = unintended consequences
I = intended consequences

Homeostatic systems: organisation through unintended consequences

The notion of homeostasis as it is used in structuration theory must be distinguished from references to homeostatic variables, as are proposed, for example, in Stinchcombe's image of functionalist explanation. For Stinchcombe (1968, p. 87), a homeostatic variable exhibits a tendency to remain stable even though there are tensions which induce it to change. In structuration theory, however, homeostasis does not refer to a variable, but rather to an entire system (or reproduction circuit) in which a transformational outcome of one activity, or set of activities, initiates a sequence of subsequent activities and transformations that eventually return to affect the first activity (cf. *CPST*, p. 78). In the most elementary homeostatic systems no single activity or constellation of activities serves to coordinate, or control, the overall course of system reproduction. Rather, the system is organised through the structuration of the reproduction circuit at large: i.e. activities are coordinated across time and space because agents know where, when, and how to relate to others during the course of their day-to-day lives, and because they have access to the resources required to transact these relations. Homeostatic cycles thus are coordinated, but they lack any specifically organised forms of control. What sets the reproduction cycle in motion are simply the motives (including motives for the maintenance of ontological security) that induce knowledgeable agents to reproduce their day-to-day routines and interactions in the appropriate, institutionalised, spatio-temporal settings (*SSPT*, p. 110; *CS*, p. 14).

Although Giddens has not spoken directly to the issue, it should be oberved that homeostatically organised systems may lack a specific homeostatic variable, but they do not lack for systemic tensions. The following illustration appears consistent with Giddens's views. Consider an exogamous kinship system involving several lineages that comprise a tribal community. In this system a cycle exists in which marriages occur in an institutionalised sequence from one lineage to another, until ultimately a marriage is made between a member of the final lineage in the cycle and a member in the first. Thus, a consequence of any given marriage between members of two lineages is that an obligation is incurred by the members of one of the lineages to make a marriage between one of its members and a member of the next lineage in the cycle. Now it might appear that no tension exists where this cycle is chronically reproduced. But consider what is involved in the obligation incurred when a marriage is made (see Leach, 1954, p. 136, for an ethnographic account). This obligation is fulfilled when appropriate matchmaking negotiations with the next lineage get underway. However, the latent tension in the system becomes evident if the negotiations are not undertaken, or are undertaken in an inappropriate way. Sanctions, institutionally constituted through the normative aspects of tribal members' mutual knowledge, now may be imposed by members of the lineage which has been spurned. Thus, a normative tension experienced as obligations by tribal members pervades the entire interlineal kinship system. Notice that no functional need regarding the tribal community must be invoked to account for this tension. It is the structuration of the kinship system through which this tension is maintained.

The preceding illustration is simplified, and it substantially understates both the complexity and the heterogeneity of activities and consequences that may serve to organise tribal communities, or other systems which may be coordinated in a homeostatic manner. Cycles of interlineal marriage in tribal communities frequently are enmeshed in more extensive cycles of political, economic, and cultural activities, with concomitant or additional obligations being incurred and fulfilled through tribal practices involving barter, gift-giving, provision of labour and holiday feasts, etc.

The prevalence of normative coordination in tribes and bands leads Giddens (*CPST*, p. 200; *CCHM*, p. 93; *CS*, p. 200; *STMS*, pp. 147, 153–4) to accentuate the role that cultural traditions may play in homeostatic modes of system organisation. However, culture cannot be set off from other aspects of the constitution of social life in this regard. Here it is important to bear in mind that a dialectic of control manifests itself even in the most basic instances of system organisation. The dialectic of control will be considered at length in the discussion of generic concepts regarding power that appears in Chapter 5. For now it is sufficient to say that even if there is no isolable form of control in homeostatically regulated systems, there generally will be some type of politico-cultural inequality among agents, or categorically differentiated groups of agents.

Whatever else may be said regarding empirical instances of homeostatically organised systems, there are two distinctive characteristics that figure prominently in the way they are conceived in structuration theory. First, both the organisation and the reproduction of such systems (which in this case are isomorphic) take place primarily via social integration: i.e. interaction in circumstances of co-presence among participants. Given the material coupling constraints which were discussed in the last chapter, the necessity to interact and engage in common activities in designated spatio-temporal settings limits both the number of agents who may be involved in such systems, as well as the spatio-temporal span of the region, which is limited to the distance agents can easily travel in order to establish their presence-availability. Therefore, most homeostatically organised systems will be relatively small, although exceptions can be found – for example, the Kula Ring, and other types of tribal federations. The second distinctive feature is particularly important to the definition of the homeostatic mode of system organisation: *they typically are organised through the generation of unintended consequences*.

At this point it becomes necessary to consider how Giddens's reformulation of the definition of intended/unintended consequences clarifies Merton's distinction between manifest and latent functions. For Giddens (*SSPT*, pp. 107–9; see also, Campbell, 1982, pp. 40–41), a basic problem with Merton's account is that he fails to distinguish with precision between an intention to produce an outcome, and a knowledge, *sans* intention, that a given outcome will ensue from a particular kind of activity or practice. A distinction between an intention, and a knowledge of outcomes, must be made because the latter may be present while the former is absent: i.e. an actor may know that an action will result in some consequence but may not intend for the consequence to occur because (a) she may be indifferent to that consequence, or (b) she may be prepared to accept that consequence in order to pursue other ends, even though she may consider the consequence undesirable in itself.

Given this argument, it should be clear why Giddens (*CS*, p. 10; *NRSM*, p. 76) defines an *intentional act* as one which its perpetrator knows, or believes (thereby allowing for faulty knowledge), will have a particular quality or outcome, *and* where such knowledge is utilised by the author of the act to achieve this quality or outcome. An *unintended consequence* of an act therefore may occur in two different ways: (i) an actor may have no knowledge that the consequences at issue will follow from the act; (ii) she may know of this outcome, but not be concerned to bring it about.

The basic distinction between knowledge of outcomes and intentional outcomes may be expanded in a variety of ways. Giddens proposes two points in this regard (see *NRSM*, pp. 75–81; *SSPT*, p. 108; *CS*, pp. 10–14). First, both knowledge of, and intentions with regard to, consequences can be, and often are, only tacitly understood on the level of practical consciousness. That is, they may be understood in a procedural sense even though agents may not discursively acknowledge that such outcomes might occur for themselves or for others. Second, how much knowledge of outcomes agents may have depends upon their awareness of circumstances and conduct in social contexts removed from their own experience. This implies that knowledge of consequences may vary not only in a spatio-temporal sense, but also with reference to hierarchies of privilege and power (*CS*, pp. 91–2).

For present purposes the most salient point regarding unintended consequences is that agents in homeostatic systems may know that they contribute consequences through their activities which serve to organise a system in which they participate *without thereby intending to produce this result*. This point is particularly important because even if agents' knowledge 'shades off' in circumstances beyond their day-to-day experience, all agents retain a more or less limited, and a more or less tacit or discursive awareness of the broader conditions in which their activities occur (see *CS*, pp. 91–2). To illustrate this knowledgeable but unintentional type of activity with reference to homeostatically organised systems, consider once again the case of a reproduction circuit involving interlineal marriage. As documented by Edmund Leach (1954, p. 36), members of a tribal community may employ a specific term or phrase for an interlineal marriage cycle in which they participate; a datum which clearly indicates their awareness that such a cycle exists. Yet this discursive recognition in no way necessarily entails that when marital negotiations are undertaken by members of two lineages, the agents involved anticipate or intend that the outcome of the proceedings will perpetuate the marriage cycle. Rather, their intentions may be confined to creating an acceptable or a rewarding match, and/or to avoiding negative sanctions which might result from failure to fulfil their culturally defined obligations. The interlineal system of marriages is organised and reproduced through these negotiations, as well as through the marriage that results, but this systemic outcome is not intended by the agents involved, even though they may recognise that the outcome occurs.

Intentional modes of system organisation: reflexive and self-reflexive regulation

In moving beyond the homeostatic mode of system organisation we do not dispense with unintended consequences. However, now intentional means of organisation must also be taken into account. *Reflexively regulated modes of system organisation* involve the introduction of intentional measures to coordinate systemic activity. *Self-reflexively regulated (administered) modes of system organisation* involve the introduction of intentional procedures to coordinate and control system reproduction.

There is nothing novel in the insight that social systems may be intentionally organised. The study of complex organisations has yielded a voluminous body of literature on the topic for well over fifty years. However, while the account of intentionally organised systems in structuration theory overlaps the field of complex organisation, there are differences in the respective objectives they pursue. Most theories of complex organisation concentrate upon bureaucracies and other modern forms of administered systems. Structuration theory, by contrast, presents an ontologically generic account of how intentionally organised systems should be conceived. The rationale for avoiding an exclusive concern for contemporary organisations turns on Giddens (*CCHM*, pp. 100ff; *CS*, p. 200; *NRSM*, p. 12; *STMS*, p. 153) recognition that intentionally organised systems of various kinds have been a part of the historical scene ever since the advent of agrarian states and systems of empire. As Weber and other historical sociologists make clear, non-modern modes of intentionally organised systems differ markedly from their modern counterparts. Hence concepts designed by students of complex organisation to apply to contemporary systems may be too restrictive to be useful in the study of non-modern modes of system organisation. Structuration theory adopts a much broader approach to encompass a wider variety of possibilities. In doing so it forsakes historical specificity – although Giddens's substantive works are studded with empirical examples – in favour of providing a conceptual perspective that facilitates analysis and comparison of the nature of organisations established and reproduced by social agents in diverse historical epochs.

The absence of empirical specificity in no way entails a simplified account. To the contrary, the concepts Giddens advances here are among the most detailed and complex in structuration theory at large. So much is this true that the set of concepts regarding administered systems warrants an independent chapter which will follow completion of the present discussion. For now I will raise three issues: (i) the nature of reflexive regulation; (ii) the role of intentions in self-reflexive (administered) systems; (iii) the extension of time–space distantiation made possible through the development of self-reflexive (administered) systems.

Giddens (*CS*, p. 28 and p. 39, n. 30) devotes relatively little attention to the reflexive mode of system organisation, but its significance is greater than his remarks would suggest. A reflexively regulated system involves an intentionally established 'apparatus' which serves to coordinate systemic activity (*SSPT*, p. 116; cf. *CPST*, p. 78). Giddens presents no generic definition of what this 'apparatus' involves except to say that it serves as a filter which exerts a regulative influence upon the elements in a circuit or cycle of system reproduction (*CPST*, p. 79). In my view, 'apparatus' of this kind should be seen as an institutionalised set of activities that corresponds to a homeostatic variable in that these activities respond to consequences of *praxis* transmitted/transported from various systemic locales. The 'apparatus' itself is established and maintained through the intentional doings of agents, but the outcomes of the workings of the 'apparatus' occur in an unintentional manner that may or may not conform to the intentions of those who are responsible for maintaining its operations.

Numerous examples of reflexively regulated systems might be offered here, many of which would involve subtle procedures and counter-intuitive outcomes. But in order to demonstrate the significance of this mode of system organisation I will use a highly simplified account of a very obvious example, albeit one to which Giddens does not refer (but see *STMS*, ch. 8). The case in point is the coordination of commodity production by a capitalist market designed and maintained for this purpose.

Consider a hypothetical system of commodity production regulated by the economic theorists' proverbially 'free' market: i.e. a market that is open to all comers, and is not dominated in any way by any group of traders. The market itself is established through the intentional efforts of its overseers. However, the market is reproduced through the unintentional consequences of the activities of those who offer and those who purchase the commodities that are designated for trade (e.g. agricultural goods, minerals, other types of extracted raw materials). The outcomes of the operation of the market are prices for commodities which no single agent can control, and hence none can intentionally establish. This price may be conceived as a 'composition effect' (*CS*, p. 10). Where a price that results from trade in the market is considered undesirable by buyers and sellers this may be regarded as a 'perverse effect' (*CS*, pp. 13–14: *STMS*, p. 10). ('Composition effects' and 'perverse effects' are instances in social life where an outcome actually does 'emerge' from the doings of many agents.)

Consider now how the coordination and control of commodity production occurs via this market. The market is intentionally established to coordinate the selling and buying of commodities. But it has the effect, through the unintentional establishment of prices, of controlling production. Thus, in standard textbook fashion (where markets are 'free' and they always are cleared), a higher price encourages producers to increase production and attracts new producers; a lower price sends a 'signal' to producers to diminish their output, and may foreclose opportunities for some producers to continue their operations.

Although reflexively regulated systems in reality often exhibit characteristics that converge with self-reflexive (i.e. administered) systems ('Commentary', p. 532), a conceptual distinction between the two can be clearly drawn. Unlike reflexively regulated systems, administered systems are intentionally coordinated *and* controlled by a group of leaders and administrators. The non-functionalist qualities of structuration theory are particularly evident here. Functionalist theorists generally prefer to accentuate the significance of unintended consequences, or latent functions (Merton, 1968, p. 122). This emphasis implicitly suggests a systemic teleology, or, at a minimum, a teleology of unintentional consequences that satisfies a systemic need. While Giddens disavows any active teleology relating system organisation to system needs via unintentional consequences, he does preserve a sense in which a system may be coordinated and controlled with reference to specifically formulated needs: needs which are formulated by the superordinate agents who regulate systemic activity. In functionalist language Giddens thereby shifts the accent to manifest functions:

> Although it is indispensable to social theory to study the involvement of unintended consequences of conduct in the reproduction of social systems, the only kind of 'functions' (or 'teleological outcomes') that are of explanatory significance in analyzing either stability of, or change in, society *are what Merton labelled manifest functions*. In other words, it is only when members of sociery themselves actively attempt to harness projected outcomes to perceived 'social needs' through the application of knowledge about the effects of conduct in reproducing social systems that teleological explanation of social reproduction has any part to play in social analysis. (*CPST*, p. 211; see also *CS*, p. 297)

Giddens's reference in this passage to the application of knowledge should not be overlooked. As will be indicated in the next chapter, knowledge – in the form of stored information – is a vital resource drawn upon by those who intentionally coordinate and control the reproduction of social systems. For the moment, only one point needs to be made in this regard. Both the intentions and the use of information by agents who attempt to coordinate and control social systems generally require a substantially greater degree of discursive awareness than is required of agents engaged in the reproduction of homeostatic systems. Even in systems that are intentionally organised, it is quite possible that many agents who participate in systemic activities may lack the degree of discursive insight maintained by superordinate agents regarding both the system at large and the consequences of their own activity.

The monitoring of stored information has a direct bearing on how self-reflexively regulated (administered) systems are intentionally organised. Indeed, the intentions of those who regulate the reproduction and outcomes of these systems depend upon the *ex ante* knowledge of the likely results of policies or plans that might be pursued. But stored information not only permits the development of (discursive) intentions, it also expands the potential level of time–space distantiation in systems beyond anything imaginable in homeostatically organised reproduction circuits. Here, again, there will be more to say in Chapter 5. But the fundamental point, in brief, is that whereas in homeostatic systems the necessity for the establishment of presence-availability among agents constrains the level of time–space distantiation to a relatively small region (see above), information relevant to the coordination and control of systems may be gathered from many different settings across time–space, transmitted to central administrative locales, and stored for future use. The information thereby extends the range of intentional plans across time–space as far beyond the central administrative locales as available means of communication and transportation will allow. The same means of communication and transportation facilitate the transmission of commands, plans, and materials associated with their implementation across time–space to remote settings of systemic activity. The significance of terming reciprocities between absent agents *system integration* should be apparent at this point.

Reflexively regulated systems, of course, also extend much further across time–space than homeostatic systems. Capitalistic markets, for example, may reach the same level of time–space distantiation as capitalistic enterprises. But the differences between reflexive and self-reflexive regulation of systemic activities are as significant as their similarities. In the reflexive mode of system organisation no centralised attempt is made to coordinate the timing and spacing of conduct, nor is any attempt made by a central group of agents to control the course and outcomes of the process of system reproduction. This difference is exemplified quite well by the contrast between the irregular and episodically unpredictable nature of market activity and the highly routinised reproduction circuits in capitalist enterprises. Clearly, the coordination and control of activities across time–space is more highly institutionalised in the latter than the former. Because self-reflexive (i.e. administered) systems routinise activities more intensively than their reflexive counterparts, they penetrate more deeply into the *praxis* of day-to-day life, and are involved more heavily in organising the time–space pathways followed by social agents.

Given the range of historical variation in intentionally established and maintained modes of system organisation, and the possibility that novel variants may be developed in the future, it would be presumptuous for Giddens to develop an exhaustive ontological classification of reflexively and self-reflexively regulated systems. Nevertheless, he does establish a generic distinction between two types of self-reflexively regulated (administered) systems (see *CS*, pp. 199–206; *NSV*, pp. 12, 313ff; *STMS*, pp. 48, 153–4). As a backdrop to this distinction he introduces the concept of *association*: a synonym for the homeostatic mode of system organisation. The two types of self-reflexive systems are *organisations* and *social movements*.

Organisations and social movements both involve the use of stored information, discursively mobilised in processes of coordination and control. With regard to social movements, this criterion rules out migrations, as well as episodes of spontaneous mass-behaviour. Giddens establishes three conceptual criteria to distinguish organisations from movements. First, in organisations efforts are made to control or alter the conditions of system reproduction, whereas in movements the objective is to de-routinise established activities, and to institute novel projects and new ways of life. Second, personnel in organisations generally conduct their activities with reference to institutionalised systemic identities, while identities are less clearly defined in social movements. Third, organisations operate within and across institutionally fixed spatio-temporal settings, whereas in movements the spatio-temporal positioning of agents is not fixed to the same extent. Although in the present account my concerns focus upon self-reflexive organisations, it should be noted that Giddens (*CS*, p. 203) introduces the concept of movements to forestall their neglect, and to correct the lopsided overemphasis on complex organisations in modern sociology (see also, Touraine, 1977). Organisation and movements, he argues, should be considered as systems of equal importance, at least in the modern era.

Counterfactual propositions: a methodological excursus

Although a great deal remains to be said with regard to administered systems, the non-functionalist qualities of structuration theory's approach to systems organisation should be evident at this point. It is important to stress that this approach is conceived as a component of structuration theory's ontology of potentials, rather than as a set of models or methods for the development of explanations. Thus, as I have indicated above, the three modes of system organisation are not primarily intended to represent forms of coordination and control of system reproduction that can clearly be distinguished in any given instance of empirical research. For example, systems organised exclusively through market-based reflexive regulation clearly do not occur very often in the real social world, notwithstanding their prevalence in economic texts. The insights into system organisation set forth in this chapter thus have only propaedeutic value; a value that hinges upon the goal to preserve the theoretical emphasis upon systemic organisation in functionalist accounts, while substituting a concern for the coordination and control of systems which occurs through social *praxis* for ontologically unnecessary or illegitimate postulates regarding collectively conceived functionalist teleologies.

Many functionalists might be inclined to respond that structuration theory's ontological approach sidesteps the virtues responsible for functionalism's appeal. They might buttress this argument by observing Giddens's acknowledgement that the postulation of collective teleologies which operate with reference to systemic functional needs is redundant in many forms of functionalist analysis. Ever since Merton's foundational essay on functionalism, scholars have found functionalism appealing on methodological grounds. While structuration theory does not concentrate on methodological themes, it would be disingenuous to neglect the significance of functionalism from a methodological point of view.

Giddens has advanced a series of reasons to explain why functionalism attracts so many exponents, despite the damaging criticism it has received over the years (*SSPT*, pp. 104–5). But however accurate these reasons may be, in my judgement he neglects the feature most responsible for functionalism's enduring appeal. Simply put, few other models of how collectivities are organised are equally stimulating to the sociological imagination. This provocative quality is perhaps less evident among Mertonians than among 'grand functionalists' (e.g. Parsons, Habermas) who propose specific functional needs which must be met if a system is to persist or survive in a given form. Assume a system to which these needs purportedly apply, and the mind springs into action with suggestions as to how the need can be fulfilled. Talcott Parsons, especially during the middle and later periods of his career, used his abstract functionalist model (the AGIL format which ultimately is incorporated in his 'cybernetic hierarchy') to speculate on the analytical interrelations between sub-systems each of which is associated with a functional need for the more encompassing analytical system in which it is incorporated. To offer a more concrete, albeit only implicitly functionalist, illustration: many Marxists covertly assume that capitalist societies have a need for a docile working class if they are to be organised in a stable manner. Given this assumption they set themselves the theoretical task of determining factors that can function to satisfy this need: for example, 'sweetheart contracts' between union and management, 'trade-union consciousness', social welfare programmes for the reserve army of the unemployed (see, for example, O'Connor, 1973).

There can be no gainsaying the need for means to jog the sociological imagination. While structuration theory rejects all imputations of functional needs to social systems, it does provide as an alternative to functionalist analysis, a methodological format to construct propositions which – although Giddens does not put matters in this light – can provoke social scientists to speculate on matters they might otherwise fail to consider.

The proposal is quite simple, but it does involve one subtle twist. Functionalist propositions, *sans* all postulates regarding teleological effective systemic needs, may be reconstructed in the form of the following question: what would have to happen for given features of a social system that are of theoretical interest to originate/persist/be altered? (*CPST*, pp. 113–14; *CCHM*, pp. 18–19; 'Commentary', p. 531; *CS*, p. 296). Now the use of the phrase 'have to happen' if it is interpreted in ontological terms might imply a paraphrase of a functional explanation: for example, if what 'has to happen' for class relations in a capitalist society to persist is the perpetuation of a docile working class, then it might be presumed that wherever a docile working class is found, it exists in virtue of its consequences for the persistence of class relations in that capitalist society. But the problem – which is clearly recognised by G. A. Cohen (1979, ch. 10; 1982, pp. 485–9) in his argument on behalf of functionalist 'consequence laws' – is that propositions which suggest that given phenomena occur in virtue of their consequences presume an antecedent hypothesis that explains how events occur. Cohen's 'consequence laws' attempt to circumvent this problem through propositions which suggest that whenever a given social item would be functional for another, the first social item is found to exist. This represents an 'unelaborated' functionalist explanation. Giddens ('Commentary', p. 530) responds to Cohen's proposal by observing that what 'consequence laws' actually propose in this 'unelaborated' form is not an explanation at all, but rather the identification of social circumstances that call for an explanation which they do not provide.

It is precisely this identification of that which needs to be explained which makes functionalism such a provocative mode of thought. Giddens preserves this asset to the sociological imagination by suggesting that the phrase 'have to' in the question, What would 'have to' happen for given features of a system to originate/persist/be altered? be construed as an implicit counter-factual. Any explanatory or ontological simplification is thereby removed. What would 'have to' happen need not be presumed to actually have occurred. It is a matter of speculation, a provisional step rather than a theory which suggests that what 'has to happen' actually comes about. The question of what would 'have to' happen' may be rendered in the past tense in speculations on the processes that brought about given features of historical systems; in the present tense for given features of contemporary systems; or even in the future tense to imagine what would 'have to' happen for hypothetically postulated features of a projected system which may be realistically conceived, or may be constructed in utopian or dystopian terms.

Counterfactual propositions not only preserve the speculative appeal of functionalist analysis, they are relevant as well to the formulation of empirical hypotheses. In order to discuss this application of counterfactual propositions it is useful to shift from a concern for functionalist methods to address a criticism of structuration theory included in a commentary by Margaret Archer. Archer writes as a proponent of sociological systems theory, and her overriding intention is to challenge the adequacy of structuration theory in general, and Giddens's account of the duality of structure in particular, to unravel the dialectical interplay between structural conditions/interaction/structural elaboration that is central to system theory's morphogenetic perspective. Several issues she raises during the course of her commentary will be addressed in Chapter 6, in conjunction with other criticisms of the structural dimension of structuration theory. The specific point I wish to discuss at this juncture concerns her remarks on the empirical analysis of the outcomes of systemic processes.

Archer's contention here (1982, p. 457) is that the structuration of systems is ever a process, and never a product. Structuration theory, she suggests (1982, pp. 461, 467), therefore avoids answering 'when' questions: e.g. when is stability more likely than change? and vice versa. On an ontological level Archer is quite correct. Structuration theory, as an ontology of the potentials of human *praxis*, addresses theoretical problems above the level of substantive inquiry in any given empirical case. It therefore proposes concepts that admit contingencies for both stasis and change; which contingencies will actually be realised depends upon the conditions, the activities, and the outcome of *praxis* in specific historical circumstances, or in given types of systems or situations. But even in substantive terms it remains correct to say that the structuration of systems and reproductions circuits is ever a process from an ontological point of view. Regardless of whether circumstances are reproduced or altered, social *praxis* never stops in its tracks when a given outcome has occurred. It may happen that the tempo of activity picks up or slows down, or that certain activities and consequences are revised, augmented, or replaced by others, but social life inexorably moves on. Perhaps only in appalling instances of devastation such as the period after the nuclear destruction of Hiroshima and Nagasaki, or the earthquake of 1906 that destroyed San Francisco, does the structuration of systems actually come to a halt. But Archer clearly does not have these radically disruptive events in mind.

But if structuration *is* ever in process, does it follow that (a) distinctions between stasis and change cannot be conceived, or that (b) specific outcomes of systemic activity cannot be determined? Hardly so. What Archer misses here is that social agents do not identify acts, outcomes, stasis or change as they occur. Rather, the identification of acts requires a reflexive moment of attention (*CPST*, p. 55; *NRSM*, pp. 82–3). The same point holds for social scientists as well. Before we can investigate outcomes, stasis, or change, we must intellectually freeze the ongoing course of structuration, or imagine that it has been frozen in the past, or will be frozen in the future. In doing so, we, and not the process of structuration, define the historical point *when* some phenomenon of interest has/will have occurred, just as social agents do during their discursive reflections on events in day-to-day life. In defining historical outcomes, investigators may assume the same criteria as those employed by lay actors, or they may adopt criteria indigenous to social scientific analysis (see *CS*, pp. 338–40; Cohen, 1984).

All of this may seem somewhat removed from the application of counterfactual propositions. But as Archer (1982, p. 467) suggests, 'when' questions call for empirically relevant propositions regarding potentials rooted in systemic stability/instability, and the conditions actors do/do not capitalise on in this regard. This is to say, in general terms, these propositions should say something regarding when reproduction or change in the structuration of systems is likely to occur, or, presuming a more fine-grained analysis, when a specific outcome of a given cycle of systemic activity is likely to occur: for example, the implementation of a bureaucratic policy, the arrangement of a specific series of marriages in a kinship system, etc.

Such propositions, obviously, can only be corroborated after the results of empirical research are in hand. But prior to the final stage of research, social scientists may entertain a variety of empirical hypotheses. Here, once again, counterfactual propositions may be put to good use. Presume, for example, that we have identified social revolutions that overturn aristocratic systems as our phenomenon of interest (e.g. Skocpol, 1979). Instead of asking When is it likely that such revolution will occur? we may speculate on what would have to have happened to bring about these revolutions. Such speculation undoubtedly will involve hypotheses concerning types of instability in specific systems or in sub-systemic reproduction circuits, conditions relevant to these instabilities that actors may or may not have capitalised on, etc.

In closing it is relevant to mention that the issue of 'when' questions, and hypothetical propositions formulated in response to these questions, involve methodological matters. As such this issue does not touch upon, nor does it in any way compromise, the structurationist ontology. Indeed, an implicit or explicit stance on ontological issues must be assumed before these questions can be proposed, and also before speculative or hypothetical responses can be entertained. It would have been extremely helpful if Archer had distinguished ontological issues from methodological matters during the course of her commentary. Unfortunately this distinction is not at all clear in her remarks.

5

Administered Systems: Power and Domination

In the last chapter I introduced the term 'administered systems' as a synonym for the self-reflexive mode of system organisation. The term 'administered systems' is appropriate because in systems of this kind the reproduction of activities, the consequences of activities, and systemic relations across time and space are coordinated and controlled through the exercise of administrative procedures which ultimately are meant to serve the intentions of superordinate agents. Administered systems therefore are power systems *par excellence*, and much of this chapter will be devoted to a consideration of their distinctive political qualities. But this is not the only theme to be developed here. To understand administered systems as power systems requires a prior grasp of Giddens's innovative approach to generic issues regarding power and domination at large. This comprises an extensive topic in itself, and the chapter begins with a clarification of the issues involved.

Power and domination: preliminary remarks

Although power and domination are among the most well-developed themes in Giddens's works, many of his insights are established in detail in his substantive writings rather than in his writings on structuration theory (see especially *CCHM*, Introduction, ch. 2; *PCST*, chs 11–15; *NSV*, pp. 8–17; *STMS*, ch. 7). Two aspects of Giddens's overall intellectual projects account for this expository separation of political themes. In the first place, in his generic theoretical writings Giddens continually emphasises the conceptual equality of the semantic, normative, and political constituents of *praxis*. To expand upon issues regarding power and domination at the expense of the others might imply a politically reductionist position which would be inconsistent with his purposes in the development of structuration theory (see *CS*, p. 283). In the second place, Giddens's substantive project includes an extensive conceptual and historical analysis of capitalism, the nation-state, and non-modern political systems, framed within an ongoing critique of historical materialism. To implement this project Giddens must set forth his views on the constitution of power, domination, and administered systems at greater length than in his ontologically oriented theoretical texts.

So as to maintain the ontological tenor of discussion, in the present chapter I shall be less concerned with substantive themes than Giddens himself. But unlike previous chapters I shall not begin with a sustained commentary on the way a single tradition of thought bears on the development of the concepts to be introduced. Part of the reason for not doing so is that beginning with Durkheim on the one hand, and Marx on the other, power and domination have slipped through the cracks in many theoretical programmes (see *NRSM*, pp. 93–102). Another reason is that those theorists who have made power and domination central to the development of social theory (e.g. Weber and Foucault), disagree so fundamentally as to make consolidation of their views a substantial task in itself. While I shall counterpose Giddens's views to those of other theorists from time to time during the following discussion, I shall begin with the position of structuration theory *per se*.

Power relations, domination, and the dialectic of control

Previously I have stressed the agency-oriented conception of power in structuration theory: i.e. the capacity all agents maintain and exercise to intervene and to thereby 'make a difference' in an ongoing course of practices, activities, and events. This concept is exceedingly broad: indeed, no instance of social *praxis* may be regarded as lacking the exercise of power in this agency-oriented sense of the term. Precisely for this reason, structuration theory includes a second conception of power, which, in effect, represents a sub-category of the first. This conception serves to specify power in a relational sense. By using this relational concept it becomes possible to consider the constitution of power in social systems in which practices and activities are related through their consequences. *Relational power* may be defined as the capability of actors to secure outcomes where the realisation of these outcomes depends upon the doings of others (*NRSM*, p. 111; *CPST*, pp. 92–4). Since administered systems involve the intentional exercise of relational power by those who coordinate and control systemic activities (this will later be conceived as administrative power), it is pertinent to add that when relational power is exercised with intent, actors know or believe that others will respond to given actions in determinate ways, and use this knowledge to bring about these responses (cf. *SSPT*, p. 348).

The relational conception of power in structuration theory cannot be properly understood without taking account of the ubiquitous presence in all power relations of the *dialectic of control*. The dialectic of control reconstructs and revises in an explicitly political manner Talcott Parsons's notion of the 'double contingency of interaction'. For Parsons (1951, pp. 10–12) this notion indicates that the reaction of each party to an interaction is dependent upon the contingent responses of others. Because each party depends upon how others respond, these responses potentially may become sanctions: each party, in effect, has reciprocal opportunities to sanction the acts of others. Parsons (1951, pp. 36ff) proceeds from this point to connect the 'double contingency' to the formation of generalised normative standards which serve to stabilise expectations of favourable responses in social interaction, and also to diminish the likelihood of negative sanctions for all parties concerned. In making this move Parsons can be faulted for treating utilitarian orientations to norms as of only residual analytical interest (*CPST*, p. 87). But this still leaves the 'double contingency' itself intact. The problem with the latter concept, however, is that Parsons fails to acknowledge that the dependence of actors upon the contingent responses of others not only involves orientations to institutionalised norms, it also involves the actualisation of power in interaction (*CPST*, p. 86).

To shift from the 'double contingency of interaction' to the dialectic of control it is necessary to expand the conceptual analysis to include the articulated interactions and reciprocities between absent agents that constitute the reproduction circuits of social systems. More specifically, attention now centres on the structuration of the power relations embedded in these circuits. The crucial insight that prefigures the concept of the dialectic of control is that *all social system and reproduction circuits involve asymmetrical distributions of resources, and therefore all systems and circuits exhibit some degree of political inequality.* A categorisation of resources will be presented during the subsequent course of discussion, but for present purposes the point to bear in mind is that resources provide agents who have access to them with a range of facilities to achieve outcomes. Now, in discrete instances of interaction it is possible that agents may have access to similar resources, and from this narrow-gauged standpoint they may achieve a rough political equality in interaction. But in systematically articulated power relations certain actors, or groups of actors, always maintain positions of superordinance and subordinance depending upon the relative quantity and effectiveness of the resources to which they have access, and the skills they have mastered to make use of these resources. Superordinate agents thus control facilities to achieve outcomes, including outcomes through the doings of subordinates, that exceed the complementary facilities of the subordinates to whom they are related during the course of system reproduction. This inequality of power relations, it should be added, is intrinsically associated with – i.e. it both influences and reflects – inequalities in the procedural and normative structuration of systems, as well as in the nature and consequences of sanctions that may be imposed by superordinates on subordinates, and vice versa.

How, then, does the 'double contingency' now appear? The key here is to recognise that a complementarity of relations persists between superordinates and subordinates. Although superordinate agents have access to more potent resources, they can never thoroughly control subordinates' activities simply by virtue of the resources they employ. Rather, in all instances in which outcomes are achieved *through* the doings of others (which leaves out of account executions, and the total immobilisation of agents), subordinate agents, by virtue of the fact that they have some degree of control over their doings, maintain at least some minimal capability to 'act otherwise' and thus at least a minimal realm of autonomy or freedom *vis-à-vis* superordinates' attempts to control their activities. Thus no subordinate agent is so coerced by, or dependent upon the resources controlled by superordinates and the sanctions associated with the use of these resources, that she loses all possibilities to respond in a manner other than superordinates would tacitly or explicitly prefer. Conversely, no superordinate agent who attempts to achieve outcomes through the doings of subordinates is so autonomous that she can achieve these outcomes without depending upon subordinates to respond in one way rather than another (cf. *CPST*, p. 93). The *dialectic of control refers to this universal presence of imbalanced degrees of autonomy and dependence that constitute power relations in systems and reproduction circuits of all kinds* (see *CPST*, pp. 6, 149; *CCHM*, p. 63; *CS*, pp. 16, 374; *NSV*, pp. 10–11).

The dialectic of control is as pervasive in social systems as the relational notion of power itself. The relative degree of autonomy and dependence among agents may vary from extremes of harsh subjugation (e.g. slave labour camps) to extremes of private liberty and public licence that surpass examples from the historical record. In addition, any historical transition or revolution, or any slower but equally effective alteration in the structure of political inequality, may shift the distribution of resources, and hence realign the relations of autonomy and dependence in complex ways. For example, as the scope of control facilitated by the resources superordinates can muster increases, thereby permitting them to intervene more extensively in the day-to-day activities of subordinates, so too opportunities may increase for subordinates to deflect, resist, or more positively to influence the activities of superordinates who depend upon their compliance (*NSV*, pp. 9–11). Giddens (*NSV*, pp. 201–21) puts this insight to good use in arguing that the unprecedented extensions of reciprocities between rulers and ruled brought about with the advent of the nation-state and capitalism created opportunities for the struggles which led to the institutionalisation of citizenship rights in nation-states. He thereby demonstrates a more balanced appreciation of power relations in the modern nation-state than either Marx and Weber – who neglect the significance of the opportunities for the advancement of democratic rights (see Cohen, 1985) – or pluralists who neglect that such rights are only a limited accomplishment in light of the superordinate–subordinate power relations which persist and are reproduced in both the nation-state and capitalism.

The dialectic of control, of course, may be implicated in stable modes of systemic organisation just as much as in periods of transition and realignment. In so far as a stable dialectic of control persists in the reproduction of power relations over the *longue durée*, it perpetuates an asymmetrical distribution of resources: i.e. a *structure of domination* drawn upon and reconstituted, in virtue of the duality of structure, as a social system is chronically reproduced (*CPST*, p. 93; *CCHM*, p. 50). In adopting this stance Giddens proposes to surmount the need to take sides in the enduring debate between exponents of individualist and collectivist conceptions of power. Unlike collectivist accounts, domination is not conceived as simply imposed upon agents who lack the resources to resist its imposition. Rather, structures of domination, as asymmetrical distributions of resources, are routinely and repeatedly regenerated as agents draw upon the more or less numerous and effective forms of resources available to them during the course of system reproduction. Unlike individualist approaches, which typically stress opportunities for individuals to choose from a wide range of possible courses of action, structures of domination prevent individuals from making, or even considering, certain decisions in this regard.

There are two points in structuration theory that forestall postulating an exaggerated freedom of decision-making power. First, as Giddens (*CS*, p. 257) puts it, power often 'flows smoothly' in the tacitly reproduced practices of day-to-day life. Tacitly accepted practices therefore serve as one basis for 'non decisions' (*CPST*, p. 89). Second, even where decision-making comes into play in the activities of rulers and others in the higher echelons of power, as well as in the activities of subordinates who contest their rule, actors are not capable of opting for all courses of action. Not only does the dialectic of control limit opportunities in this regard, these opportunities also are shaped by the limits of resource-based facilities agents do or do not possess to implement decisions. One need only consider the parallel failure of US intervention in Vietnam and Soviet intervention in Afghanistan to illustrate these decision-making limits on a grand scale. The inability of union leaders to win concessions from capitalist managers illustrates the limits on decision-making opportunities in the more recurrent activities of day-to-day life. Where those in position to make decisions are discursively aware of the limits to their capabilities stemming from the limits of the resources they can employ, the decision-making options which they perceive to be beyond their grasp represent a second category of 'non-decisions': a category which involves the shaping of agendas.

As mentioned above, the resources asymmetrically distributed in structures of domination do not stand apart from either the procedural or normative elements (rules) that comprise mutual knowledge. Agents not only must have access to resources, they must know how to use them to achieve outcomes, and they must know the appropriate circumstances in which they may be used. Having said this, however, there is one significant difference between resources and mutual knowledge. Mutual knowledge, however unevenly it may be distributed in the political hierarchy of a given system, cannot be accumulated and stored for future use. Resources, by contrast, often can be gathered, preserved, and retrieved in various ways (*NRSM*, pp. 111–12). As will be made evident during subsequent sections of this chapter, this property of resources is of central importance to the exercise of power in administered system.

To this point, power and domination have been presented without reference to how power is exercised. Here there is a theoretical division which must be addressed. The two basic positions are respectively established in the works of Max Weber and Michel Foucault. Most conventional conceptions of the exercise of power in some way are informed by Weber's classic ideal types of domination (for Giddens's commentaries in this regard, see especially *CPST*, pp. 146–50; *PCST*, pp. 200–5). But the underpinnings of Weber's concepts offer a highly skewed view of the exercise of power. For Weber (1968, pp. 53–4; see also, pp. 212, 941–8), power (i.e. the probability that an actor will be able to carry out his will in a social relationship, despite any resistance, and regardless of the basis of the probability) is a 'sociologically amorphous concept applicable to all personal qualities and all conceivable combinations of circumstances'. Weber therefore narrows his conceptual aperture to focus on domination (i.e. the probability that commands will be obeyed). Weber thus assumes a conceptual position in which power relations originate from the commanding heights of power (see Cohen, 1985, pp. 292–4). The pervasive exercise of power in more mundane socially constituted contexts and locales never comes into focus.

As opposed to Weber, Foucault accentuates the polymorphous techniques, procedures, and mechanisms of power intensively institutionalised in the activities of agents at the peripheries of centralised hierarchies of dominion (for Giddens's reflections on Foucault, see especially *PCST*, ch. 15; for a comparison between Weber and Foucault, see *CS*, pp. 145–58). In summarising the intellectual strategy of his various research projects in this thematic domain, Foucault (1980, pp. 95–103) avows his intent to invert all orientations to the exercise of centralised command over others. Unlike Weber, the institutionalised power for which he expresses concern is neither centralised nor appropriated in anyone's hands. Rather, it is 'employed and exercised through a net-like organization' (Foucault, 1980, p. 98). For Foucault, conclusions regarding the question of how these dramatically effective, yet enormously subtle, procedures of power are appropriated through more global forms of domination is indefinitely deferred.

If the contrast between Weber and Foucault were exclusively a matter of assuming a 'top down' or a 'bottom up' starting-point for the analysis of power, then the dialectic of control would serve as an appropriate conceptual means to reconcile their respective positions. But there is more at stake here. The contrast between Weber and Foucault actually involves differentiation in the types of procedures involved in power relations. Power-holders on the one hand, and those at the peripheries of power on the other, can be observed to engage in different modes of *praxis* even if their activities are interrelated in the reproduction of any given system. Giddens recently has advanced a set of concepts that distinguish the diverse modes of *praxis* to which Weber and Foucault respectively refer:

All social systems of any duration involve an 'institutional mediation of power'. That is to say, domination is expressed in and through the institutions that represent the most deeply embedded continuities in social life. But in the context of any collectivity, association or organization domination is expressed as modes of *control* whereby some agents seek to achieve and maintain the compliance of others. I shall refer to stable forms of control as types of *rule*. Forms of rule are (more or less) stable relations of autonomy and dependence in social systems and are sustained by the routine practices that those in super-ordinate positions employ to influence the activities of others. As such they are to be analytically separated from the institutionalized mediation of power. (*NSV*, p. 9)

Giddens does not present this distinction in response to the division between Weber and Foucault, but its relevance should be apparent. It is noteworthy that, for once, Giddens does not propose a reconciliation of the diametrically opposed standpoints they represent. Instead he implicitly accepts that a distinction must be made before the two can be interrelated. But in doing so he also implies that this interrelation must be established if power relations in social systems are to be conceived in their entirety. Forms of rule without an institutional mediation of power would make rule itself a superfluous term. An institutional mediation of power in the absence of rule would neglect the degree to which forms of rule penetrate the day-to-day activities of agents. Hence the two concepts must be seen as complementary to one another in the constitution of power relations, as well as in the structuration of domination in social life at large.

Administrative power

No civilisation, world-system, or society ever has been organised solely through the reproduction circuits of administered systems. Capitalist enterprises are geared into various markets in multifarious ways, and they may, in effect, exercise some degree of control over markets, just as markets may also shape entrepreneurial options to an empirically determinable extent. Even the most well-organised nation-states do not fully coordinate or control nuclear families, informal neighbourhood associations, organised religious groups, social movements of various kinds, and other civic groups. What is remarkable is not that institutionalised and articulated relations between agents remain partially independent of administered systems, but rather that administered systems coordinate and control so much of the day-to-day activity of social agents in the modern world. Giddens stresses this theme in his substantive work. But unlike Habermas (1984, 1987), Giddens is less concerned with the cultural ramifications of administered systems, and more concerned with the problem of administrative power. This theme does not define the sum total of his substantive interests, nor does administrative power somehow represent the basis for his ontological views on power at large. Nevertheless, there can be no gainsaying that administrative power is a prominent motif in both the substantive and ontological segments of his works.

But what exactly is administrative power? As a first step to answering this question it may be useful to distinguish the issue to which Giddens's concept of administrative power responds from the issue to which Max Weber's 'law of small numbers' is addressed. The 'law of small numbers' (Weber, 1968, pp. 952–3), which represents a generalised reformulation of Michels's 'iron law of oligarchy', stresses the unsurpassable effectiveness of rule which is generated by the concentration of decision-making powers and the control of administrative personnel in the hands of a small group of leaders who comprise a ruling minority. Although structuration theory expands Weber's 'top down' orientation in the 'law of small numbers' to include the dialectic of control, it says nothing to deny the validity of Weber's insight. Rather, the concept of administrative power retains Weber's focus on the significance of ruling minorities. However, it also refers to an issue that does not arise in Weber's 'law of small numbers', or, for that matter, in any of Weber's other ideal-types. This issue couples Giddens's novel conception of systems patterned across time and space with his concern for systemic forms of rule, and by bringing together these two previously unrelated themes it establishes a basis for a number of Giddens's most important theoretical contributions, as well as substantive insights into the organisation of social life in the modern world. Stated in the form of a question, the issue is: how can a relatively small group of agents in the upper echelons of an administrative hierarchy coordinate and control the extension and reproduction of systemic activities and relations patterned across time and space? The shift away from Weber's position should be clearly spelled out. *Unlike Weber, the exercise of rule, rather than the effectiveness of rule stands at the heart of this question*. Thus, this question brings us back once again to the fundamental concern for social *praxis* that pervades all aspects of structuration theory.

Administrative power refers to the coordination and control or, more broadly, capabilities of coordination and control, over the timing and spacing of human activities (*NSV*, p. 47). Administrative power, as thus conceived, appears in structuration theory as logically anterior to insights regarding the effectiveness of rule. Indeed, this effectiveness may vary to a considerable extent depending upon the spatio-temporal 'reach' of administrative power. If power-holders lack the facilities required to coordinate numerous activities in different settings across time–space, this clearly limits the effectiveness of their rule. If they maintain facilities to coordinate activities, but lack the capabilities required to control these activities, the effectiveness of their rule is still restricted and compromised in many ways.

The specific resources and procedures rulers employ to coordinate and control activities transacted within and between spatio-temporal settings must be determined through historical/empirical inquiries focused on specific systems, or kinds of systems. Thus, to take one of Giddens's recurring themes, the administrative power exercised by rulers of systems of empire and traditional states bears little resemblance to the far more extensive coordination and control of spatio-temporal activities and relations exercised by power-holders in the nation-state and capitalist enterprises. But if every instance or type of administrative power must be studied in substantive terms, this does not imply that administrative power is an infinitely variable form of rule. To the contrary, within broad limits certain types of resources may be conceived as supplying fundamental capabilities without which rulers and leading administrative officials would be unable to secure outcomes through the doings of others across time and space. Through the use of these resources, administrative power-holders establish distinctive kinds of power relations which may more or less intensively structure and control the day-to-day lives of subordinate agents, by virtue of both the practices which are thereby institutionalised in diverse spatio-temporal settings, and the forms of sanction that may be imposed or manipulated as threats.

While the notion of administrative power as the coordination and control of activities across time–space is easily understood, Giddens's account of the exercise of administrative power is multi-faceted, and incorporates many novel insights. Rather than moving directly to the details of this account, it will be helpful to develop a theoretical context as a means to portray its departures and continuities with established theoretical traditions. But in order to do so it is necessary to first have at hand an expanded version of the generic categories of resources of domination which informs Giddens's thought on the exercise of power in systems of all kinds. Conceived from this vantage point, resources are fundamental constituents in the structuration of systems which supply agents with two kinds of facilitating capabilities: allocative resources analytically identify capabilities that can be used to generate power over the naturally constituted world; authoritative resources do the same with regard to the socially constituted world. Table 5.1 expands upon these categories (from *CCHM*, pp. 51–2; *CS*, p. 258).

Table 5.1

Allocative Resources supply capabilities of control over:
- I.A.   Material features of the environment (raw materials, material power sources)
- I.B.   Means of material production/reproduction (instruments of production/technology)
- I.C.   Produced goods (artifacts created by the interaction of I.A. and I.B.)

Authoritative Resources are media that supply capabilities of control over:
- II.A.   Organisation of social time space (temporal-spatial constitution of paths and regions)
- II.B.   Production/reproduction of the body (organisation and relation of human beings in mutual association)
- II.C.   Organisation of life-chances (constitution of chances of self-development and self-expression)

This classification of resources is generically applicable to systems of all kinds, and it does not speak to the specific constellation of resources involved in the exercise of administrative power. It is a matter of no small importance that all categories of resources in Table 5.1 can be analytically specified in any and all types of social systems. Having said this, it is equally important to note that certain categories of resources will figure more prominently in different types of systems. Since administered systems presuppose the intentional coordination and control of activities reproduced across time–space, activities which are aspects of the socially constituted world, authoritative resources take on considerable significance in the exercise of administrative power. This emphasis upon authoritative resources applies regardless of whether the type of administrative system in question is an imperial state, a nation-state, or the administrative organisation of a capitalist industrial enterprise or commercial firm.

Giddens's emphasis upon authoritative resources in his account of the exercise of administrative power both informs and is informed by his conceptual and substantive critique of historical materialism. Not surprisingly, many Marxists have been disturbed by his views in so far as they contravert claims that all forms of power directly or indirectly depend upon control over the forces of production and the extraction of material surplus which results from this control. Given the theoretical scope of both structuration theory and historical materialism, no single issue can distil the critical response by Marxists to Giddens's polemically expressed opposition to a number of their most basic tenets and historical principles. However, one criticism which has a particular bearing on the issues involved in Giddens's account of administrative power turns on the contention that he accords primacy to Weberian themes regarding the exercise of dominion (see especially, Callinicos, 1985, pp. 134, 162 *passim*).

This contention is true in the sense that Giddens, like Weber, denies that the capabilities over socially constituted activities supplied by authoritative resources necessarily and always are shaped, regulated, or can be reduced to the capabilities over the forces of production, even in some ever-receding final analysis or historical conjuncture. But if this point is true it also is trivial. The Weberian rubric employed here appears as a residual category (residual to Marxist theory, that is), and like all residual categories the rubric is too obtuse to admit precise definition. It is much the same as saying that Marx should be regarded as a Ricardian simply because he is concerned with the labour theory of value. But this is not all. It should be recognised that nothing in the generic categories presented in Table 5.1 suggests or implies that allocative resources must be subordinated to their authoritative counterparts in any given substantive analysis. Thus where capitalist systems are in question structuration theory need not underestimate the centrality of the control of the forces of production and the extraction of surplus, as Weber arguably did in his ideal-types. Moreover, even in systems where authoritative resources must be ascribed a prominent role, this in no way suggests that allocative resources can be treated as superfluous to the exercise of power. Finally, it must be borne in mind that administered systems always overlap and intersect homeostatic and reflexively regulated systems where the constellation of resources employed in the exercise of power may involve different balances in the relative significance of the materially and socially constituted resources of domination. Hence to label Giddens a Weberian, if by this is meant that authoritative resources inevitably take precedence over allocative resources, or to subsume his thought on power and domination under a similar label such as 'managerialism' (Alford and Friedland, 1985, pp. 169–70), not only is obtuse, it is also incorrect.

Since the topic is administrative power I shall not set forth a thorough examination of the difference between Giddens's and Weber's respective analyses of power and domination. However, I already have noted certain differences between the two with regard to the dialectic of control and the institutional mediation of power, and in order to forestall the impression of an alignment between them with regard to administrative power I shall establish further differences below. To this end my discussion begins with some critical reflections on Weber's views on legitimation, which is the closest he comes to considering how administrative superordinates exercise rule over others. These remarks amplify my previous claim that by stressing the significance of administrative power, i.e. the coordination and control of systemic activities across time and space, Giddens augments and, in important respects, moves beyond the thematic focal points of Weber's ideal-types.

The critical contrast between Weber and Giddens anticipates themes regarding resources of domination and power relations in administered systems which will be developed throughout the remainder of this chapter. So as to avoid a possible source of confusion it should be noted that the following critical remarks, which stress oversights in Weber's views on legitimate domination, in no way imply a neglect of the significance of legitimation on

Giddens's part. This will be made clear in the closing stages of the chapter where Giddens's position on legitimation in administered systems will be examined in some detail.

Weberian legitimation and the exercise of administrative power

For Weber (1968, p. 31), legitimacy, in the most general sense, refers to social actions and relationships in which at least some actors are guided by an orientation to determinable maxims or norms which are regarded by the actors as in some way obligatory or exemplary. In the first instance, the question of legitimate domination is: 'When and why do men [and, women – IJC] obey? Upon what inner justifications, and upon what external means does this domination rest?' (Weber, 1946, p. 78). The issues Weber raises here are more complicated than they may initially appear. In the first place, it frequently is overlooked that throughout his writings Weber (e.g. 1968, pp. 31, 213–15, 946–7) is careful to indicate that in addition to, or apart from, voluntary assent to legitimating maxims or norms, actors may obey commands on the basis of motives ranging from sheer weaknesses and helplessness, to fear, to calculations of hope for advantages or the realisation of interests, to custom or convention. Ultimately, Weber (1968, p. 31) accepts that only some of the actors in a legitimate order must consider the norms or maxims to be obligatory or binding. Weber's (1968, p. 215) most general conception of obedience then refers only to a *formal* sense of obligation: i.e. without regard to the actor's own attitude or evaluation of the content of the command. What matters is that the content of the command becomes the basis for the actions which the actor carries out. Or, in other terms, the command influences the conduct of the ruled '*as if* [my emphasis] the ruled had made the content of the command the maxim of their conduct for its very own sake' (Weber, 1968, p. 946). In assuming this stance toward obedience, Weber establishes a much broader range of social and psychological bases for compliance than is evident in the way legitimation is dealt with by Talcott Parsons (1969, pp. 361ff; see Cohen, Hazelrigg and Pope, 1975, pp. 238–9) and Jurgen Habermas (1987, pp. 268ff), both of whom establish an analytical baseline in which power is legitimised with reference to justification for obedience tied to agents' expectations regarding the pursuit of collective goals.

If Weber's stress on the formal obedience to legitimate commands implies only a contingent link, in any given concrete instance, between obedience and the justification of commands, the reason why legitimacy figures so prominently in his ideal-types is that, by contrast with interests, customs, or conventions, elements of actors' orientations which are formally oriented to legitimating maxims or norms provides a far more reliable basis for domination to occur (Weber, 1968, p. 213). In addition, the relationships between rulers, administrators, and the ruled, i.e. the organisational distribution of powers of command, can be most easily typified by the legitimating claims made by power-holders with regard to the obedience of others (Weber, 1968, p. 953). An implication of this Weberian point of view is that legitimation, even when it only results from formal obedience to commands, organises and stabilises the hierarchically structured power relations throughout any given system of domination (cf. Weber, 1968, p. 31).

Considered in terms of the subjective definition of social action which informs all of Weber's ideal-types, it would appear to make perfectly good sense to conceive obedience (formal or voluntary) to legitimate commands as a primary basis for stabilising and organising the control rulers and administrators exercise over the ruled. However, in emphasising the subjective orientation to commands Weber neglects the fact that actors are embodied, and that their actions involve interventions in spatio-temporally situated activities and events. The stability of rule depends in substantial measure not only upon superordinates's reliance upon the obedience of the ruled, or more broadly upon how the activities of the ruled are *controlled*, but also upon how superordinates *coordinate* the spatio-temporal sequences and outcomes of the activities in which subordinates engage during the course of system reproduction. Thus Weber's insights into the contribution of legitimation to the stability of domination eclipses a concern for administrative power in much the same way as do his insights into the effectiveness of rule undertaken by ruling minorities in virtue of 'the law of small numbers'.

But Weber's account is deficient in another respect that also is accentuated in the concepts regarding administrative power Giddens incorporates in structuration theory. Here, attention turns from coordination to control. While Weber's epistemology allows for empirical departures from ideal-typical images, and while his views on domination allow for motives of fear, interest, and hopes for advantage as subjective bases for obedience, he rather surprisingly does not spell out in conceptual terms possibilities that agents will disobey commands. That is, he only briefly (e.g. Weber, 1968, p. 651) attends to how administrators manage to keep disobedient agents in line. Even Weber's extensive discussion of the origins and nature of discipline mentions the ubiquitous presence of 'compulsory integration' (i.e. coercive control) only as a residual category (Weber, 1968, p. 1150; see also pp. 1148–56 *passim*).

Subsequent works that explore the 'informal structure' of modern bureaucracies (e.g. Selznick, 1949, p. 251; Burawoy, 1979) raise doubts regarding the eclipse of disobedience in Weber's works. These works foreshadow, and may be interpreted in terms of, Giddens's concept of the dialectic of control. Indeed, a central implication of the dialectic of control suggests that the formally legitimated obligations incorporated in bureaucratic rules (and traditional maxims) rarely conform to actual practice (*PCST*, p. 204). The exercise of coercive control over potentially recalcitrant subordinates is, of course, by no means confined to administered systems. However, the spatio-temporal extension of administered systems does render coercive control particularly problematic. The question here is: how can superordinates who operate in one systemic locale establish means to control the doings of others situated in a variety of spatio-temporally remote settings who may not necessarily be inclined to obey?

The preceding remarks by no means exhaust the oversights in Weber's works with regard to the exercise of power by rulers and officials in administered systems. However, they do underscore two issues that figure prominently in Giddens account of administrative power. The first refers to the resources required by upper-level administrators in order to coordinate the activities of agents across time and space. The second refers to the ways in which administrators may exercise control of activities in remote locales. Although I shall deal with these issues *seriatim* below, it must be understood that the two are closely related, and the ways in which they combine must be established before any account of forms of rule in an administered system can be considered complete.

Stored information: an authoritative resource of administrative power

Despite the manifest differences between Weber's views on legitimate domination and the structurationist account of administrative power, there is one issue where a thematic intersection does occur. According to Weber (1968, pp. 223, 225, 952, 957), 'secret' knowledge regarding administrative policies and plans, and technical knowledge of administrative activities coupled with access to facts contained in office files, are primary sources of the superiority of modern bureaucratic administration. These insights appear at prominent points in Weber's ideal-types. But he fails to expand upon the contributions that specific forms of knowledge make to the exercise of dominion over the activities of others, or to processes of policy formation and management of administrative affairs.

While Giddens (*CS*, pp. 151–2; *STMS*, pp. 155–6) acknowledges Weber's insights in this regard, he presents a far more robust and specific account of stored information as an authoritative resource employed in the exercise of administrative power to coordinate, and, to some extent, to control systemic activities articulated across time and space. Unlike Weber, Giddens includes non-modern administered systems within the ambit of his conceptual insights regarding information. One of the most dramatic discontinuities between non-modern systems and those characteristic of modernity consists in the enormous expansion of stored information that reciprocally has been generated by, and has contributed to, the growth of capitalist enterprises and the nation-state (*NSV*, pp. 144–5, 172–81). By contrast, the information employed in non-modern systems of empire and traditional states was of an inferior quality, and the available means for the storage and communication of knowledge were both cumbersome and inefficient (*NSV*, p. 178).

Stored information may supply power-holders with a range of capabilities. Knowledge of the doings of subordinates, for example, may be skilfully employed to coerce or induce compliance from subordinates, thereby influencing their life-chances in so far as their participation in systemic activities is concerned. But from the standpoint of the *coordination* of systemic activities, stored information contributes facilities of an entirely different kind. Indeed, this coordinating application of stored information may be considered as a necessary condition of administered systems. The information in question refers to the spatio-temporal sequencing of systemic activities, the spatio-temporal movements of agents involved in these sequences, and the articulation of the outcomes of these activities across time and space. With this information in hand, those in the upper echelons of power in administered systems may establish, regulate, and alter the organisation and outcomes of activities in systems or reproduction circuits, they may designate settings where specific activities are to be performed, assign specific agents to those settings at designated times, and they may monitor the activities and outcomes produced in those settings, thereby accumulating more information relevant to the coordination and control of system reproduction.

The collection and accumulation of information obviously is as vital to the exercise of administrative power as the ways in which this information is applied. For this reason, Giddens (*CCHM*, pp. 5–6; *NSV*, p. 14) places a great deal of emphasis upon administrative surveillance, a concept which must be distinguished from supervisory surveillance which will be discussed below. Giddens draws much inspiration from the works of Foucault in developing these concepts. However, given Foucault's neglect of centralised hierarchies of power, no direct analogue for administrative surveillance appears in his works, and, in general, as Giddens observes (*PCST*, p. 129), Foucault did not distinguish one mode of surveillance from the other.

Administrative surveillance is a compound concept that refers on the one hand to the gathering of pertinent data, and on the other hand to the coding and collation of this data which transform them into information suitable for administrative applications. The nature of the codes and classificatory schemes employed varies, both historically and with reference to the kinds of information required for the coordination and control of activities in any given system, or type of system. Having said this, a ubiquitous prerequisite for administrative surveillance is that power-holders must be literate, where literacy is defined in terms of the symbolic codes employed. Thus, non-modern administrators might be literate by virtue of their capability to read rather rudimentary signs, whereas modern administrators may be literate by virtue of their capability to engage in sophisticated techniques of interpretation, statistical inference, and computer programming. In most instances literacy also involves a familiarity with applications of conventional metrics which more or less precisely establish standardised units for the discrimination of duration across time and space. Administrative surveillance also requires means to store and retrieve coded and classified information, as well as to transmit or transport information both from and to remote locales. The nature of all of these various means obviously may differ from one historical period to another, and from one type of system to another.

To put some content into this conceptual account of the utility of stored information as a resource of administrative power, and simultaneously to illustrate some of the distinctive features of the modern exercise of administrative power facilitated by the use of this information, consider the political implications of the development of Occidental chronometric conventions and mechanical techniques for the measurement of these conventional units of time. Most theories of power would be hard-pressed to conceive chronometry as a substantial resource of domination. Yet, as Lewis Mumford (1934, pp. 16–18) suggests, the clock may be regarded as a piece of 'power machinery' without which modern social life would be immediately disrupted, and would eventually collapse. Although mechanical measurement of time was not invented for political reasons, it did originate for purposes of regulation of disciplined activities in Christian monasteries during the thirteenth century. It was first applied as a 'power machine' by fourteenth-century capitalists who used clock-time to coordinate and regulate the activities of some of the earliest forms of truly proletarian labour. The workers subjected to this application of chronometry as a resource of domination responded in conflicts that anticipated the not altogether unrelated rebellion of their Luddite counterparts several centuries hence (see Landes, 1983, pp. 71–9). Undeterred by these events, capitalists continued to find more fateful applications for the clock, which culminated in the precise time-zoning of industrial activity on the one hand, and the commodification of labour-time on the other. From an administrative standpoint it is easy to see that the coordination of industrial production would be profoundly impaired if tasks were not demarcated into temporal units, and if the participation of workers in these tasks was not also defined in temporal terms. However, it requires no more than a basic familiarity with Marx to see that these same temporal demarcations are implicated in the alienation of workers from production processes established by and for capitalist purposes, as epitomised in the profit-oriented emphasis upon temporal efficiency in Taylor's techniques of 'scientific management'. Temporal demarcations are equally fundamental to the capitalist exploitation of labour-power from Marx's point of view, which crucially depends upon wages paid for labour-time rather than for commodities produced. (For Giddens's views on the commodification of labour-time, see *CCHM*, pp. 133–5).

In speaking of chronometric technique it may appear that we have strayed from the topic of stored information. Clocks, after all, do not store information relevant to the coordination of systems (although with the advent of microchip technology the day when they do may be close at hand). However, along with calendars – which already facilitated the coordination of activities in administered systems prior to the advent of modernity (see *CCHM*, pp. 131–2; *NSV*, p. 174) – clocks establish the conventional temporal units that permit such information to be coded, collated, and stored. The device that stores this temporally coded information relevant to the spatio-temporal coordination of systemic activities today is known as an administrative timetable:

> A timetable may seemingly consist of a description of events or activities given independently of it. *But all timetables are essentially time–space organizing devices.* A timetable does not just describe how events or activities are fixed in relation to one another, it is the medium of their very coordination. *STMS*, p. 160; see also *NSV*, p. 174)

By storing information regarding the coordination of systems, timetables serve as an authoritative resource under category II.A. in Table 5.1, i.e. capabilities relevant to the control over time–space pathways followed by agents. Timetables may be more or less precise, and their existence in no way ensures that the intentions of those in the upper echelons of administered systems which are built into the timetable will be carried out by subordinates. Nevertheless, by serving as the medium through which activities are coordinated, timetables must be regarded as 'power machines' to the same extent as the clocks and calendars to which they are closely related. But timetables do more than coordinate the articulated spatio-temporal pattern and tempo of systems and reproduction circuits. They also are vital for purposes of administrative surveillance. For example, timetables which establish delivery dates (a quintessentially spatio-temporal notion) also establish means to gather information on the reliability of those who supply various goods. By the same token administrative files may be developed on the quantity or quality of output by systemic personnel in specific systemic locales over given periods of time, and administrators thus may identify, and formulate plans to reorganise, operations they deem ineffective in this regard.

If timetables are an administrative resource based upon stored information, they are not the only such device that may be regarded in this way. Giddens, for example (*CCHM*, p. 117; *NSV*, pp. 123–6; *STMS*, pp. 155–6), treats money, *inter alia*, as a medium to code and store information regarding the value and profitability of material production in capitalist enterprises and as a medium facilitating the transmission of this information across time and space. Rational capital accounting procedures collate and store information regarding production and profitability in monetary terms, thereby dramatically enhancing the coordination of entrepreneurial systems, and extending the potential time–space distantiation of the entrepreneurial control over circuits of reproduction. Giddens thus puts rational capital accounting in a decidedly more political light than it appears in Weber's account of the formal rationality of the capitalist enterprise (on Weber's account see Cohen, 1981).

In closing on the topic of stored information and administrative surveillance it must be re-emphasised that administered systems quite literally would not exist in the absence of these vital authoritative resources. While the preceding example illustrates this point with regard to capitalist enterprise, stored information plays an equally vital role in administered systems of all kinds. In establishing this theme Giddens lends new meaning to the cliche that 'knowledge is power' by stressing the link between knowledge and the time–space distantiation of administered systems. Indeed the span of administered systems across time and space, the differentiation and regionalisation of systemic activities within and between systemic locales, and the sequential coordination of these activities across time and space, all depend upon the quantity and quality of coded and collated information involved in the exercise of administrative power.

Administrative power, allocative resources, and Marxist theory

Despite the substantial importance of stored information, to concentrate on it to the exclusion of all else would entail a highly reductionist view of the resources implicated in the forms of rule of administered systems. As I previously mentioned, the exercise of administrative power depends upon allocative as well as authoritative resources, and the significance of these resources will be considered in the sections which follow. Three different allocative resources will be dealt with during the course of those sections: 'surplus production', the means of violence, and territorial containment.

It must be clearly understood that the ordering of sections with regard to these resources has been adopted for expository reasons. In particular, this ordering in no way implies that 'surplus production' is a more fundamental allocative resource than the means of violence. As I shall indicate below, one of Giddens's most important ambitions is to correct the substantial neglect of the means of violence by social theorists. But having said this, when the topic of allocative (material) resources is raised most readers initially will interpret it with reference to Marxist theoretical categories. For this reason I shall defer discussion of the means of violence until Giddens's views on the connection between 'surplus production' and administrative power have been examined in some detail. The account begins with an overview of Giddens's position *vis-à-vis* Marxist theory at large.

In certain respects to concentrate upon administered systems is to obscure Giddens's position on central elements in Marxist theory. Such is the case, for example, with regard to social classes. For Giddens, classes are not administered systems, although their existence may depend upon the fact that certain kinds of administered systems exist (e.g. capitalist industrial enterprises). Classes may be most clearly conceived in terms of power relations which cut across systems, and which are structured by large-scale asymmetries in the control and distribution of allocative resources (see *CCHM*, pp. 113–14; *NSV*, pp. 69–71; see also *CPST*, pp. 110, 115). It is preferable to use the term 'allocative resources' rather than 'property' here, because the *social* constitution of property, including its institutionalised definition, as well as the procedures, rights, and obligations associated with its ownership and control, varies to such a great extent between non-modern and modern societies that the term 'property' ultimately loses its precision. Land, which falls under category I.A. in Table 5.1, served as the basis for class relations in non-modern societies. But with the advent of abstract capital (exchange value), class relations in capitalist societies came to be based upon an array of allocative resources which can be alienated from their producers and owners far more easily than land as a natural resource.

The distribution and control of allocative resources, and hence the structuration of class relations, may be aligned with, or diverge from, administered systems in various ways. Tracing out these alignments comprises one basic task Giddens sets himself in the substantive analysis incorporated within his 'contemporary critique' of historical materialism. Since the topic at hand is administered systems, I shall not be concerned to delineate these alignments. However, it is worthwhile to establish in more general terms the basis for Giddens's objection to the historical materialist tradition in Marxist thought.

On the deepest level of the structurationist ontology, Giddens (*NRSM*, pp. 102–3; *CCHM*, pp. 155–6) is opposed to the narrow limits of the Marxist account of human *praxis* in which human beings are regarded first and foremost as tool-making and tool-using animals. *Pari passu* he also denies that the need – regardless of whether it is interpreted in functionalist or in praxiological terms – to master the environment so as to acquire the material prerequisites for human survival serves as the fulcrum, even in the last analysis, for all other aspects of social life (*CCHM*, pp. 21–2). His objections to these premises further entail (*CCHM*, pp. 1–2) that: (i) human history cannot be understood in terms of the progressive augmentation of the forces of production; (ii) that human history cannot be regarded as the history of class struggles; (iii) that Marx's historical materialist evolutionary scheme is indefensible, and therefore must be abandoned. It therefore follows that Giddens (*CPST*, pp. 154, 162) cannot accept the historical materialist conceptual format for the analysis of modes of production as the lynch-pin of a theory of administered systems. Rather, Giddens insists that the administrative control of human beings figured *more* prominently than class relations in the organisation of non-modern states and systems of empire; and even in the capitalist era, where class relations do play a pivotal role, the fundamental significance of administered systems cannot be ignored. If Marx never fully acknowledged as much, this may have been because entrepreneurial bureaucracies, and state-intervention in economic affairs, were less well-developed in his immediate surroundings than in any other set of circumstances which have arisen during the capitalist era.

Giddens's harsh indictment of the fundamentals of historical materialism belies many points where he derives insights from Marx's work. Throughout his substantive analyses Giddens (*CCHM*, pp. 7–8) stresses that Marx's analysis of capitalist exploitation and accumulation, as well as Marxist analyses of class relations, are indispensable assets to his own substantive conception of the structure and structuration of capitalism. But even on the ontological level many loose affinities exist between structuration theory and Marxist theory. If the concept of *praxis* in structuration theory is not formulated in materialist terms, it nevertheless sustains Marx's implicit connection between agency and power. If the trans-historical centrality of class struggle is rejected, a sense of the tacit or overt struggles in practice between power-holders and subordinates persists in the broader terms of the dialectic of control. Finally, as I have already said, if structuration theory disavows a reduction of structures of domination to the ownership and control of the forces of production, it nevertheless insists that allocative resources and the capabilities they supply *always* play some role in the exercise of power (*CS*, pp. 258–9).

The extent to which Giddens writes in the spirit of Marx may be gauged by the fact that several of his Marxist critics (see especially, Wright, 1983) have grasped the gist of his thought, both in terms of structuration theory and in terms of his substantive analyses, far better than most other commentators. So much do Marxist undertones reverberate in his work that even his conceptual analysis of administered systems, which seemingly opposes Marxist theory at every turn, is by no means devoid of variations on

Marxist themes, albeit variations which alter and augment Marxist ideas to a considerable extent. A fundamental point on which Giddens concurs with Marxist theory is that the control of material resources serves as a necessary condition for the exercise of administrative power. Variations on Marxist themes that proceed from this point concern the nature of 'surplus production' and how it is extracted.

Allocative resources and administrative power: the appropriation of 'surplus production'

That administrative power cannot be exercised in a material vacuum already is evident in the media required to transmit and store information resources. Even the transcription or recording of information requires some kind of material base (*NSV*, p. 178; see also Callinicos, 1985, p. 150). But of greater importance, the exercise of administrative power involves the assembly of a corps of administrative officials disengaged from direct participation in processes of material production (*NSV*, p. 15). The material support for these officials, in turn, must be derived from the indirect or direct appropriation of part of the fruit of the labour of others.

The point is as obvious as it is significant, and few Marxists, no doubt, would be inclined to dissent. But Giddens handles the details of the issue with a great deal of caution in order to avoid two problematic aspects of Marxist theory. In the first place, appropriation need not involve direct control of the means of production, nor need it involve the immediate supervision of the processes of production. Indeed, in non-modern systems the limited capabilities of rulers and administrators to coordinate and supervise activities across time and space severely limited their capacity to engage in either form of control. In many instances day-to-day routines, including labour itself, were not implicated in systemic activities (*CCHM*, p. 102). Peasants, in particular, whether 'free' or bonded, retained much control over their life-style and labour (*NSV*, p. 70). Thus, whoever controlled the land (i.e. the means of production) did not control it in anything more than a nominal or legal sense. The most prevalent way in which appropriation occurred was via the imposition of taxation and rent backed not by ownership of the means of production, but rather by the use of force (*CCHM*, p. 112; *NSV*, p. 158). The modern nation-state, of course, also relies upon taxation backed by sanctions which revert in the end to physical force, and, at least in capitalist societies, the nation-state itself neither owns the bulk of the means of production, nor controls the labour process through the auspices of its own supervising agents.

In the second place, Giddens takes pains to avoid proposing a narrow definition of 'surplus production' as the *sine qua non* for appropriation to occur. To do so would dispose structuration theory toward the Marxist view that the course of human history, and the development of administered systems in particular, hinges upon the augmentation of the means of production through which 'surplus' can be generated. But 'surplus', Giddens argues (*CCHM*, pp. 110–11), is itself an ambiguous term, and instances may be found in which appropriation has occurred in its absence. 'Surplus' is ambiguous because it cannot be defined with reference to the minimal material conditions for human survival. On the one hand this definition is vacuous: few human commodities can be identified in which a surplus above these conditions has been lacking for a substantial segment of the population. On the other hand it is not always clear that those who are capable of production beyond the minimum must strive to realise this potential. This is especially evident where productive activity and exchange are embedded in traditional webs of institutionalised relations, rather than in the class relations inherent in the capitalist organisation of labour (*NSV*, p. 67; also Polanyi, 1944). But even if the minimum material conditions for survival are not attained, the appropriation of material goods still may proceed. This eventuality is not confined to non-modern settings. It is at least arguable that Stalinist policy during the 1930s was to build the administrative, military and industrial organisation of the Soviet state at the expense of driving large segments of the peasantry to destitution through the appropriation of the bulk of their production. Mobilisation for war in other twentieth-century societies, at times, has resulted in similar degrees of material deprivation for workers and peasants, although rarely officials of the state, or members of the military forces.

While Giddens continues to refer to 'surplus production' (*NSV*, p. 15), the foregoing remarks suggest that the term may be misleading in certain historical situations. However, the point remains that administered systems do require sources of foodstuffs and *matériel* if they are to coordinate and control activities of any kind. Modern capitalism stands out in this regard because it transposes the appropriation of allocative resources from a support for administrative power to an open-ended process of accumulation. But modern capitalism differs from all other systems in terms of its mode of system organisation as well, a contrast that includes all non-modern forms of profit-oriented enterprises, as well as state systems of all kinds. From this vantage point, capitalism appears as a concatenated system comprised of intentionally administered enterprises that are unintentionally regulated through the networks of labour and product markets in which they are enmeshed. What fuels these complex reproduction circuits – and here Giddens (*NSV*, p. 133) adheres closely to the Marxist position – is the commodification of both property and labour power. By disengaging exchange value and abstract labour from their material embodiments in goods and corporeal human activity, capitalist reproduction circuits can extend articulated relations between absent agents around the globe at a tempo no previous economic system can match. One (but not the only) distinctive aspect of Giddens's substantive analysis of capitalist systems and their ramifications for modernity at large involves his insights into the epochal transformation of the timing and spacing of activities and relations associated with their commodification. This ultimately involves the commodification of both time and space *per se* (see *CCHM*, ch. 6).

Allocative resources and administrative power: the means of violence

As I previously have said, one of Giddens's leading objectives, both in his substantive works and in structuration theory at large, is to prise open a theoretical space to establish the significance of the means of violence as a resource of administrative power (for a like-minded historical project, see McNeil, 1982). Capitalist systems represent something of an anomaly here, since, as Giddens (*NSV*, p. 71) points out, one of the great historical discontinuities of the modern era is that the dominant (capitalist) class no longer directly controls the means of violence. Nevertheless, if capitalism (and certain traditional systems such as the church) do not marshal any weapons as resources, the indirect influence of control of the means of violence still cannot be denied. For systems that do control the means of violence typically pacify populations and maintain territorial domains within which non-violent systemic activity may be institutionalised, coordinated, and controlled. States, which represent the leading systems that have access to means of violence, not only use them to pacify populations, but also as sanctions to support their appropriation of 'surplus' production via various modes of taxation and fees.

One of the great flaws of the classical traditions that continue to influence even the most recent programmes in social theory is their silence on the significance of violence as a resource of power. Even Habermas reflects this classical inheritance in so far as violence is dealt with only *sotto voce* in his works. Giddens not only proposes to rectify this fundamental oversight in social theory, he also suggests two reasons why it may have originated. Understood in terms of the history of ideas, Giddens (*CCHM*, pp. 206–9) suggests that the opposition to utilitarianism shared by otherwise antithetical classical theorists such as Marx and Durkheim led to the assumption that the era of violence in social relations had come to an end. This occurred indirectly, rather than in a straightforward manner, in so far as both theorists absorbed from utilitarian political economy the notions that industrialism stood at the centre of modern modes of social organisation, and that industrialism was inherently a pacifying social force. Considered from the standpoint of the sociology of knowledge, Giddens (*CCHM*, pp. 177–8) also suggests that the 'seven decades of European peace' during the nineteenth century re-enforced a sense shared by Comte, Spencer, and Durkheim that militaristic violence no longer figured prominently, as it previously did, in the constitution of social life. Of course not all classical theorists were similarly persuaded of this turn of events. Weber, for one, never denied the significance of violence, although it is regrettable that his death deprived us of the conceptual approach to issues related to the means of violence, which no doubt would have been a matter of great concern in his projected work on the sociology of the state. As it is, theorists and historians of state violence such as Karl von Clausewitz and Otto Hintze barely appear on the sociological horizon. The same can be said for Raymond Aron's contribution, which has begun to influence a still relatively small-scale renewal of interest in violence on the part of certain British social theorists (see Shaw, 1984).

Giddens's substantive concern with the means of violence as a resource of administrative power in both traditional and modern state-systems is far better developed than his conceptual account. His basic definition poses no difficulties: *the means of violence* are simply material devices of any kind that supply capabilities to do harm to the human body through the use of force (*NSV*, p. 343, n. 20). But, from here, matters become considerably more complex. In the first place, although the means of violence comprise an allocative resource since they are material goods, they also may be regarded as an authoritative resource in so far as their use, or the threat that they might be used, represents the most extreme, albeit not the most effective, form of coercive sanction that may be employed to bring agents to comply with commands. In the second place, the means of violence vary quite widely both in their nature and in the way they are used. Moreover, their use, in itself, depends upon the establishment of various types of administered systems.

Giddens has only begun to scratch the surface of this topic, and his remarks for the most part focus on the use of violence in the modern nation-state as contrasted with the use of violence in traditional states. To this end, he suggests (*NSV*, p. 16) a dichotomous classification. The means of violence may be applied either in the form of *military power*, or *policing power*. Military applications of the means of violence supply capabilities to extend boundaries as frontiers, to defend these perimeters from threats of invasion, and to preserve the position of states in inter-state systems. In addition, military power may be applied within the boundaries of states in lieu of well-developed administrative control of subordinate groupings (e.g. in Third World states) (*NSV*, p. 251). Policing applications of the means of violence almost always occur within state boundaries or frontiers, and are directed toward the pacification of subordinate groups. Policing thus involves the sanctioning of 'deviance' from established routines as defined by legal codes and regulated by juridical systems (*NSV*, p. 16). The enforcement of taxation demands in modern states illustrates an application of policing power where tax collectors who have access to arms are not supported by military forces.

Allocative resources and administrative power: territorial containment

As indicated in the discussion of the generic concepts regarding power and domination presented earlier in this chapter, one aspect of resources that sets them apart from mutual knowledge is that they can be stored. Subsequently it was noted that stored information, including official files as well as timetables, capital accounting books and so forth, provides capabilities crucial to the exercise of power in administered systems. It now should be added that the material 'surplus' appropriated from producing classes also must be stored to provide a dependable reserve of material support for rulers and their administrative staff. This storage may involve actual stockpiles of goods (e.g. granaries, warehouses, etc.) and/or it may involve 'liquid' instruments of credit. In either case, material storage depends, in part, on stored information, since goods must be coded according to an inventory scheme so that they may be retrieved and transported across time–space to the administrative personnel which they serve to support.

Administered systems of all kinds generally maintain locales or regions in which resources are concentrated, and made available for administrative applications as required. In structuration theory these locales or regions are known as *power containers* (*STMS*, pp. 157–8; *NSV*, pp. 12–13; *CS*, p. 262; *CCHM*, pp. 5–6, see also pp. 35, 94). The concept is more complex than it initially may seem. Like all locales, power containers are socially constituted by a variety of articulated procedures and relations. But if power containers are socially constituted as arenas of activity, they also are territorially demarcated settings which may be internally regionalised in various ways. Intuitively obvious examples include the headquarters of bureaucratic organisations and capitalist enterprises, military barracks, and capital cities in traditional states and imperial systems. All of these territorial centres of established administrative systems stand in complex relations to peripheral arenas of power, for example branch offices and factories, consumer markets, theatres of battle, outer realms of the empire, the countryside beyond the walls of city-states, and these centre–periphery relations are constituted by various modes of system integration, as well as supervisory control through face-to-face interactions. (On the distinction and the relations between central regions and peripheral regions, see *CS*, pp. 130–2).

In all of these instances the territory occupied by the administrative headquarters may be conceived as a material resource in itself (under category I.A. in Table 5.1). The same holds for the nation-state as a power-container in the modern era. But to construe the nation-state as a power container requires a shift in territorial levels of analysis. This shift is warranted by the fact that with the dramatic expansion of administrative capabilities to coordinate and control spatio-temporally remote activities, heads of state, legislators, and administrative officials now extend the purview of their administrative power so that they may regulate and appropriate resources across vast territories, and equally vast populations of agents. The centre and peripheries of administrative power here are demarcated by politically defined borders, whereas in traditional states boundaries were defined territorially as frontiers. (On borders and frontiers, see *NSV*, pp. 49–53). Modern nation-states may be conceived as internally and externally regionalised systems. Externally they are enmeshed in various ways in the politically regionalised relations of the global inter-state system (*NSV*, p. 267, ch. 10 *passim*). Internally they are regionalised by the distribution of industries, population concentrations, and variations between neighbourhoods and locales in the modern 'created environment' (*NSV*, pp. 193–4). What makes both the external and internal regionalisation of nation-states difficult to discern in a conceptually or empirically precise manner is that the capitalist world-economy, national and trans-national enterprises, and markets for labour, goods, and real estate, cross-cut the boundaries of nation-states in a multitude of ways. This complexity in the regionalisation of modern power containers illustrates why a major objective of Giddens's substantive analysis is to describe and explain the peculiar nature, development, and consequences of the insulation of economic and political relations in modern capitalist societies (see *CCHM*, pp. 125–8). Nation-states may be territorially defined as power containers, but their inner regionalisation, and much of the activity that constitutes specific regions and locales, is subject to the administrative power of capitalist enterprise and the unintentional regulation of capitalist markets.

A note on technology

All who are familiar with the historical materialist emphasis upon the augmentation of the forces of production as the piston in the engine propelling historical progress will have noticed the absence of productive technology as a resource of administrative power. The reason for this omission is simply that, for Giddens (*NSV*, p. 146), prior to the advent of capitalism productive technologies did not greatly transform nature. He therefore regards industrialism as an indigenous feature of modernity rather than a resource of domination that appears in all instances of administrative power.

In a broader sense, technology, of course, is implicated as a resource of administrative power *per se*. But it is so polymorphous as to defy definition. One can hardly discuss the means of violence as a resource without taking military technology into account. Similarly, the information resources that supply capabilities to coordinate and control the timing and spacing of activities would not exist were it not for technologies of communication, transportation, and information storage and retrieval. The architecture that shapes and facilitates supervisory control relies upon forms of engineering that are difficult to conceive under the same rubric as either military or informational technologies. And this list is far from complete. Given that all of these technologies were developed and advanced at different tempos, and to some extent in different eras prior to modernity, it seems an exceedingly difficult, and perhaps unrewarding task to conceptualise technology as a resource unto itself. Only in the modern epoch, where research and development regarding technologies of all kinds has been routinised in administrative systems through a set of generalisable relations between scientists, engineers, and administrators does it seem reasonable to conceive technology *tout court* as a resource of domination. But even here, the applications of technology to the coordination and control of activities across time and space is so varied that a unitary definition rendered in parsimonious and unambiguous terms necessarily would be so broad as to lack theoretical precision.

Supervisory control: power relations in administrative systems

The preceding discussion has established the significance of authoritative and allocative resources for the exercise of administrative power, i.e. for the organisation by superordinate agents of systemic activities across time and space. As I have stressed in several ways, stored information, 'surplus production', sanctions (or the threat of sanctions) backed by the means of violence, and territorial 'power containers', may assume different forms, and be diversely combined in various types of administered systems (e.g. non-modern empires, capitalist enterprises, modern nation-states). In addition the quantity and quality of these resources has a direct bearing on the effectiveness of administrative power, and hence on the overall organisation of administered systems across time and space. However, despite the considerable contribution of these resources, they pertain primarily to the forms of rule in administered systems. What has been left out of account to this point are the institutional mediations of power, the ways and means through which the intentions of superordinate agents are implemented, and the doings of subordinate agents are controlled in the power relations of administered systems.

Giddens's thoughts on power relations in administered systems pick up a number of themes initiated in Michel Foucault's studies of discipline and supervisory control (see *CCHM*, pp. 170–4; *PCST*, pp. 221–5; *CS*, pp. 153–8; *NSV*, pp. 185–6; *STMS*, pp. 157–8). However, while Giddens regards Foucault as the most original contributor to the theory of administrative power subsequent to Max Weber, it is important not to push the affinities between Giddens and Foucault too far. Giddens specifically objects to Foucault's neglect of the acting subject, and the holistic notion that power relations operate on, rather than through, agents' practical or discursive consciousness. He also dissociates his perspective, both in structuration theory as well as in his substantive work, from Foucault's exaggerated and reductionist view of power in social life. But for present purposes, Giddens's most salient objection to Foucault involves the latter's neglect of the hierarchical aspect of administrative power. While Foucault's investigation of supervision and surveillance in sequestered settings suggests that power is coterminous with small-scale locales. *Giddens conceives direct supervision as, so to speak, a 'remote control' exercised by upper-level power-holders over the activities of agents across time and space.*

Supervision by proxies for those at the pinnacle of power relations is essential to the time–space distantiation of administered systems. In systems where reproduction circuits extend across small-scale regions, supervision and sanctioning of subordinates may be carried out by superordinate agents on a face-to-face basis (*CCHM*, p. 161). Supervision, in effect, becomes one element among others in the reproduction of day-to-day life. But when the exercise of administrative power occurs through modes of system integration, rulers and officials in one physical setting lack access to absent agents, and must rely upon others to see that systemic activities are carried out, and that outcomes are achieved.

While this supervisory mode of surveillance and control serves to implement administrative power, it is by no means a mechanistic process, and it indeed represents a considerable topic of investigation in itself, as students of 'informal structures' have recognised for many years. What appears from the standpoint of administrative timetables and accounting books as a routinised series of activities and relations, actually involves a complex dialectic of control between supervisors and subordinates which may conform to the upper-level image of coordinated activities only to a limited extent (*NSV*, p. 186). Supervisors frequently establish circumstantial 'effort bargains' or *quid pro quos* in which subordinates preserve some latitude in their doings in return for their compliance with the general course of systemic activities. Where these activities are routinised they become elements of mutual knowledge shared by supervisors and subordinates alike. This works to the advantage of supervisors who now have an institutionalised baseline of compliance which they may use to monitor agents who deviate from routines, and subsequently to issue cautions and sanctions. Supervisory sanctions will vary depending upon the type of system and the resources to which supervisors have access, but in general they affect the life-chances of the agent (authoritative resource category II.C.). The most extreme sanction, obviously, is the use of physical violence culminating in capital punishment. But Giddens (*NSV*, pp. 10, 16) – who is by no means alone in this regard – observes that the power to put subordinates to death provides very limited means to control day-to-day conduct. Indeed, the fact that this sanction figured so prominently in the supervision of activities in non-modern administered systems limited the degree of control exercised in such systems to a point that falls far short of the potentials for control established by the more mundane forms of sanction drawn upon by supervisors in modern bureaucracies and capitalist organisations: e.g. termination of employment, status degradation, impediments to promotion, etc. The latter modes of sanction are, in turn, facilitated by the storage of information on the life-histories and career-histories of agents which are ubiquitous elements of all modern forms of administrative surveillance.

Beyond sanctioning *per se*, the physical configurations of systemic locales also serves as a resource of supervisory surveillance and control. Drawing upon both Foucault and Erving Goffman, Giddens (*CS*, pp. 122–9; *NSV*, pp. 12–13, 185–6; *STMS*, p. 162) observes that the zoning of locales into front regions and back regions creates areas of disclosure utilised by supervisors, as well as zones of concealment from supervision utilised by subordinates. Architecture, a topic that seldom enters the pages of theoretical texts on power, thus becomes in structuration theory a matter of no small importance to the exercise of supervision in administered systems.

Legitimation in the upper echelons of administered systems

To this point only a broad overview has been presented of the institutionalisation of power relations in administered systems. To enter into this topic in more detail it is useful to return to the problems to which Weber's account of legitimation responds: when and why do actors obey commands and how does this obedience contribute to whatever degree of stability exists in the power relations embedded in administered systems? Accepting that Weber overlooked the significance of administrative power in no way entails that his questions should, or can, be dismissed. The skilful use of stored information and supervisory control permits rulers and upper-level officials to coordinate, regulate, and monitor systemic reproduction circuits. But administrative power still must be mediated through the doings of others, and negative sanctions alone are not sufficient to ensure that this mediation will proceed in a stable manner. Having said this, however, there are several respects in which the structurationist approach to the questions of obedience in administered systems moves along lines that alter the Weberian approach to legitimation. For one thing, given the praxiological principles of structuration theory it is as important to establish *how* actors obey commands, as it is understood *why* commands are obeyed. Whereas Weberian legitimation is conceived as a passive and subjective readiness to comply, *structurationist legitimation is conceived as an active engagement in the production of compliance.* An immediate implication of the latter point of view is that the nature of legitimation may be substantially influenced by whether legitimation occurs in face-to-face interactions, or whether it occurs where agents do not establish presence-availability.

There is also another issue where structuration theory alters the terms of Weber's problem. In the structurationist account of administered systems, a much sharper distinction is drawn between the legitimation of obedience among those in the higher echelons of power, and the legitimation of compliance among subordinates who engage in activities which power-holders establish, and attempt to maintain. For the moment my remarks are confined to legitimation among rulers and officials in the higher realms of power. Here we immediately encounter one point on which Weber (1968, p. 952) and Giddens (*CPST*, p. 190) agree. Power-holders in administered systems typically have an *interest* in maintaining the existing order of domination, or at least those aspects of the order which provide for an asymmetrical distribution of resources that works to their advantage. In subsequent remarks I shall be critical of Giddens's views on unacknowledged interests. In anticipation of these criticisms it should be noted that the interests power-holders have in maintaining the existing order of domination pose no special problems. Such interests may be presumed to exist because, in general, power-holders acknowledge these interests in discourse and writing, and because they infuse their interests in activities which manifest their concern to maintain their advantaged positions.

As Weber well understood, interests in political advantage generally do not serve as a singular basis for obedience to orders within the higher circles of power. Instead they generally are combined in some way with acceptance of legitimating maxims and norms (in Giddens's terms, symbolic orders and legitimating codes). It is precisely for this reason that attention must turn to how, as well as why, obedience occurs among rulers and administrators. Here we must contend with the fact that however matters may have been in the German bureaucracies with which Weber was familiar on a first-hand basis, an assent to legitimating norms can be coupled with interests that may dispose upper-level officials to disobey specific commands, or to bend their obedience to serve their own ends. Court intrigues and inner-circle struggles for power in executive boardrooms and presidential offices, after all, are ever-present possibilities in administered systems.

How obedience occurs among power-holders very much depends upon the time–space distantiation of their interactions. Giddens (*STMS*, pp. 164–5) draws a distinction between traditional relations of legitimation and relations of legitimation in modern organisations in order to show that the presence of formal rules in the latter instance enhances the potentials for modes of system integration between absent administrators. This is a highly pertinent insight in light of his conception of administrative power, and I shall return to it below. However, I believe that his insights regarding traditional legitimation should be regarded as pertinent to modern types of organisation as well. These insights focus on obedience to legitimate orders transacted among power-holders on a face-to-face basis. Giddens stresses that such transactions were vital to the exercise of power in traditional systems in lieu of formal rules, and he also acknowledges that such relations may occur in modern organisations. In my view these face-to-face relations among agents at the apex of political hierarchies are more prevalent and consequential than Giddens allows in modern administered systems as well.

To properly appreciate the significance of face-to-face relations among power-holders it is important to understand that modes of legitimation as conceived in structuration theory do not always involve tacitly maintained procedural and normative rules (mutual knowledge) regarding reproduced modes of conduct. Administrative activity often is discursive in nature, and legitimating symbolic orders establish concepts embedded in interpretative schemes that circumscribe and facilitate political discourse among power-holders with regard to the nature of the dominion they exercise (see *NSV*, pp. 75–6, 209–10 on traditional and modern states). Now in so far as all discourse is subject to divergent interpretations (*STMS*, pp. 99–102), the *terms* of obedience are subject to negotiation, and may be contested in various ways. Face-to-face interactions among power-holders permit the terms of obedience to be established in an indexical manner during the course of conversation. Close and continuous contact among power-holders also permits agents to monitor the extent to which the terms of obedience are realised in conduct. In this way rulers and leaders may gain knowledge of the officials upon whom they can rely to carry out their intentions, and they also may dismiss, or otherwise sanction, officials whose discourse signifies a degree of disloyalty. Ultimately, in stable forms of rule a bond of trust may be discursively established between power-holders in which the negotiation and monitoring of the terms of obedience established within the prevailing codes of legitimation may be taken for granted on a day-to-day basis. This, however, is a rather more complicated process than Weber's subjective conception of obedience based upon the acceptance of legitimating norms would suggest.

The problem with establishing the terms of legitimate obedience among rulers and officials on a face-to-face basis is that it does not ensure that when administrators are far removed from the presence of rulers they will continue to act upon the rulers' intentions in instances where to disobey these intentions would serve their own interests. This was particularly true in the case of traditional states and imperial systems. Personal relations facilitated by the presence-availability of power-holders were important in such systems because, given the slow and difficult procedures of communication and transportation, few means of administrative surveillance were at hand. Given the discursive investment of legitimate power in the person rather than in the office of the rulers, and given the slow and undependable media of communication, administrative officials removed from the presence of rulers therefore retained a wide latitude of discretion in their activities. This accounts for the frequent assertions of autonomous power by officials whose activities carried them to remote physical settings, as well as various practices (e.g. the frequent rotation of officials) intended by rulers to forestall this possibility (*NSV*, p. 558; *STMS*, p. 164.

The legal–rational organisational codes characteristic of modern organisations substantially enhance the time–space extension of administrative power in this regard. They do so because, as Weber emphasised for different reasons throughout his works, these codes legitimate impersonal obligations to adhere to clearly defined procedures and tasks. Now since administrators (e.g. supervisors, branch managers, etc.) in remote locales are not monitored on a face-to-face basis, they too retain some latitude in their activities. However, legal–rational codes may lead to impersonal bonds of trust that supplant face-to-face negotiations of legitimate obedience (*STMS*, pp. 164–5). The difference here from a praxiological standpoint is that the trust is established in the performance of tasks, rather than in an establishment of loyalty through personal encounters. Impersonal trust is, of course, not a foolproof technique to ensure that orders are carried out. Disobedience in the upper echelons of power among officials who do not meet on a face-to-face basis undoubtedly is more frequent than Weber's ideal-types of legal–rational bureaucracy would suggest. Nevertheless, impersonal trust on the basis of legal–rational codes often is sufficient to permit the exercise of administrative power across spans of time–space to an extent that surpasses systems in which bonds of obedience are generated exclusively on a face-to-face basis. Nothing in Giddens's account of legal–rational legitimation denies Weber's accentuation of the comparatively greater degree of organisational effectiveness and stability facilitated by a compliance with impersonal rules. But in attending to the ways in which the bonds of impersonal trust are established in virtue of these rules Giddens introduces an accent on the spatio-temporal 'reach' of administrative power in modern organisations which does not appear in Weber's work. In doing so, Giddens creates new opportunities for theorising and analysing the manifold ways in which modern administered systems such as the state and trans-national corporations coordinate and control activities through the agency of officials situated at great distances from the centres of power. The question of the scope of rule (*NSV*, p. 10), which appears only as a leitmotif in Weber's ideal-type, thus becomes a dominant theme in Giddens's substantive theory of modernity.

Exploitation, ideology and interests: an unresolved problem

To turn from the obedience of officials in the higher circles of power to the compliance of subordinates is to enter a realm of power relations that typically is constituted at some distance from the central locales of administrative power. This spatio-temporal distancing coincides with a distancing in the procedures and orientations associated with the activities carried out (*CCHM*, pp. 66–7). On the one hand, rulers and upper-level officials may try to conceal actual procedures of power behind a veil of nominally legitimate or ritualised political routines (*CPST*, pp. 190–1; *STMS*, p. 163). On the other hand, subordinate agents who are both politically and spatio-temporally distanced from these actions may see through the veil, thereby acquiring a cynical or pragmatic regard for legitimate orders and commands. This cynicism and pragmatism, and the potential for disobedience they entail, accounts for the presence of supervisory surveillance, and the latter, in turn, re-enforces the detached outlooks subordinates maintain toward power-holders and their doings.

By accentuating subordinates' cynical and pragmatic regard for legitimate commands, Giddens does not mean to suggest that the potential for disobedience among subordinates is realised on a day-to-day basis in administered systems. The reproduction of administered systems depends upon the fact that subordinates comply with the orders and routines set forth by superordinates. As previously mentioned, supervisory surveillance alone cannot ensure that this compliance occurs. However, far more than is true among those in the higher echelons of power, it cannot be presumed that subordinates comply on the basis of their interests in maintaining the system as it stands. The advantages of upper-level positions, after all, do not necessarily redound to the benefit of subordinate agents. This circumstance places the questions of how and why subordinates comply with commands in a distinctly non-Weberian light. For if subordinates' interests do not neces-

sarily correspond to those of superordinates then it w
that some degree of exploitation may occur as su.
comply with superordinate directives. And if exploitation uc
occur then the legitimation of these directives must be conceived
from an ideological point of view.

Giddens is one of the few scholars unaffiliated with the Marxist
tradition to express concern for the concepts of exploitation and
ideology. Before turning to the issues involved in the compliance
of subordinates it is worthwhile to introduce his definition of these
concepts. In doing so, however, we encounter an unresolved
problem in his work, a problem which involves the status of
unacknowledged interests. Ever since Marx established his classical definition of the term, exploitation has been considered primarily with reference to the usurpation of surplus production from
producing classes by those who control the forces of production.
But while Giddens's concept of exploitation subsumes the Marxist
slant (*CCHM*, pp. 110–12), for Giddens (*CCHM*, pp. 58–61,
239–47) this concept also refers to power relations beyond the
circumstances of material production. Giddens defines exploitation and relates it to ideology in the following terms:

> Exploitation . . . is more aptly conceptualized in relation to
> domination or *power*. In defining exploitation itself, we need
> not depart far from conventional England usage. According to
> the Oxford English Dictionary, 'to exploit' is to 'turn to account
> or utilize for one's own ends.' This is essentially the usage I shall
> suggest here. Exploitation may be regarded as domination
> *which is harnessed to sectional interests* (domination over nature
> or domination over human beings).
>
> This viewpoint links to the framework for the analysis of
> ideology . . . The analysis and critique of ideology are concerned
> with showing how structures of signification are mobilized to
> legitimate the sectional interests of dominant groups, i.e. to
> legitimate *exploitative domination*. All forms of domination can
> be adjuged in terms of how far they are harnessed to sectional
> interests of particular social categories, collectivities – or classes
> – and how far they serve the universal (generalisable) interests
> of communities or societies of which they are a part. *The concept
> of interest raises numerous difficulties, which I shall not attempt
> to confront in this context* [my emphasis]. But it can be taken as

axiomatic that sectional and universal interests are never wholly exclusive. (*CCHM*, pp. 60–61)

It is crucially important to note that exploitation is a *contingent* feature of power relations. The nature of this contingency hinges upon and accentuates the centrality of *interests* to Giddens's concept of exploitation, and by extension his concept of ideology as well. Simply put, exploitation exists only to the extent that the interests of dominant groups of superordinate agents diverge from generalisable interests which superordinates share in common with subordinate agents. By hinging the concept of exploitation on agents' interests, Giddens adopts a sophisticated perspective in which exploitation co-mingles with non-exploitative aspects of power relations. Unlike some varieties of Marxist theory, he therefore does not hold that exploitation necessarily presupposes a thoroughgoing opposition of interests. But conversely, unlike some varieties of pluralist theory, he does not hold that a degree of common interests precludes the existence of exploitative relations. Considered in terms of the structurationist ontology, non-exploitative power relations based upon shared interests, and exploitative relations based upon divergent interests, potentially may be combined in varying degrees in any given system. The exact degree to which they are combined therefore can be determined only on the basis of empirical research, and substantive theories of historical systems.

In many respects this interest-based conception of exploitation appears quite appealing. But its utility for purposes of the development of sociological research projects, and theories of exploitation in specific kinds of systems, depends upon how interests are identified in social life. The identification of interests, of course, poses no problems – at least in principle – in so far as agents discursively acknowledge, or are discursively aware of, what their own interests are. This discursive acknowledgement, as I have previously indicated, is quite widespread among superordinate agents. But exploitation cannot be defined in terms of the interests of superordinates alone. For exploitation to occur the interests of superordinates and subordinates must diverge. However, the identification of subordinates' interests can be a more difficult matter. As Giddens makes clear, the possibilities for discursively formulating interests frequently are limited in the lower echelons of social groupings. Such limitations may arise from numerous circumstances, including, but not restricted to, inferior education opportunities, familiarity with a limited range of *milieu* of action, and/or the inaccessibility of relevant information (*CS*, p. 342). Given these limitations it would severely curtail the utility of the concept of exploitation to insist that it occurs only when discursively acknowledged interests that diverge from interests held by superordinates can be empirically identified with reference to subordinate agents.

It is at this point that the problem of unacknowledged interests becomes apparent in Giddens's account of power relations. Giddens is quite willing to accept that agents are not always aware of what their interests are. Therefore, the identification of interests on the part of the theorist must involve an imputation of interests to social agents. The concept of interest, in brief, must be understood to occupy a metatheoretical status (on this point, see *SSPT*, p. 348). The problem here is that theorists who impute *unacknowledged* interests to agents necessarily are dealing (on a metatheoretical basis) with interests that play no active part in the constitution of social life. In the history of social theory, imputations of this kind have always been exceedingly difficult. Prime examples are evident in the endless problems Marxists have encountered in attempting to impute to the proletariat an unacknowledged interest in a classless social order. Giddens is well aware of the pitfalls of these Marxist imputations, and he denies their validity (*CCHM*, pp. 240–41). But he has laid down few ground-rules for how acceptable imputations of unacknowledged interests can be made.

One procedure he mentions in passing ('Interview', p. 72) is to treat questions such as those regarding unacknowledged interests from a counterfactual point of view: i.e. to ask what sort of response people would make if they knew what a social scientist claims to know about their behaviour (and the circumstances and relations of which they may be unaware which social scientists claim are implicated in the conditions associated with the behaviour). This strategy, although undoubtedly useful from the standpoint of critical theory, has serious disadvantages with reference to Giddens's interest-based conception of exploitation. Exploitation, after all, is not a counterfactual matter, but rather an aspect of power relations that is an ongoing reality in the course of system reproduction. It follows that if unacknowledged interests are to be admitted as a basis for a conception of exploitation, then these interests must be in some way treated as aspects of reality.

Another way to introduce a basis for unacknowledged interests might be to ground structuration theory in a philosophical anthropology. Giddens, in fact, briefly alludes to this strategy as a basis for the analysis of ideology, which, it is important to bear in mind, is regarded by Giddens as based upon interests to the same extent as the concept of exploitation (*CPST*, pp. 189–90). However, while every social theory implicitly presumes a philosophical anthropology of some kind, if Giddens's intent were to develop structuration theory along philosophical anthropological lines, its present character as an ontology of potentials would be substantially altered. As Jeff Livesay implies in a recent commentary (1985, p. 75), a philosophical anthropology which incorporates a transcendental (or, at least, a trans-historical) account of interests grounded in characteristics of the human condition, would provide structuration theory with normative foundations while limiting its openness to historical contingency. That is, instead of supplying concepts which might inform the analysis of whatever interests exist in any given socio-historical domain, structuration theory would become engaged in sorting out which interests are correct or incorrect from a philosophical anthropological point of view, and proposing explanations to account for why agents fail to acknowledge the interests which structuration theory accentuates and upholds. Here again, this strategy might be advantageous (albeit highly speculative) for the development of critical theory. However, Giddens, to date, has shown little inclination to formulate structuration theory along these lines, and only the briefest programmatic hints of his views on philosophical anthropology appear in his works (e.g. *CCHM*, pp. 155–6, 251).

The only thing that can be safely said about Giddens's approach to unacknowledged interests is that it remains an unresolved problem in his development of structuration theory. Since his concepts of exploitation and ideology are based upon interests, many of which may be unacknowledged by subordinate agents, it follows that these concepts must be regarded as problematic as well. Is it possible then to dispense with exploitation and ideology as central concepts in the structurationist account of power relations in general, and, more specifically, power relations in administered systems? To be sure, Giddens never claims that exploitation must be regarded as ubiquitous to all administered systems in the same sense as power and domination. It also bears repeating that exploitative relations incorporate an admixture of interests shared in common between power-holders and those in the lower echelons of power relations. These contingencies apply to the concept of ideology as well, in so far as Giddens indicates that ideology is not co-extensive with culture *per se* (see *CPST*, p. 187). But for all of this, I do not believe that exploitation and ideology can be set aside, or treated as subsidiary concepts. Giddens's accounts of how and why subordinates comply with orders and commands are suffused with references to ideology (see especially *CCHM*, pp. 64–8). And if he does not consider exploitation to be as ubiquitous as power and domination, his post-Marxist expansion of the concept makes exploitation appear as a prominent characteristic of power relations in the past as much as in the present, and Giddens does not foresee that exploitation will end in the future (see *CCHM*, pp. 241–2). Giddens adopts an equally open-ended view toward the prevalence of ideology in social life as well (*CPST*, p. 197; *CCHM*, p. 277). He thus puts himself in the awkward position of emphasising the potential for exploitation and ideology to exist in social life, while his definitions of these concepts do not admit empirical specification, at least in so far as they are based upon interests unacknowledged by subordinate agents which diverge from interests maintained by superordinate rulers and administrators.

The compliance of subordinates in administered systems

Despite the foregoing problem, there is simply no way of avoiding the concept of ideology in addressing Giddens's views on subordinates' compliance. Indeed, while the possibility remains open in structuration theory for agents to comply based upon interests shared in common with those who coordinate and control administered systems, most of Giddens's accounts of subordinate compliance appear in conjunction with his exposition of the role of ideology in the constitution of social life. Since this is the case, and since the concept of ideology involves the problematic imputation of unacknowledged interests to subordinates, the only practical way to set forth Giddens's views on subordinates' compliance is to bracket the issue of interests at this point. This expository strategy narrows the significance of ideology *per se*. But what remains in view is none the less a significant issue from a praxiological standpoint: how subordinates are mobilised to engage in activities that contribute to the reproduction and outcomes of systems coordinated and controlled through the exercise of administrative power. How, that is, this mobilisation occurs above and beyond the threat of sanctions associated with supervisory surveillance.

Given this issue, a distinction can be made between two modes of ideology: ideology implicated in institutionalised routines, and ideology as discourse (*CPST*, p. 183; *CCHM*, pp. 66–8). While Giddens does not slight the second mode, he does consider the first to be a more potent basis for the mobilisation of subordinates' conduct. Compliance with institutionalised routines involves a tacit 'acceptance as real' on the level of practical consciousness of pre-established procedures and relations (*CS*, pp. 331–2). Agents, in effect, tacitly construe the routines in which they engage on a day-to-day basis as 'fixed': i.e. as circumstances they are unable to change (see the following chapter on structural constraints). In the absence of feasible options that do not involve participation in these routines, compliance becomes accepted as the line of least resistance. Resistance here has a twofold meaning: suggesting on the one hand that subordinates' behaviour is channelled by the available routines in which they may participate without exerting an unusual type of effort, and suggesting on the other hand that a failure to comply would be considered by others an act of resistance or defiance which might be subject to sanctions.

Subordinates' acceptance of the 'facticity' of systemic procedures is illustrated in strikingly similar terms in Marx's (1967, p. 737) reference to the 'dull compulsion' involved in the subjection of workers to the capitalist organisation of production, and Weber's (1968, pp. 946–7) description of the 'dull custom' which may motivate the ruled to obey commands. The 'acceptance as real' that accounts for this 'dull' compliance is ideological because it obscures other praxiological options that, although not institutionalised, nevertheless might be feasible if they could be perceived. Thus the 'facticity' of routines may be more apparent than real, but it is no less effective in disposing or accustoming subordinates to comply.

Although the tacit acceptance of institutionalised activities may be unaccompanied by discourse as a form of ideology, discursive forms are not thereby ruled out (*CS*, p. 332). Much of social life may be enacted via tacitly performed procedures, but nevertheless actors also always maintain a reflexive theoretical understanding of the grounds of their activity (*CS*, p. 5). This understanding itself may be tacit, but it typically depends upon the discursive terms and symbolic codes that are available to agents as means to comprehend the circumstances associated with the systems they encounter, and to which they contribute through the course of their activities in day-to-day life. As Weber (1968, p. 953) suggests, such codes often arise from the justifications power-holders proffer to establish a cultural basis for their dominance over others. For Giddens (*CS*, pp. 25–6, 180), the significance of these codes, considered from the standpoint of subordinate agents, is that they reify in discursive terms the apparent 'facticity' of prevailing systems, and the power relations embedded within them.

Reification here retains the Lukacsian sense of the appearance of social phenomena endowed with the properties of objects or things. But because reification in structuration theory is attributed to forms of discourse and symbolic codes, the emphasis shifts from Lukács's neo-Kantian stress upon subjective apprehension of something 'objectively given', to modes of thought and conversation in which terms are used that treat the properties of social phenomena as equivalent to phenomena of nature, without referring to their social origins, or to the ways in which they are socially reproduced (*CPST*, pp. 195–6; *CS*, p. 180). Hence systemic power relations not only are considered to be unalterable in practice when reified symbolic codes are employed, they also are regarded as immutable in principle in the same way as the weather, or the law of gravity.

Giddens does not address the issue of whether reified discourse not only re-enforces the 'facticity' of social circumstances and events, but also engenders an attachment to social systems. However, inferences can be drawn in this regard from various segments of his work, especially those concerned with his substantive analysis of anomie and nationalism in modern societies (see *CCHM*, pp. 191–6; *NSV*, pp. 209–21, 323–4). At first glance these concepts may appear to be mutually inconsistent: either anomie *or* the presence of bonds to nation-states established with reference to the symbolic codes of legitimation proffered by those in the upper levels of power. But Giddens suggests that nationalistic sentiments may be a concomitant of anomie, rather than its opposite. The point, in brief, is that nationalistic sentiments tend to focus on circumstances removed from day-to-day activities. Lacking moral meaning in their quotidian routines, agents find the communality supplied by national symbols appealing (*NSV*, p. 218). Hence they bond with a reified discursive image of the nation-state while they retain a cynical regard for the exercise of power during their participation in (or forbearance from) systemic activities (e.g., taxpaying, voting, etc.).

It would be entirely misleading to close these remarks before noting that in structuration theory symbolic codes of legitimation need not necessarily dispose subordinates to comprehend their circumstances in reified ways. Once again, it must be underscored that symbolic codes are ambiguous and embody multi-variant traits. Considered with reference to the dialectic of control, legitimating symbols may be interpreted in a manner that dissolves the reification of systemic circumstances, and exposes the short-comings of power-holders via internal critiques, employing those symbols to point the way to possibilities for the realisation of new ways of life.

Concluding remarks

Administered systems, as I mentioned at the head of this chapter, are regarded in structuration theory as the most powerful mode of system organisation. But it bears repeating, as well, that the political themes presented in this chapter neither entail nor imply that Giddens develops structuration theory by reducing social life to power relations. A distinction must be made in this regard between Giddens's writings on structuration theory and his histor-ically oriented substantive writings, for it is true that in the latter he does concentrate upon political themes to a significant extent. That this is not the case for structuration *per se* should be evident in the following chapters, where attention shifts from Giddens's approach to systems to his views on the role of structure in the constitution of social life.

6
Structure, Position-Practices, and Enablement/Constraint

In this chapter and the next I shall be dealing with topics regarding the nature and implications of structural concepts in structuration theory. The present chapter considers issues involved in institutionalised activities and relations as conceived from a structural point of view, while the following chapter considers the analysis of structure and conditions that foster structural change with special attention to the structural properties of societal systems. Giddens's account of structure has drawn considerably more critical attention than any other aspect of structuration theory. So much is this the case that I have organised much of the discussion in the present chapter so as to take fundamental criticisms into account, and in several instances I shall propose conceptual means to deal with problems to which these criticisms refer. In developing these lines of thought I shall set aside references to the bearings of the French structural tradition upon structural concepts in structuration theory. This omission, however, requires a brief explanation.

If Giddens is taken at his word, his approach to structure stands in a line of descent from the French structuralist tradition. Even in his more recent writings (e.g. *CS*, pp. 16–17) he makes it appear that such is the case. But his assertions belie the limited extent to which he actually invokes structuralist insights. While his initial thoughts on structure clearly were stimulated by critical confrontations with structuralist theory and research (see especially *CPST*, ch. 1, and pp. 59–65, 155–160), in more recent works it has become increasingly clear that he owes a smaller debt to structuralist ideas than, for example, he does to time-geography, or to analyses of the production of social action. Thus, other than a commentary of Foucault – which, in itself, does not concentrate upon structural themes – few remarks on French structuralist scholarship appear in *The Constitution of Society*, while commentaries on the views of Goffman, time-geographers, American structural sociologists, Parsons, and others, are developed at some length. Giddens's most recent essay on structuralism and post-structuralism, although complimentary in certain respects, re-enforces the sense that he is distancing himself from the tradition. This essay (*STMS*, ch. 4) does not so much present a 'positive critique' or a 'non-structuralist manifesto' as a commemoration of an honourable intellectual movement which made a difference to the modern theoretical agenda, but which ultimately succumbed to serious internal defects. Hence, while Giddens (*STMS*, pp. 97–8, 108) praises the structuralist and post-structuralist movements for the issues they raised, he begins by pronouncing their perspectives to be dead and gone (*STMS*, p. 73).

It would be going too far to suggest that French structuralism left no imprint on how Giddens's views structure in structuration theory. The French notion of structure as a series of underlying codes that must be inferred from their surface manifestations did, after all, provide a basis for Giddens's initial distinction between social systems as patterns of activities and relations reproduced across time and space, and the structural properties drawn upon and regenerated during the course of system reproduction. But once this point of departure is acknowledged it is difficult to identify insights Giddens accepts or rejects from the works of specific scholars associated with the structuralist and post-structuralist traditions: e.g. Saussure, Lévi-Strauss, Althusser, Barthes, Derrida, *et al*. Indeed, given the heterogeneity of views on conceptual and methodological issues which these scholars expound it is no simple matter to determine exactly what they share in common. While Giddens attempts to extract common themes from structuralist and post-structuralist works at two points in his writings (*CPST*, ch. 1; *STMS*, ch. 4), his way of dealing with these themes has drawn heavy fire from at least one structuralist critic (see Gane, 1983, pp. 378–85). Moreover, his periodic invocation of analogies between structuralist views on language and his own views on the structural properties of systems (e.g. *NRSM*, pp. 118–19; *SSPT*, p. 126), are by his own admission loose and prolegomenal, and they obscure the fact that linguistic codes comprise only one aspect of structure from his analytical point of view (see Chapter 7).

In my opinion, then, there are good reasons to proceed directly to Giddens's account of structural themes in structuration theory, rather than engaging in what would necessarily be lengthy consideration of Giddens's departures as well as the affinities which remain between his views and those of scholars associated with structuralist and post-structuralist schools of thought. An additional advantage in following this route is that it makes it unnecessary to deal with some of the more recondite structuralist figures of speech Giddens employs (especially in *Central Problems*). While those conversant with structuralism may recognise notions such as 'syntagmatic' 'paradigmatic', 'différance', etc., my informal attempts to explain these concepts to others who are unfamiliar with structuralist nomenclature lead me to believe that they may obscure more than they clarify, thereby impeding a direct understanding of the insights and arguments internal to structuration theory that Giddens means to propose.

Structure and the continuity of social systems

The first thing that must be understood with regard to all concepts pertaining to structure in structuration theory is that structure *qua structure* does not *produce* patterns, nor does it *actively* coordinate and control social systems. All of these activities involve the exercise of agency, and in structuration theory the exercise of agency is confined to the practices undertaken by social agents. Nor does structure *qua* structure articulate systems across time and space. This articulation, as I have previously stressed, occurs in the various modes of social integration and system integration through which the consequences of social *praxis* are transmitted in circumstances of co-presence and communicated or transported between points in distant regions and locales. Given these points, it cannot be stressed too strongly that collectivities are defined in structuration theory not as structures *per se*, but rather as systems that are structured (by virtue of the duality of structure). This principle is so important that it is worthwhile to quote Giddens at length:

> A structure is not a 'group', 'collectivity', or 'organization': these *have* structures. Groups, collectivities, etc., can and should be studied as systems of interaction. (*NRSM*, p. 121)

> Social systems, which are systems of social interaction, are not structures, although they necessarily *have* structures. There is no structure, in human social life, apart from the continuity of processes of structuration. (*SSPT*, p. 118)

> [A] 'structural approach' to the social sciences cannot be severed from an examination of the mechanisms of social reproduction. It is perfectly correct, of course, that society is not a creation of individual actors and that the structural properties of social systems endure beyond the lifetime of individuals. But structure, or structured properties, or structural parameters, exist only in social reproduction across time and space. (*CS*, p. 212)

Now if systems are reproduced through processes of structuration, and if, therefore, they are patterned and organised in and through the doings of agents, then the nature and contribution of structure to system may not be clear. It is evident, of course, that structure must play a significant role in structuration theory, for, as I indicated in Chapter 1, the duality of structure is a crucial move in Giddens's efforts to overcome the untenable ontological implications of the division between theories of action and theories of collectivities. The role of structure in the constitution of collectivities can be established by posing the following question: if systems are patterned and regulated through series and cycles of practices and relations articulated across time and space, what quality of systems remains to be addressed?

The answer is that to concentrate upon the situated production of social systems does not immediately make clear the conditions that permit systemic patterns and modes of organisation to be reproduced. Such conditions are absolutely vital, for in their absence systems would not and could not be maintained. Instead, social life would consist of an inconstant flux of events: an unpatterned and disorganised chaos in which social life in any recognisable form could not occur. Structural properties in social systems may not reproduce systems, but they shape, channel, and facilitate system reproduction whenever it occurs by providing agents with the practical awareness of the practices, relations, and spatio-temporal settings they require in order to participate in the reproductive process. In institutionalised systems, practices, relations, and articulations which are central to system reproduction may be regarded as structured processes; processes, that is, which are reproducible by an indefinite number of knowledgeable agents. Since this is the case, systems consisting of structured processes may be reproduced by succeeding cohorts or generations of agents. The system thus endures even though agents who contribute to its persistence come and go.

The preceding remarks presume that the concept of the duality of structure is well understood. To re-enforce previous accounts of this notion I would like to here dispel a misguided interpretation of it which appears in the context of a recent critical polemic by Joseph Smith and Bryan Turner:

> The notion of the duality of structure seems to us to involve a vitiating circularity. According to Giddens, social structures are constituted by human agency as well as simultaneously being the medium of such constitution. We will show that action is taken as a (prior) necessary condition for structure, and structure as a (prior) necessary condition for action, so that we are forced to turn in an impossible circle. (Smith and Turner, 1986, p. 127)

Smith and Turner correctly perceive that structure and action stand in a relation of reciprocal necessity in the duality of structure. But they are entirely mistaken in their conclusion that any kind of 'vicious circle' is thereby created. Any given practice is structured by the skills required to reproduce the practice, including the skills involved in the manipulation of relevant resources. Now any agent – or any given grouping, or cohort, or generation of agents – who engages in the reproduction of this practice obviously does not reinvent these skills on the spot every time they engage in the practice in question. If this were the case for all social practices the result would be the kind of chaos to which I earlier referred. (Which is why, Giddens (*CPST*, pp. 216–17) contends that continuities in *praxis* persist even in periods of radical change.) Having arrived on the scene with institutionalised skills intact, agents proceed to reproduce the practice. As they do, they re-enforce their awareness of the skills themselves, and also the identity of these practices as they are recognised by themselves and others as enduring activities in social life. This is what the duality of structure means, and it should be evident that *it is an historical process rather than any kind of 'vicious circle'*. Indeed the same practice may be conveyed from the past (ordinarily by means of agents' memory regarding 'how things are done') into the present, and through reproduction transmitted into the future for periods that may extend across decades, or even centuries.

To shift from individual practices to systems comprised of practices articulated across time and space raises certain methodological issues which I shall presently discuss. However, from an ontological standpoint all that is involved are ongoing processes of structuration: i.e. the structuring of social relations across time and space, in virtue of the duality of structure (*CS*, p. 376). The historically dynamic quality of the structuration of systems which occurs through the duality of structure is characterised quite well in the following terms:

> [S]ocial systems would plainly not exist without human agency. But it is not the case that actors create social systems: they reproduce or transform them, remaking what is already made in the continuity of *praxis*. (*CS*, p. 171)

Conceiving the structural properties of systems: the double hermeneutic and institutional analysis

It is, of course, more difficult to conceive the structuration of social systems than the reproduction of a single institutionalised practice. In so far as systemic practices and relations are actively articulated, coordinated and controlled during the course of system reproduction, there obviously will be various interconnections between structural properties (a topic which is discussed at length in the following chapter). But the study of the structural properties of systems at large encounters problems which stem from the fact that these properties are not emergent 'social facts' *sui genesis*, which is to say that they do not exist or persist as phenomena or objects unto themselves. In the first place, structural properties of systems never exist all at once, but instead continually disappear and reappear through the ongoing course of system reproduction. In the second place, structural properties, as previously mentioned, do not retain any powers of agency. As Giddens suggests:

> [I]f the relations between structural properties, once isolated, are treated as having their own 'inner dynamics' . . . rather than as continually reproduced conditions, the activities of individuals . . . seem redundant. The overall conditions of system reproduction are in no way 'guaranteed' by the structural relations upon which (counter-factually) they depend. (*CS*, p. 192)

But having granted these points, it remains to be said that if the interconnected structural properties reproduced during the course of system reproduction are not ontologically emergent, they nevertheless are 'real' aspects of social life. That is, so long as the structuration of a system across time and space proceeds in a routine manner, the system is a structured system, and its structural properties may be conceived in collective terms.

To conceive structural properties in this way a number of methodological measures are required. The first measure involves moving from analyses tied to agents' awareness of the practices and circumstances implicated in their participation in the constitution of social life, to second-order analyses which both preserve and surpass forms of mutual knowledge of which agents are aware. This move comprises *part* of what Giddens terms the *double hermeneutic* in social scientific theory and research (*CS*, pp. 284–5, 328–30; *NRSM*, pp. 79–81; *CPST*, pp. 245–53; see also Cohen, 1984). The move from first-order to second-order levels of analysis is only part of the double hermeneutic, because Giddens is also concerned with the ways in which second-order descriptions and explanations of social circumstances, relations, institutions, and events relevant to specific domains ultimately infiltrate these domains and, by altering agents' knowledge, foster changes in how the constitution of social life occurs. The influence of social scientific knowledge on the procedures and outcomes of social conduct, and the structuration and organisation of social systems, should not be underestimated. As Giddens observes (*CS*, pp. 348–54), 'discoveries' in the social sciences, if they are at all of interest or illuminating to social agents, will not remain 'discoveries' for very long. Indeed, while the influence of social scientific knowledge on the constitution of social life substantially differs from the technologically mediated influence of knowledge produced in the natural sciences, the practical connotations and implications of social scientific theory and research, Giddens argues, are at least equal in extent to the practical relevance of scientific insights into the operation of the natural world. In one sense the influence of social scientific knowledge exceeds that produced in the natural sciences, because social scientific knowledge uniquely has the potential to contribute to the constitution of the subject-matter it studies. On the one hand, social scientific knowledge may directly influence the policies and plans of those in the upper echelons of administered systems. This is why, for example, schools of management today typically offer courses in the social scientific study of complex organisations, etc. On the other hand, social scientific knowledge may be used in the formation and mobilisation of movements for social change, as well as in the development of cultures of resistance. The latter application points to the pivotal role Giddens ascribes to the double hermeneutic in establishing the inherently critical potential for social theory and research (for more extensive discussions, see *CS*, pp. 334–48; Cohen, 1984, pp. 94–5 *passim*).

For present purposes, however, it is the movement from first-order to second-order analysis which is of greater concern, since this move facilitates the analysis of structure. One presumption here is that social scientists may wish to identify and study aspects of the constitution of social life which cannot be grasped through concepts and tacit forms of mutual knowledge to which agents have access in their day-to-day lives. To this end, second-order analyses of structure routinely involve theoretical meta-languages and professional procedures for the collection and interpretation of empirical data. But the double hermeneutic also presumes that second-order analyses are never radically divorced from the first-order discursive knowledge and tacit knowledgeability which social agents maintain. Thus, while structural concepts may refer to circumstances which lie beyond the cognitive horizons established in agents' knowledge of their own social circumstances, these concepts nevertheless always are informed by ethnographic insights into first-order modes of knowledge and knowledgeability. Indeed, because structure exists only in so far as it is reproduced in social *praxis*, structural concepts, in effect, represent reconstructions and consolidations of first-order knowledge, albeit reconstructions and consolidations undertaken from distinctively social scientific points of view.

Second-order analyses of structure clearly would be impossible if the application of concrete forms of mutual knowledge in the day-to-day constitution of social life was to be the focal point of concern. While the analysis of structure involves those properties of practices and relations which are chronically reproduced, the day-to-day reproduction of these properties *in situ* may involve many aspects of social life which do not endure in the *longue durée* (e.g., short-term outcomes of situated conduct and outcomes of a given cycle of system reproduction, episodic deviations from established routines, etc.). Here we arrive at a second methodological measure which facilitates the analysis of structure: the invocation of brackets involved in *institutional analysis*. As opposed to the study of *praxis* in day-to-day life, which Giddens refers to as the analysis of strategic conduct, in institutional analysis it is assumed that all practices and relations of interest are chronically reproduced (*CS*, pp. 30, 288). It must be emphasised that the brackets on strategic conduct which are thereby imposed are purely methodological: it is crucial to bear in mind that from an ontological standpoint the structural properties of practices, relations, and collectivities always are reproduced through the duality of structure (*CPST*, p. 80; *CS*, p. 190). But by treating the institutionalised course of reproduction in a state of suspended animation, as it were, social scientists are able to conceive and investigate enduring structural properties in a logically precise and parsimonious way.

In Chapter 3, I introduced systems analysis as a mode of bracketing designed to facilitate the study of the patterning and articulation of systems across time and space. However, it would unduly complicate matters to simultaneously analyse the spatio-temporal patterning and the structural properties of social systems. This establishes the need for a third methodological measure in the analysis of structure, a measure which treats structural properties as if they have no locations or relations in social contexts reproduced across time–space. Although Giddens does not underscore the methodological significance of this measure, it is a clear implication of his remarks in this regard (*NRSM*, p. 119; *CPST*, p. 65). Its effect is to conceive structural properties on a second-order basis as if they were reproduced in a 'virtual' (i.e., in effect, but not in reality) space demarcated only by categories and relations relevant to institutional analysis. Here, again, methodological limits must be stressed. The analysis of structural properties in no way negates the need to take account of the reproduction of systemic patterns across time and space, just as it in no way negates the grounding of the institutional analysis of structure in forms of knowledge and knowledgeability which agents employ.

Various critics have been troubled by the methodological qualifications required in order to conceive the structural properties of systems. Margaret Archer (1982, p. 467), for example, suggests that once brackets have been imposed upon strategic conduct in order to study structural properties (or vice versa), the temporal relations between the two cannot logically be examined. Archer argues that this is because structure and action must be temporally co-terminous by virtue of their reciprocal relations in the duality of structure. But she misunderstands Giddens's intention here. The analysis of institutionalised properties of systems is meant to address properties that are chronically reproduced so that they persist in the *longue durée*. Strategic conduct, or articulated processes of structuration which involve strategic conduct, re-generate (or alter) the institutionalised properties of systems on a different time-scale, the *durée* of day-to-day life. This difference in time-scales in no way compromises the logical possibility of examining the recursive relations between structure and action. Just because the structure of a practice, say the filing of an income-tax return, is initially conceived as an enduring procedure does not mean that in a given study the analyst cannot shift time-scales to study how an historically situated tax-payer, or aggregate of tax-payers, draw upon their knowledgeability (or the knowledgeability of others) to file their tax returns for a specific year. Indeed many theoretically informed ethnographic studies (e.g. Willis, 1977; Burawoy, 1979) and in-depth analyses of social *praxis* (e.g. Hochschild, 1983) proceed, at least implicitly, in precisely this way. That is, they presume from the start that a set of highly structured practices exists, and proceed to investigate how these practices are actually performed by social agents in specific settings as they carry on with their day-to-day lives. In doing so they offer evidence of a central insight implicated in the duality of structure: each instance of the reproduction of an institutionalised activity comprises an intersection between structural properties of conduct inherited from the past and the situated exercise of agency by social actors.

Social positions or position-practices? the 'missing institutional link'

Once methodological issues are properly understood, a basic conceptual issue with regard to the association between structure and action comes into view. Despite Giddens's call for an 'institutional theory of day-to-day life' (*CPST*, p. 81; 'AI', pp. 164–5), at least one well-informed commentator, Nigel Thrift, argues that Giddens has left a 'missing institutional link' in structuration theory. Writing with specific reference to *The Constitution of Society*, Thrift (1985, p. 618) contends that Giddens by and large is silent on the institutions that establish the linkage between structure and agency implied by the notion of the duality of structure. While I believe that Thrift overlooks Giddens's attempt to forge a link of this kind, I also believe that Thrift has spotted a link which, if it is not entirely missing, is not very well developed in Giddens's textual accounts.

The closest Giddens comes to providing an 'institutional link' between structure and agency is in his conception of social position. Social positions are conceived within the brackets of institutional analysis, and are specifically designed to surmount problems in the way social roles are typically defined (*CPST*, pp. 115–17; *CS*, pp. 83–4). According to Giddens, the problem with role-concepts is that they generally assume role prescriptions as 'given', thereby giving short shrift to role performance which occurs in social *praxis*. Curiously, however, Giddens's alternative conception of social positions fails to accentuate the enactment of conduct in structured practices to a greater extent:

I shall define a social position . . . as a social identity that carries

with it a certain range (however diffusely specified) of prerogatives and obligations that an actor who is accorded that identity
(or is an 'incumbent' of that position) may activate or carry out:
these prerogatives and obligations constitute the role-
prescription associated with that position. A social identity is
essentially a category, or a typification made on the basis of
some definite social criterion or criteria: occupation, kin relation, age-grade, etc. (*CPST*, pp. 117–18; cf. *CS*, p. 84)

Given this definition, social roles then become a specific sub-
category of social positions which involve face-to-face encounters,
well-defined identities, and normative definitions of 'expected'
behaviour which are more pronounced than is generally the case
(*CS*, p. 86). Social positions at large may be conceived from a
structural point of view as an institutionalised framework of social
relations which refers to the 'positioning' of individuals within an
analytically formulated 'social space' comprised of symbolic categories and ties (*CS*, p. 89).

Now because of the reference to prerogatives and obligations
Giddens's conception of social positions does not altogether fail to
acknowledge the reproduction of positions in institutionalised
practices. Nevertheless, positions are defined less by the kind of
structured conduct they involve than by the kinds of identity which
position-'incumbents' hold by virtue of their position. Yet, positions should serve as the institutional link agents encounter as
structured practices, and whereby through the reproduction of
these practices in the duality of structure they contribute to the
perpetuation of structure. This is the link I believe that Thrift
would like to find, and the concept of position as it is presently
formulated does not fill the bill.

In saying this I do not mean to suggest that identities associated
with the performance of structured practices should, or can, be left
out of account. It is, after all, an undeniable aspect of many
practices in all social systems that certain modes of conduct can
only be performed in an effective manner by agents who exhibit
criteria which, when acknowledged by others, establish their more
or less clearly defined obligations and rights. But there is no
reason, as far as I can see, why the *exhibiting* of these criteria, and
the *enactment* of rights and obligations, should not be included in
the primary definition of positions. In this regard, Giddens would

have been wise to consider the utility of the concept of position-practices introduced by Roy Bhaskar. As it is, he alludes to Bhaskar's concept only briefly (*CS*, pp. 83, 282–3), without pausing to establish its relevance for his work.

Although Bhaskar's work corresponds to structuration theory on many issues and while his conception of position-practices manages to keep the intersection between structure and action clearly in view, this concept must be modified in certain respects, and elaborated in others, if it is to be rendered useful for, and consistent with, the structurationist ontology. Modifications are required because, as I mentioned in an earlier chapter, while Bhaskar (1979, p. 48) recognises that social structures do not exist independent of social activities, he also (1979, p. 26) begins with a general ontology of structures, and postulates structures as enduring 'generative' components of societal totalities which 'govern' their substantive activities of production (Bhaskar, 1979, p. 48). Position-practices therefore appear in Bhaskar's work (1979, p. 51) as 'slots', into which active subjects must slip in order to reproduce structure. These 'slots' are positions in so far as they refer to rights, duties, tasks, etc., and practices in so far as they refer to activities in which occupants of these positions engage. Bhaskar also stresses that position-practices must be conceived on a relational basis, a point to which I shall return.

Now Bhaskar fundamentally departs from Giddens by originating his work in collectivist terms: i.e. by ascribing primacy to structure rather than structuration (a point Bhaskar implicitly acknowledges in 1983, p. 85). As a result, although he takes practices associated with positions into account, he spends very little effort considering the nature of these practices and how they are carried out. That is, to borrow a term from symbolic interactionism (see Turner, 1962), Bhaskar like Giddens substantially neglects the activities involved in 'role-taking' (or 'position-taking').

Having said this, I believe that a revised and elaborated conception of position-practices can serve as a more robust link between structure and institutionalised modes of conduct than Giddens presently provides. Positions may remain as 'markers' in the virtual perspective from which structure is analysed (cf. *CS*, p. 282), but they may be conceived more concretely as position-practices, and the relations between positions may be conceived as position-practice relations (see below). The following items comprise what I believe to be a minimum definition of position-practices as institutionalised (i.e. structured and reproducible) constituents of social life.

(1)   a positional identity embedded in one or more systemic reproduction circuits defined in terms of identifying criteria (e.g. observable attributes, documented qualifications, etc.) and associated with a series of prerogatives and obligations;

(2)   a cluster of practices through which identifying criteria, prerogatives, and obligations are made manifest in ways that others can and do acknowledge in institutionalised modes of interaction;

(3)   a range of other position-practices with which a given position-practice must be, or contingently may be, interrelated as 'incumbents' enact their prerogatives and obligations;

(4)   the institutionalised aspects of reciprocities (including politically asymmetrical aspects of reciprocities involving a dialectic of control) through which position-practice relations occur. These reciprocities may involve modes of social integration and/or system integration.

If position-practices are conceived in this way they establish basic units of institutionalised systems which agents encounter and reproduce (through the duality of structure) as they contribute to the structuration of that system. Put in another way, position-practices (and position-practice relations) endure as structured clusters of institutions even as successive cohorts or generations of agents participate in system reproduction. Of course this allows for the fact that circumstantial variations will occur in any given instance of the reproduction of position-practices. Situational contingencies, matters of 'style', mistakes in conduct, and strategic forbearance from engaging in conduct – all must be taken into account. Nevertheless what we now have at hand is an alternative to social roles which stresses the enactment of identities, prerogatives and obligations so as to form a link between structure and agency. To speak, for example, of a father or a doctor, of a priest or a chief executive officer, is not only to refer to a positional identity, but also to a set of structured practices which position-incumbents can and do perform.

Position-practice relations

As indicated in items 3 and 4 of the foregoing definition, position-practices are always interrelated with others. These relations are reproduced via diverse modes of social integration in circumstances of co-presence, as well as via modes of system integration between absent agents. However, in the institutional analysis of the structural properties of systems, position-practice relations may be traced out while holding the spatio-temporal patterning of these relations out of account. Although Giddens does not work with the extended definition of position-practices introduced above, his image of social relations is consistent with the notion of position-practices relations. To indicate this I have replaced each reference to social relations in the following passage with a reference to position-practice relations:

> Social interaction refers to encounters in which individuals engage in circumstances of co-presence, and hence to social integration as a level of the 'building blocks' whereby the institutions of social systems are articulated. [Position-practice] relations are certainly involved in the structuring of interaction but are also the main 'building blocks' around which institutions are articulated in system integration. Interaction depends upon the 'positioning' of individuals in the time–space contexts of activity. [Position-practice] relations concern the 'positioning' of individuals within a 'social space' of symbolic categories and ties. (*CS*, p. 89)

Giddens does not discuss in detail what he has in mind by a 'social space' of symbolic categories and ties, but it is none too difficult to construe it as a kind of 'mapping', within the brackets of institutional analysis, of all of the various relations between position-practices within (and between) social systems; a 'mapping', that is, of the structured properties of position-practice relations which presumes that all position-practices and the relations between them are chronically reproduced in broadly similar forms. As I shall indicate in the next chapter, this 'mapping' may be decomposed from a concrete image of position-practice relations into analytically conceived structures and institutional orders. However, even from a concrete point of view a mapping of position-practices relations may be quite complex.

Many of the complexities in 'mapping' concrete position-practice relations arise from the fact that position-practice relations are comprised of *clusters* of institutionalised modes of conduct through which identities are established, obligations fulfilled, and prerogatives exercised. Naturally, all of these activities are not enacted simultaneously nor do they all necessarily occur through reciprocities with only one corresponding symbolic category of position-practices. From a structural point of view, then, any given position-practice may be related (in 'social space') to numerous other position-practices, although the nature of these relations may vary in many ways. Consider here the case of workers who participate in the factory assembly of automobiles. On the shop-floor there are position-relations among a group of workers and lower-level supervisors (foremen, section managers, etc.). Beyond the shop-floor, 'vertical' position-practice relations also exist between workers and upper-level administrators of the plant, and less directly of the enterprise. 'Vertical' position-practice relations may also be traced out between the workers and the administrators of union organisations. 'Horizontal' position-practice relations also exist between the assembly-line workers, and workers who extract raw materials and build component parts through labour transacted in a variety of remote work sites. In addition, following the insight into social relations which underlies Marx's analysis of the 'fetishism of commodities', position-practice relations may also be identified between the workers who produce automobiles and the agents who purchase and use these automobiles during the course of their daily lives. Even this, however, may not exhaust all possibilities. By virtue of the fact that taxes or social insurance fees are withheld from their paychecks, as well as by virtue of legal rights which may be invoked to forestall certain unsafe or 'unfair' managerial procedures, the position-practice of workers may also be related to position-practices in various 'branches' or bureaucracies of the state (i.e. position-practices in the relevant reproduction circuits of the state system).

Needless to say, the various relations between position-practices will vary in their 'intensity' (cf. Granovetter, 1973, on 'weak ties'), in their more or less direct implications for the day-to-day activity of position-practice 'incumbents', and also in the extent to which those agents who reproduce a given position-practice are aware that such relations exist. The latter is an extremely important point, in so far as it indicates the second-order status of analyses of position-practice relations. Workers most definitely will be aware of their relations in circumstances of co-presence with fellow workers, and with their immediate supervisors. But their awareness of the relations between their position-practice as workers and the consumers of the commodities they produce is, as Marx suggests, often obscured by the way such commodities are assembled, distributed, and sold through the agency of capitalist enterprises, and the mediation of market-based bargaining between wholesalers, retailers, and consumers.

To round out this discussion, it should be noted that this structural 'mapping' of position-practice relations only superficially resembles the formal images of social relations developed by network analysts and other contemporary morphologists. True, the notion of 'social space' is shared in common from both points of view. But as I have indicated above, the structural mapping of Giddens relations is never entirely an abstraction of relational forms from the context of social *praxis*. Position-practice relations are not simply formal 'ties' between 'nodes'. Instead they always retain substantive definitions based upon the most general qualities of position-practices and position-practice relations as they are enacted in social life (see Giddens's critique of Blau on this point, in *CS*, pp. 210–13).

The complementarity of enablement and constraint

From an institutional point of view it would be possible at this point to move immediately to the analysis of the structural properties of collectivities. However, issues of great importance with regard to the linkage between structure and action remain to be discussed, a discussion that will absorb the rest of this chapter. All of these issues revolve around Giddens's novel approach to the nature of constraint in social life. Without any doubt this is the most controversial and heavily criticised aspect of structuration theory. Prior to the publication of *The Constitution of Society* Giddens dealt with the topic only in passing remarks, most of which involved the contention that all constraints are also enablements (*NRSM*, p. 161, also 75, 93; *CPST*, pp. 69–70, also 51). This proposal departs in obvious ways from the prevailing view that constraints should be regarded primarily as limits and obstructions to the kinds of conduct in which agents may engage in their day-to-day lives. Because Giddens did not seem to adhere to this perspective, critical commentators sensed that this might be a weak spot in his attempt to supersede the division between collectivist and action-oriented accounts of social life. Some (e.g. Carlstein, 1981; Thompson, 1984) treated the issue as one problem among others that Giddens had yet to resolve. Others (e.g. Layder, 1981, pp. 62–70, 102–3; 1985, pp. 139–44; Archer, 1982) held it to be symptomatic of overall deficiencies in structuration theory.

Giddens took this criticism quite seriously, and he now has responded at length (*CS*, pp. 169–80, 304–10; *STMS*, pp. 11, 61, 219–22). His argument divides into two stages: in the first stage he identifies multiple sources of constraint in social life; in the second stage he considers structure as a specific source of social constraint. Regardless of how one regards his account of structural constraint – and, as I shall indicate below, I am not entirely satisfied with it in all respects – his recognition of the heterogeneity of constraints in itself represents a notable contribution not only to the development of structuration theory, but also to theoretical discourse on constraint in the social sciences at large.

Before distinguishing between different forms of constraint it is necessary to establish the nature of Giddens's claim that all constraints are also enablements, or, to be more precise, all constraints are *complemented* by enablements. To see what is involved here consider how social life would be constituted if constraints were unaccompanied by enablements. This would be as if one were to try to teach a child about some aspect of social life by showing her the kinds of activities and outcomes which she is unable to accomplish and achieve. No matter how well she learns that these options are foreclosed, the child's education inevitably remains incomplete because, while she may know the limits of her freedom, she does not know how to proceed. In saying that all constraints are complemented by enablements, structuration theory underscores the insight ignored in exclusively negative definitions of constraint, that no matter how severe constraints may be they always establish opportunities for some more or less extensive range of activities which enables actors to intervene in social life. As I shall indicate below, material and structural constraints immediately entail enablements, while the enablements associated with negative sanctions may, or may not, be established by those sanctions in and of themselves. Nevertheless, *all* constraints – save the complete immobilisation of the agent, for example by drugs or material bondage – must be complemented by enablements in order for the constitution of social life to occur.

Material constraints

In *The Constitution* (pp. 174–6), Giddens identifies in conceptual terms three basic sources of constraint in social life: material constraint, negative sanctions, and structural constraint. Since the first two sources have been introduced in previous chapters, my discussion of them will centre upon certain oversights in Giddens's account. Material constraints were dealt with in conjunction with the physical and biological limits on the spatio-temporal movement and interactive capabilities associated with the corporeality of human beings and the obdurate qualities of the material world. *Coupling constraints* delimit human communication and perception in face-to-face encounters; *capability constraints* delimit opportunities for such encounters and establish time–space distantiation as an obstacle to reciprocities, which has only been partially overcome since the advent of modern technological mechanical means of transportation and communication.

It should be none too difficult to recognise how coupling and capability constraints are conceivable in and of themselves as forms of enablements as well. Simply put, if human corporeality and the biologically given capacities of human perception and communication restrict opportunity for interaction among agents, they also provide conditions necessary for interaction to occur. But Giddens, I believe, unnecessarily skirts (except in passing: e.g. *NRSM*, pp. 110–11) another material form of constraint/enablement arising from the natural environment (see also Carlstein, 1981, p. 52). This oversight, I believe, should not be identified from a Marxist point of view. As Giddens (*CCHM*, pp. 59, 245–6) observes, Marx, in company with other theorists of the

Victorian era, adopted an instrumental stance toward the natural environment as the material medium of human social development. Here nature, in effect, is defined as an enablement, and all constraints result from the 'social metabolism' with the environment. But the natural environment not only expedites social life, it also restricts it in ways that were clearly evident to all actors prior to the advent of modern technology. Today, we are once again gradually recognising, as the evidence of the unintended consequences of modern technology becomes clear, that nature is not simply an endless storehouse of resources and opportunities which humans may exploit in any way they choose.

Given that natural topographies, resources, and climates vary markedly around the earth, and given historical variations in how humans have coped with and employed these aspects of the environment, there can be no simple, unitary definition of constraints and enablements in the environmental domain. Indeed the complexities of environmental sociology have recently attracted the attention of a number of scholars who still disagree on many of the most basic issues in the field (see Catton and Dunlop, 1978a, b; Schnaiberg, 1980; Buttell, 1987). Nevertheless, that opportunities and limitations on social life are established by material surroundings – even in the midst of the modern 'created environment' – becomes quite clear if one considers that only a seemingly small shift in climatic conditions can substantially alter opportunities for activities such as agriculture, marine navigation, population migration, and military manoeuvres (which is why all modern military organisations engage in meteorological surveillance). Of even greater importance are the limits on natural resources such as potable water, construction materials, sources of energy, and arable land. Even if, in the long run, modern forms of science and technology potentially can develop alternatives to exhausted environmental resources, this was not true in the past, and it is not true in the short run today.

It should be noted, *pace* Margaret Archer (1982, p. 467), that constraints issuing from the natural environment are never simply brute 'material existents' which constrain social life in direct and immediate ways (i.e. 'in their own right'). Land, for example, no matter how abundant or scarce it may be, need have little influence on the nature of institutionalised activities undertaken in a community organised for fishing and/or maritime trade. Moreover, the significance of land as a resource is quite different for a military organisation, as opposed to, say, a hunting and gathering tribe. The point here is that all environmental constraints and enablements can be defined only in connection with their implications for social *praxis*. An obvious exception is environmental circumstances such as the inexorable advance of deserts, glaciers, or rising water tables, which threaten the very existence of social life over large regions of the earth. But one can understand very little regarding the opportunities opened and foreclosed by environmental circumstances by concentrating exclusively on how human beings manage to avoid being overwhelmed by the environment. If Giddens overlooks environmental constraints and enablements, Archer's suggestion that these factors are 'brute existents' vulgarises the complexities involved in sophisticated social scientific studies of topics under this heading.

Negative sanctions

Negative sanctions refer to constraints deriving from the punitive responses on the part of some agents toward others. Although negative sanctions generally are imposed in social interaction, as indicated in Chapter 4, many negative sanctions also may involve more extensive institutional mediations of power. Thus, while the conceptual purview of negative sanctions includes responses to violations of cultural folkways, mores, and taboos, it also includes responses to violations of administrative commands in administered systems, and – given the dialectic of control – the counter-responses of subordinate agents as well.

Because negative sanctions are historically constituted in different ways, they are subject to enormous variation in the extent to which they may limit and restrict social conduct. Although formally codified penalties and punishments may be the most obvious forms of negative sanctions, more frequently imposed informal sanctions often delimit conduct to an equal, if not greater, extent (*CS*, pp. 22–3, 176). The constraining qualities of negative sanctions are evident in the extent to which specific forms of conduct are deterred through their imposition. However, negative sanctions pose something of a dilemma *vis-à-vis* Giddens's claim that all constraints are complemented by enablements. Giddens (*CS*, pp. 175–6) acknowledges that there are major asymmetries in the constraint/enablement relation here. But he attempts to preserve the complementarity of enablement and constraint by holding that a constraint for one person may be an enablement for another (this can be expressed in elliptical terms for aggregate groups as well). The problem with this argument, however, is that it fails to address the question of how the imposition of negative sanctions is complemented by enabling opportunities for action on the part of the individuals upon whom they are imposed. It may be, of course, that negative sanctions are imposed to generate compliance with a specific course of conduct; e.g. when military officers impose, or threaten to impose, physical or symbolic punishment upon those who disobey their commands. Here constraints preserve an opportunity for compliance which enables social conduct to proceed in the rather loose sense that no penalty will be incurred for the obedient performance of conduct under orders. But the outer limits of Giddens's proposal of a ubiquitous association between constraints and enablements appear to be breached in cases where negative sanctions are imposed without any complementary indication of alternative forms of appropriate conduct. For example, police or military personnel may threaten to impose punitive measures on actors who fail to cease and desist from certain types of conduct (e.g. street demonstrations, publication of subversive documents, etc.). Now it might be said that here forbearance by agents subject to sanction can be loosely defined as an activity which complements the negative sanction as a constraint. But beyond this point the negative sanction may leave open no positive course of action, except, of course, to defy the order to cease and desist. It is as if I were to tell my daughter to stop making noise in the house or I will punish her in some way. Her quite appropriate reply might be: 'But Dad, what am I supposed to do that doesn't make any noise?' Only if I come up with a positive proposal can it be said that my constraint is, for her, also an enablement, and even then the sense of enablement at issue is far weaker than enablements which issue, for example, from the corporeal capabilities of interaction and movement which complement coupling and capability constraints.

Structural constraint/structural enablement

Disengaging material constraints and negative sanctions from structural constraint serves to clarify the qualities of social life to which the latter concept refers. Unlike material constraints, structural constraints originate exclusively in socially established conditions for action, and like all features of the social world these conditions are subject to variations, both historically as well as within given systems. Structural constraints, of course, share this quality of historical variability with negative sanctions. But whereas negative sanctions originate in punitive responses imposed in interaction among agents, structural constraints originate in the institutionalised qualities of practices and relations simply by virtue of their (reproduced) persistence during the ongoing course of social life. For example, whether or not negative sanctions are imposed on workers who fail to meet production quotas in a capitalist (or state-socialist) factory depends upon the specific contingencies of the dialectic of control between workers and supervisors, contingencies which may vary from one shop-floor to another, or even on the same shop-floor during different historical periods. But the fact that factories are administered systems in which production techniques and the pace of production are controlled and coordinated by superordinate officials, implies historically enduring structural constraints on activities associated with the position-practice of workers. Because any given actor who enters an industrial enterprise as a worker must engage in manufacturing practices which are instituted by others, these practices may be said to be 'pre-structured' *vis-à-vis* the individual. But in so far as workers adhere to these practices they also contribute to their reproduction through the duality of structure, even if this reproduction frequently occurs in a tacit and unacknowledged manner.

Giddens's conceptual definition of structural constraint summarises the qualities touched upon in the foregoing example: structural constraint derives from the contextuality of action, i.e. from the 'given' character of structural properties, *vis-à-vis* situated agents (*CS*, p. 176). I would add here that these structural properties may be regarded as aspects of position-practices and position-practice relations. In a related passage Giddens expands upon this definition in the following way:

To say that society pre-exists the lives of its individual members at any given moment is only to identify a source of constraint insofar as its pre-existence in some way limits possibilities open to them. To emphasize that individuals are contextually situated within [position-practice] relations of a greater or lesser span is similarly only to identify a source of constraint if it is shown how this limits their capabilities. In each case constraint stems from the 'objective' existence of structural properties that the individual agent is unable to change. (*CS*, p. 176)

Two related points implied in this passage deserve special mention. First of all, the issue of structural constraint requires attention to the standing of the individual agent. That is, we cannot be concerned exclusively with the institutionalised practices and relations through which structuration occurs, but rather we must also address the obduracy of structured practices and relations as tacitly or discursively monitored by the agent. But second, as opposed to the disposition among collectivist theorists who endow 'objective' social constraints as properties of social groups with powers analogous to natural forces that somehow determine the course of social life as experienced by individuals (see DiTomaso, 1982; Alexander, 1984, pp. 22–3), structural constraint in structuration theory lacks any capacity to intervene in social conduct. If structural constraint shapes any aspect of social conduct undertaken by individuals it does so by shaping their capabilities as social agents, i.e. by establishing the potential kinds of actions or relations in which they may engage in so far as they adhere to established routines.

It directly follows from viewing structural constraints as implicated in opportunities for action that they not only limit possibilities for activity and the generation of outcomes *vis-à-vis* individuals, but they also appear to the agent as pre-structured enablements associated with opportunities for action which remain open to them. For example, contemporary institutionalised relations of production in capitalist manufacturing firms may constrain workers' opportunities to set their own rates of productivity, determine the kinds of goods they produce, and the industrial techniques they employ. But without denying that these constraints may be quite onerous to workers, it is also the case that the same capitalistically structured activities enable workers to participate in production and 'make a living'. Marx undoubtedly would immediately heap scornful derision on the enabling options which workers encounter in capitalistic activities and relations of production. But the point is that no matter how anyone may evaluate structural options, they always involve a balance between opportunities for activity (and the achievement of outcomes) which are foreclosed or obstructed, and opportunities which enable other forms of activity and outcomes to be produced.

Giddens expresses this point in a rather subtle way when he suggests that the 'could have done otherwise' which is a fundamental quality of human agency should not be juxtaposed to constraints on behaviour which derive from the structural properties of collectivities (*STMS*, p. 220). To do so would make it appear that agents would be 'free' to engage in an indefinite range of activities if only structural constraints did not exist. But a suspension of all structural constraints would logically entail the suspension of all structural properties of social conduct and relations which enable individuals to engage in activity as well. The result would therefore not be 'freedom' in the sense that actors could 'do otherwise', but the kind of unremitting chaos to which I referred in introducing the concept of structure above. For this reason, structural constraint/enablement is never completely absent in the constitution of social life. The question of whether an agent 'could have done otherwise' therefore must be treated as a matter of degree when considered with reference to structural enablement/constraint.

The restrictive qualities of structural constraints

When is a constraint truly restrictive? At first glance it might seem that restrictions can be theoretically defined in structural terms alone. But this can lead to absurd conclusions. For example, the structural attributes of position-practices in capitalist societies foreclose opportunities for agents to work as slaves in bondage, or as members of nomadic tribes. Yet few would argue that these limitations are structural constraints because few, if any agents, would want to follow either course of action. However, the structuring of position-practice relations in capitalist systems also forecloses opportunities for workers to manage their own industrial activities, and because many workers might want to do so if presented with the option, this appears as a true structural constraint. The point here is that structural constraints cannot be fully defined unless the individual's (or group of individuals') regard for pre-structured options is taken into account. Consider here a second example. While peasants may be constrained from engaging in commercial agricultural activities, the restrictions they encounter in this regard may not appear to them to be constraints in so far as the major aims of peasants typically involve the preservation of their material subsistence, and a commitment to the status gained within a narrow range of social relationships (see Wolf, 1969, pp. xiv–xv). Given these objectives, peasants may regard constraints on commercial activity as imposing no restrictions whatsoever on their ongoing conduct. However, if modern commercial farmers establish markets for both arable land and agricultural produce, these newly institutionalised activities may begin to foreclose options available to peasants to reproduce their established ways of life. Thus, from the peasants' point of view, rather than appearing as a source of enabling opportunities, capitalistic institutions (and their consequences) may be regarded as structural constraints.

Giddens is fully aware that structural constraints cannot be dissociated from actors' motives and wants, and he establishes the point in the starkest of terms by addressing the situation where constraints rigidly reduce an actor's options to a logical extreme:

Identifying structural constraint in a specific context or type of context of action demands consideration of actors' reasons in relation to the motivation that is at the origin of their preferences. When constraints so narrow the range of (feasible) alternatives that only one option or type of option is open to an actor, the presumption is that the actor will not find it worthwhile to do anything other than comply. The preference is a negative one of wishing to avoid the consequences of non-compliance. If the agent 'could not have acted otherwise' in the situation, it is because only one option existed, given that agent's wants. This *must* not be confused . . . with the 'could have done otherwise' that marks the conceptual boundary of action [i.e. agency – IJC]; it is exactly this confusion that structural sociologists tend to make. Where only one (feasible) option exists, awareness of such limitations in conjunction with wants, supplies the reason for the agent's conduct. (*CS*, p. 309; see also pp. 177–8)

Although this passage speaks for itself, two rather significant points must be stressed. First, Giddens's example here need not be considered a prototypical case of constraint. In many instances the range of feasible options open to the agent does not reduce to a single course of action. Second, the term 'feasible' here signifies that structural conditions *always* allow certain options which agents may regard as unfeasible given their motives and wants (cf. *CS*, pp. 177–8). But even after these clarifications are made, there are several implications of this passage which must be considered at length. This will be the topic in the following discussion.

Structural constraints and the 'dissolution of the agent'

As I earlier mentioned, structural constraint has been the focal point of a number of critical commentaries by scholars such as Margaret Archer, Derek Layder, and John Thompson. I join these critics in the belief that certain problems remain in Giddens's account. Although each critic develops an independent argument, ultimately the points they raise overlap to a significant extent. Among the various critical arguments, those provided by John Thompson will serve here as the basis for my remarks. An important reason for considering Thompson's arguments is that he deals more extensively than any other critic with the account of structural constraint that appears in *The Constitution of Society*. With specific regard to structural constraint, Thompson (1984, pp. 168–70) raises three issues on which I shall comment below. (i) He suggests that in extreme instances, such as the stark case established in the foregoing passage, structural constraint effectively 'dissolves' social agency into structure. (ii) He suggests in passing that Giddens's views on constraint are weakened by his views on agents' wants and desires. (iii) He argues that Giddens provides no adequate account of the differences and distribution of various forms of structural constraints within a given system or collectivity, and that Giddens therefore cannot conceive relative degrees of freedom from structural constraint. My position is that Thompson is correct on points two and three, but misses the mark with respect to point one.

Thompson's argument regarding the dissolution of agency by structural constraint focuses exclusively on instances where an agent encounters only one feasible option. The question then is: if an agent has but one feasible option is there any sense in which the agent 'could have done otherwise' than follow the course of action which does not engender negative consequences that the actor seeks to avoid? Thompson (1984, p. 169) proposes that the agent, indeed, could *not* 'have done otherwise', and hence agency, which Giddens defines with reference to this 'could have done otherwise', is effectively dissolved. Structure thus appears, in this extreme situation, to be antagonistic to agency, although in less restrictive structural conditions it is appropriate to speak of structural 'degrees of freedom'. During the course of his remarks Thompson denies the relevance of Giddens's distinction between feasible structural options, and options *per se*. Given the individual's wants, he argues, the feasible option is the only *practical* option the agent can pursue.

Although Thompson nowhere acknowledges the point, his argument for the structural dissolution of agency leaves the door ajar for theories which would impute a deterministic force to structural conditions. At least in extreme circumstances it would appear on his account that agents might be conceived as structurally strait-jacketed 'bearers' of structure (Althusser). Moreover, while Thompson indicates that in less extreme conditions greater 'degrees of freedom' may exist, collectivist theorists might expand the deterministic implications of his argument by proposing that structural constraints typically reduce many agents' options to a single course of action given their desire to avoid negative consequences of various kinds.

It would be unrealistic to deny that agents sometimes do find themselves in extreme predicaments where only one option is open that minimises negative consequences, and callous to propose that they have more than one feasible option from a practical point of view. Yet, to forestall the appearance of structural determinism it is important to preserve the 'could have done otherwise' of agency. And, *pace* Thompson, it also is important to note that unfeasible options always exist even for agents in the most dire straits. Why is this important? Because agents' wants may be subject to change in diverse situations, so that what appears unfeasible given situation A, may not be unfeasible given situation B. Consider the case of suicide, which Giddens (*CPST*, p. 149) regards as the 'ultimate refusal' (to comply). Thompson might argue that *given* an agents' wish to avoid destruction, any course of conduct which would not result in her demise is a feasible alternative to suicide, and that suicide itself is no option at all. Yet agents who, throughout most of their lives, remain averse to self-destruction, may encounter circumstances in which suicide itself appears to them as less undesirable than their continued existence: for example, 'altruistic' suicides (Durkheim), in which an individual sacrifices her own life so that another may live, or so that her honour, or the honour of some other agent or principle, is upheld. Of course the 'degree of freedom', or the range of structured courses of action and their outcomes, must be reduced to an extreme either/or choice between suicide and one other option before suicide itself may shift from an unfeasible to a feasible strategy to pursue. Still, in so far as at least two options exist, *the 'could have done otherwise' of agency is never radically dissolved*. Indeed, even in circumstances where agents perceive and acknowledge that they are doomed to die, they still may find alternative ways to end their lives (for example, in the case of the defiance of Nazi extermination procedures by members of the Warsaw Ghetto).

The preceding arguments may preserve a *structural* sense in which agents always potentially have some latitude to 'act otherwise', no matter how great or small that latitude may be. But it is by no means equally clear that agents potentially have a latitude to 'act otherwise' from a *subjective* point of view. Here, I believe, is the real source of difficulty in Giddens's argument regarding structural constraint. The problem occurs because in addressing structural constraint Giddens shifts the accent in his conception of agency from *praxis* to the motivations associated with *praxis*. The generic conception of agency in structuration theory presumes that the power to intervene in a course of affairs is logically prior to all matters regarding subjectivity and the reflexive monitoring of social conduct (*CPST*, p. 92; *CS*, p. 15). From this point of view, the restrictions imposed by structural constraint also should be conceived prior to taking agents' subjectivity into account. However-er, it should be evident now that Giddens does not define structural constraint in this way. Rather, structural constraint exists with reference to the ways in which structured (institutionalised) courses of action impinge upon the extent to which agents may engage in modes of *praxis* which are associated with their subjectively held motives. Structural constraint therefore is not exclusively a structural concept, nor one which may be defined with exclusive reference to the duality of structure. Rather it is defined as a social-psychological concept, i.e. as an aspect of the constitution of social life defined by agents' subjective regard for the institutionalised options they encounter during the course of their lives.

By defining structural constraint in this way Giddens incurs the obligation to provide a robust ontological account of how subjective wants and desires are formed in his theory of the acting subject. However, Thompson (1984, pp. 169–70) suggests that Giddens has not met this obligation to date, and I believe that he is quite correct on this point. To expand upon Thompson, consider first how structural constraint appears from the standpoint of one of the central elements of Giddens's views on the acting subject (see above, pp. 51–4). According to Giddens it is often the case that large areas of social life are not *directly* motivated (*CPST*, pp. 59, 218). Agents, of course, tacitly know what they are doing, they also tacitly recognise at least some of the outcomes engendered by their conduct, and they can give reasons for their conduct upon request (*CS*, p. 6). Nevertheless, in routine situations (which specifically excludes stark and dramatic circumstances such as those in which suicide may appear to the agent as an available option) agents may maintain nothing more than generalised motivation to the integration of their conventional practices during the course of their day-to-day routines. This motive is grounded in an unconscious need to maintain 'ontological security', i.e. a confidence or trust that the natural and social worlds are as they appear to be (*CS*, pp. 64, 375).

I do not wish to impugn the validity of this insight. Indeed, I regard it as one of Giddens's most important and valuable contributions. However, in so far as motives based upon an unconscious need for ontological security are at issue, the significance of the concept 'structural constraint' appears to be minimised to a great extent. The point here is that where agents are motivated only by a need to maintain a generalised trust in the circumstances implicated in their routine ways of life, they may have no occasion to reflect upon alternative institutionalised courses of action which they might pursue, unless pre-established routines are disrupted in some way. This is not to say that other options do not exist from a structural point of view, i.e. from the standpoint a social scientist might adopt in a second-order analysis of structure. But from the agents' perspective, given her need for 'ontological security', all of these options would appear to constrain her desire to carry on with her routine ways of life. Conversely, the option to continue with these routines may not appear *to the agent* to constrain her actions in any way whatsoever.

Giddens might well reply at this point that motives based upon a need for ontological security are generally associated with motives which supply overall plans or projects (in the Schutzian sense of the term). That is, even if much day-to-day activity is not directly motivated other than by a generalised need for ontological security, the range of conduct which is motivated in this way appears to the agent as part of an overall course of action related to a given purpose or end of which she is aware (cf. *NRSM*, pp. 78, 84; *CS*, p 6). Thus what may not appear to the agent as a structural constraint based upon her need for ontological security, may nevertheless appear as a structural constraint in light of her overall project. For example, a factory worker may not be directly motivated to go to work on a day-to-day basis, but rather merely follow her daily routine. Therefore the limited opportunity available to workers to advance their careers may not appear to her as a constraint from this day-to-day vantage point. However, if the worker is motivated by a long-term ambition to be promoted to a managerial position, then the limited opportunities for advancement she confronts may appear to her as substantial constraints indeed.

But at this point we encounter what I believe is the most serious problem with Giddens's view of structural constraint, and a considerable gap in structuration theory at large. The problem is simply that *to date Giddens has proposed no account of the nature or development of motives above and beyond the need for ontological security.* This gap in his work does not compromise the overall integrity of the structurationist ontology because, as I mentioned in Chapter 1, throughout most of his work Giddens is concerned with the constitution of social life as it occurs in social *praxis*, and to this end he 'decentres' the theory of the acting subject in favour of issues pertaining to the production and reproduction of social conduct and relations. *But the topic of structural constraint, in effect, 'recentres' the subject, and issues which Giddens has yet to address begin to arise.*

I shall not attempt here to cover all of the issues which would be involved in the development of the kind of theory of motivation that Giddens's account of structural constraint requires. But the importance of such a theory can be made clear with reference to the process of socialisation or acculturation through which motives are formed. In this regard, structural constraint may be conceived as a disalignment between motives that agents have established as they have been socialised into their institutionalised ways of life, on the one hand, and, on the other, the structured opportunities (courses of action) they encounter which limit their capabilities to pursue plans or projects based upon these motives. A theory of socialisation, from this point of view, thus becomes a necessary element of an account of structural constraint. However, to date, Giddens has done nothing more than offer insights into the formation of ontological security in this regard (*CPST*, pp. 120–23; *CS*, pp. 51–60). (My remarks on the need for a theory of socialisation in structuration theory have been informed by a forthcoming essay by Jeff Livesay.)

The distribution of structural options

The third criticism by Thompson I wish to discuss points to Giddens's neglect of the differential distribution of structural options. Thompson (1984, p. 170; see also p. 168) correctly observes that in order to deal with structural constraint the distribution of options must be correlated with the distribution of motivating wants and desires. However, having noted the absence of a comprehensive account of motivation in Giddens's writings I shall treat the distribution of structural options here as an issue unto itself. While this move entails that we are no longer speaking of structural constraint according to Giddens's social-psychological definition of the term, the distribution of structural options remains relevant to constraints in so far as it refers to the number and kinds of institutionalised courses of action which actors may pursue in their day-to-day lives, as well as in their long-term projects, and to the consequences for actors who opt for, and reproduce, these structured courses of action.

As Thompson suggests, Giddens does not discuss the distribution of structural options in any great detail. One basic reason undoubtedly is that distributional images of any kind do not represent the constitution of social inequality from the standpoint of structuration theory. Rather, as is the case for all aspects of social life as they are conceived in the ontology of structuration theory, inequalities exist only in so far as they are reproduced in social *praxis* by virtue of the duality of structure. The reproduction of inequalities, it should be added, is difficult to conceive so long as attention remains focused on the structured options available to individuals. Rather, regardless of whether the inequalities at issue occur in small systems (e.g. status groups in communities) or large collectivities (e.g. classes in capitalistic societies), inequalities are reproduced in and through institutionalised social relations, and more specifically the power relations which incorporate a dialectic of controls (see Chapter 5). Distributions of structural courses of action thus do not represent the constitution of inequality, but rather only the institutionalised conditions which agents encounter during their participation in the reproduction of inequality. To concentrate exclusively on these distributions can easily lead to a neglect of the relational aspects of inequality, as is the case, for example, in status attainment models of social mobility. (It can also lead to a neglect of agents' motives to engage in these relations; see *CS*, pp. 212–13, 304–10.)

But the fact that accounts of the distribution of structural options can be misleading, does not necessarily mean that they have no theoretical value so long as suitable qualifications are made. Social agents, after all, do encounter during the course of their lives a set of options to engage in the reproduction of relations of inequality, and their life-styles as well as their material standards of living are substantially affected by the options they ultimately can and do pursue. Thus, once the reproduction of relations of inequality is acknowledged it remains useful to consider how these options are distributed in any given system or collectivity.

Although Giddens does not provide a conceptual account of the distribution of options, there is no reason why such an account cannot be developed in structuration theory. This can be done, within the methodological brackets of institutional analysis, by means of positional concepts which permit options available to agents in those positions to be identified as institutionalised aspects of social life which are reproduced and endure in the *longue durée* (and which may be altered during periods of social change). In Marxist studies (e.g. Wright, 1985), class location exemplifies a concept of this kind. However, class location appears in structuration theory as a substantive, rather than a generic, concept, since Giddens denies that classes are always the most basic categories in hierarchies of inequality. What is needed, then, are ontologically generic categories which can inform substantive studies of the distribution of options not only in class hierarchies, but also in hierarchies of inequality of all kinds – for example, hierarchies based upon status, gender, ethnicity.

In my view, the notion of position-practice, which I introduced above as an augmented version of Giddens's concept of position, provides the kind of concept which structuration theory requires for the identification and comparison of distributions of structural options. The advantage of this concept over Giddens's concept of positions is that the institutionalised courses of action available to agents who 'occupy' (and reproduce) a given position-practice are clearly spelled out, as are the kinds of relations in which they may engage. Hence, this concept is very well-suited to serve as a basis for determining the structural options to which agents have access. There is a question of scale to be addressed in applications of this concept. If position-practices were to be confined to the purview of conventional conceptions of social role, they would be too specific to address large-scale groupings such as social classes. However, there is no reason why position-practices necessarily must be conceived in this way. One may, for example, conceive a social class as a position-practice identified in terms of a broadly defined set of structural options and relations shared in common by a large grouping of agents. Within this broad category more detail can be added by decomposing the larger position-practice category into more precisely defined position-practices. Ultimately the purpose and subject-matter at issue in the analysis of a particular distribution of options will determine how broad or detailed these position-practice categories must be.

One final point: it is extremely important to bear in mind that the distribution of options to position-practice categories is conceived here exclusively in structural terms. One reason to stress this point is that during the course of day-to-day life, a given individual may 'occupy' several different position-practices as she moves from participation in one system to another, and her options as an agent may be influenced by the conjunction of these position-practices. Individuals and position-practices therefore are not necessarily homologous concepts from a theoretical standpoint. A second reason to stress this point is that, as I have indicated earlier in this chapter, a concern for the kinds of structural constraints associated here with position-practices, leaves out of account material constraints as well as contraints which derive from the threat of enforcement of negative sanctions.

Giddens's critics, I believe, have correctly spotted structural constraint as a weak point in his development of structuration theory. In my view these weaknesses arise from two gaps in his work: first, the absence of a full-scale account of the development of agents' motives, and second, his neglect of the distribution of structural options. I have tried to show how the second gap can be filled, while I have left the first for future development. But in closing I wish to indicate my belief that both gaps can be filled within the overall conceptual framework of structuration theory as it stands. Put in another way, whatever weaknesses there may be in Giddens's account, they may be eliminated without compromising the ontological account of the constitution of social life which Giddens provides.

7

Structural Analysis, Societies, Societal Change

The analysis of structure: preliminary remarks

While the present chapter sustains an interest in structural themes, the issues to be discussed are conceived from a point of view that departs considerably from the way structure was dealt with in Chapter 6. In the first instance this is because attention now shifts from the implication of structure in specific practices and position-practices to the structural properties of collectivities. But the more significant point is that in making this move there is a shift in perspective. Instead of viewing structure as the institutionalised properties of concrete activities and relations, these structural properties now will be analytically decomposed and reconceptualised. This analytical perspective was briefly introduced in Chapter 1, where it was indicated that structural properties of social *praxis* may be conceived in terms of rules and resources. The discussion of resources in Chapter 5 implicitly adopted this point of view. However, as will be evident in the first part of this chapter, there is a wide array of concepts pertaining to the structural analysis of systems that remains to be introduced.

Following the discussion of structural analysis, the remainder of the chapter provides an overview of Giddens's approach to the analysis of societies and societal change. The reason for dealing with these topics in a chapter devoted to structural themes is that two basic structural concepts – structural principles and structural contradiction – play central roles in Giddens's analysis of societies. However, societies cannot be conceived in structural terms alone, and therefore a number of systemic issues and substantive themes will be taken into account.

Structural analysis

The ambition to isolate aspects of social life which are not clearly evident in its concrete manifestations because they are embedded in, or combined with, other aspects of many different kinds has inspired leading figures in both classical and contemporary social theory. Marx's distinction between use-value and exchange-value represents a good case in point. Neither of these concepts can be discussed in concrete terms. Rather, use-value and exhange-value refer analytically to diverse qualities or appearances of a commodity in its concrete form (Marx, 1967, pp. 35–41; 1975, p. 198). Marx's method for analysing the underlying properties of commodities, and deep-seated properties of other social relations as well, remains controversial, and it is not clear that he maintained a consistent methodological position throughout his career, or even in his 'later' writings on political-economy. Nevertheless, some insight into his method of analysis may be gained from a passage in the *Grundrisse*, which, it should be mentioned, subsequently has influenced developments in structural Marxist methods and epistemology (see Althusser, 1970, pp. 185–6, and n. 22):

The concrete is concrete because it is the concentration of many determinations ... It appears in the process of thinking, therefore, as a result, not as a point of departure, even though it is the point of departure in reality and hence also the point of departure in observation and conception ... the method of rising from the abstract to the concrete is only the way in which thought appropriates the concrete. (Marx, 1973, p. 101)

Marx's classical interest in decomposing concrete reality into its many determinations is sustained and enlarged – albeit in concepts which are radically at odds with Marxist thought – in the more contemporary project of Talcott Parsons. Parsons, of course, launched his theory through an analytical decomposition of 'social action' into means, ends, norms and conditions, all of which are organised in his model of the structure of social action. But even before presenting this model he already insisted upon the relevance of analytical techniques:

> Human life is essentially one and no concretely possible degree of functional differentiation can destroy its unity. But tho its concrete reality is a unity, it can, like all other complex phenomena, be broken down for purposes of analysis into different factors. (Parsons, 1935, p. 660)

I have cited Marx and Parsons here in order to indicate the prevalence of an interest in the analysis of factors embedded in the concrete reality of social life. While Giddens also has an interest in analytical theory, it is important to underscore one rather substantial difference in his approach. Unlike Marx and Parsons, Giddens does not *begin* the development of concepts in structuration theory from an analytical point of view. To the contrary, he begins with a deep respect for the fact that social life is constituted in the production and reproduction of concrete forms of practices and relations, and this is why so many of his concepts do not involve the decomposition of *praxis* into structural elements such as rules and resources.

But if analytical decomposition is an undesirable way to initiate structuration theory, there can be no gainsaying its necessity. As Marx and Parsons clearly recognise, social life is too complex, too fraught with diverse factors (e.g. economic, political, cultural), to be fully conceivable in concrete terms. Moreover, factors and elements considered as structural properties do not necessarily appear in independent social systems. Addressing the question of how the economic, political, legal/normative and symbolic institutional orders of societies should be conceived, Giddens argues that:

> 'Substantive' conceptions presume concrete institutional differentiation of these various orders. That is to say, it is held, for example, that 'politics' exists only in societies having distinct forms of state apparatus and so on. But the work of anthropologists demonstrates effectively enough that there are 'political' phenomena – to do with ordering of authority relations – in all

societies. The same applies to the other institutional orders. (*CS*, p. 34)

Although I shall not dwell at length upon epistemological issues in structural analysis, a word should be said regarding the status of concepts which will be under discussion in subsequent remarks. While it is evident that all concepts in structural analysis (e.g. rules, resources, etc.) are second-order concepts, and while it is evident as well that Giddens treat these concepts as analytical abstractions from concrete procedures of structuration, he has not provided a ful-fledged epistemological argument in this regard such as Parsons provides with reference to 'analytical realism'. If we sever Parsons's argument for analytical realism from the connotations of neo-Kantian transcendentalism which may be inferred from his writings (see Bershady, 1973; Münch, 1981), I believe that the general epistemological position Parsons adopts is consistent with Giddens's analytical perspective. It is consistent, that is, provided that concrete reality is granted greater respect than Parsons concedes at any point in his work.

Parsons's (1968, p. 730) most basic claim for analytical realism is that his concepts pertaining to 'elements' or 'factors' are not fictitious but, rather, 'realistic', in the sense that they 'grasp' aspects of the objective world, albeit aspects which must be analytically separated from others before they can be discussed. Giddens can be seen to concur with this claim in so far as he contends that structural concepts in structuration theory should not be understood – following Lévi-Strauss – as a model invented by an observer (*CPST*, p. 63). It also follows from his brief, programmatic allusions to the possibility of interpreting the status of structuration theory at large in terms of a realist epistemology (*SSPT*, pp. 75–7; *PCST*, p. 14). But there is one extremely important difference to be underscored between Parsons and Giddens on the 'realist' interpretation of structural concepts. For Parsons (1968, p. 750), analytical elements have *causal* rather than simply descriptive significance. However, in structuration theory, structural concepts cannot be construed as causal in the immediate sense that they intervene in the production of social life, although they may contribute to causation as enablements/constraints. This follows since, while structural conditions may be necessary for the reproduction of practices, relations, systems, and collectivities, only social agents retain the capacity to generate these practices, relations, etc., in and through their doings. Parsons's imputation of causal significance to analytical elements hypostatises analytical abstractions into concrete forces. Giddens insists, to the contrary, that agents' strategies of conduct, their reasons for following these courses of action, and the various consequences (intended and unintended) of social activity must be taken into account, along with structural and situational conditions, before causes can be discussed in social life. Hence in structuration theory there can be no such thing as an autonomous category of structural analysis (see *CS*, pp. 211–13, 216, 328–9, 345).

Structural analysis of rules

Structural analysis in structuration theory begins by decomposing the institutional properties of modes of *praxis* into categories defined as rules and resources. While I shall not rehearse the discussion of resources presented in Chapter 5, the notion of rules requires some elaboration at this point. Giddens's views on rules have shifted somewhat during the course of his work. Whereas his early writings (see *NRSM*, pp. 123–4; *SSPT*, p. 118) distinguish two different *types* of rules – semantic and moral – his later writings conceive rules as a unitary concept, and analytically isolate two *aspects* of rules rather than two types (*CPST*, pp. 64–8, 82–3; *CS*, p. 18). The *semantic, or constituitive* aspect grasps the performative elements of *praxis*, with specific reference to the discursive and tacit meanings agents ascribe to their own activities as well as to the activities of others, and with reference as well to the socially constituted contexts generated as meaningful to agents when activities are established and maintained. The *regulative* aspect of rules refers to the appropriate or legitimate manner in which activities may be carried out, as well as to the positive and negative sanctions which are tacitly or self-consciously applicable to the activities. An additional shift in Giddens's account should be noted in the latter regard. Whereas initially Giddens equated normative rules with a Durkheimian notion of moral obligation, by placing a greater emphasis upon sanctions in his later works he proposes to treat morally obligating norms as a sub-heading under the heading of normative rules *per se* (*CPST*, pp. 270–71, n. 63). He thereby allows for the psychic detachment from norms which is evident when agents regard norms as amoral (or immoral) conditions of social life which they cannot overlook, but to which they remain uncommitted.

We now arrive at an important point regarding the conception of rules. In the present discussion I treat rules as *analytical* aspects of *praxis*. This, as I shall indicate below, appears to be Giddens's intention as well. However, there are moments when Giddens appears to suggest that rules may be conceived in *concrete* terms. This contention is epitomised by Giddens's analogy between rules and algebraic formulae (*CS*, pp. 20–21). What Giddens means to suggest is that rules and algebraic formulae both refer to generalisable procedures which may be applied in an indefinite number of specific situations. However, what he fails to make clear is that algebraic formula, unlike praxiological rules, may be taken as concrete procedures which are not implicated in any larger or more complex context. Thus, in solving an equation I may become so absorbed in its application that, at least for a moment, I do not engage in any other cognitive procedures at all. Giddens's analogy between formulae and rules thus suggests that the generalisable procedures to which rules refer may be regarded as instances of concrete, institutionalised practices. Critics such as John Thompson (1984, pp. 157–8), who find Giddens's conception of rules loose and obscure, can find ample support in this vacillation between rules as analytical constituents of *praxis*, and rules as concrete practices in themselves.

The main tendency in Giddens's writings, however, is to conceive rules from an analytical standpoint. Rules remain generalisable, but the crucial point is *that any given practice involves an overlapping and loosely connected set of rules* (*CPST*, pp. 65, 82; *CS*, p. 18). In dealing with rules (and resources as well) we therefore reverse the direction taken in the conceptualisation of position-practices and position-practice relations: instead of combining practices into a composite structural concept, we focus on specific procedures embedded in these practices. A seemingly straightforward practice such as, say, voting in a formal-democratic election, may be decomposed into rules regarding strategies of voting which may be institutionalised in various political parties, rules regarding designated periods of voting which may be institutionalised in the state system, rules regarding the confidentiality of each individual's vote, and also resources, which in this case may include citizenship as an authoritative resource. Another practice, such as obtaining a loan from a bank, may involve interactional rules regarding appropriate dress and non-verbal demeanour, status displays (e.g. displays of trustworthiness, deference), bureaucratic and economic rules to establish qualifications, and so forth.

When individual practices and position-practices are decomposed into various rules it becomes impossible to trace out concrete relations and concrete articulations across time and space. However, a compensating advantage in adopting this analytical point of view is that specific rules may be understood, from the second-order perspective adopted in institutional analysis, as interwoven or embedded in a variety of diverse practices and relations both within and beyond the practices and relations which constitute any given concrete system. Rules pertaining to the confidentiality of voting, for example, may extend beyond state elections to the election of offices in many other systems – for example, unions, professional associations, social clubs, high school and university student councils, etc.; rules regarding the manipulation of financial resources may extend beyond arrangements for loans to arrangements for investments, the creation of capitalist enterprises, etc. More 'cultural' rules may be generalisable to an equal extent. Displays of trustworthiness and deference, for example, may be implicated in practices ranging from arranging for a loan, to applying for a job or admission to a university, to interviews involved in conducting job-evaluations, etc.

Relations of conversion between structural properties

One of the most important tasks in structural analysis is to trace out the relations between the institutionalised structural properties of systems. However, the relations between structural properties must not be confused with the relations between agents (see *CS*, p. 192). It must be underscored here that rules and resources represent analytical abstractions from the concrete 'content' of social relations which are reproduced in and through social *praxis*. Hence the actual 'content' of relations between agents will be richer and more complex than the relations between structural properties. It follows that a knowledge of a specific set of relations between structural properties is insufficient to understand how concrete relations between agents are generated and reproduced. Having said this, the central assumption that ties relations between structurally conceived rules and resources to the reality of social life as constituted in social *praxis*, is that:

> Rules and regulations are not distributed in a random form in society, but are coordinated with one another in and through the coordination of the systems of interaction in whose production and reproduction they are implicated. (*SSPT*, p. 132)

Relations between structural properties involve the 'convertibility' of rules and resources, or relations of conversion between analytically conceived sets of rules and resources. Just as rules may be implicated in a variety of concrete practices, so too conversion relations between rules and resources may summarise relations that are implicated in a variety of concrete reciprocities between agents. The notion of 'convertibility' refers to the transformation of structural properties that transpires during the reproduction of concrete relations carried out by social agents (cf. *CPST*, pp. 103–5; *CCHM*, p. 53).

In order to illustrate the nature of relations of conversion in the analysis of structure, we can turn to the following prototype Giddens develops based upon Marx's theory of social relations in the capitalist modes of production (*CPST*, pp. 104–5; *CCHM*, p. 55; *PCST*, p. 36; *CS*, pp. 186–7, 301–3).

private property: money: capital: labour contract: profit

The first thing to be said about this prototype is that each concept involves a combination of rules and resources. Private property, money, and capital, for example, each involves a form of allocative resource, but in each instance these resources are subject to semantic definitions and normative regulations which are implicated in the practices through which the manipulation of resources occurs in social life. The conversion relations represented in the prototype should be relatively easy to understand. Through a variety of different practices (e.g. market activity, collateral-based loans), private property is converted into money. Money, in turn is converted into the control of capital (for example, through direct purchase, capital investment). The labour contract (which, again, may take a variety of concrete forms) permits the control of capital to be converted into the control of labour-power (the only 'property' which workers possess). Finally, the control of capital in conjunction with the control of labour-power is convertible into commodities which yield a profit to the entrepreneur (via the exploitation of labour-power and marketing activity).

This, of course, is not the only set of conversion relations involving property which can be analytically traced out in capitalist systems. The conversion relations in the following set indicate that through the labour contract capital also ultimately is converted into the asymmetrical industrial domination of the proletariat by the bourgeoisie:

private property: money: capital: labour contract: industrial authority

Yet another set of structural relations represents a set of conversion relations involved in the intergenerational transmission of position-practice identity in the capitalist class:

private property: educational advantage: occupational position

Here again, it is important to bear in mind that each of the conversions in this set of structural relations abstracts analytical aspects from a variety of practices and interactions. Thus the conversion of educational advantage into occupational position may actually occur in social *praxis* through the strategic use of the prestige of job applicants' educational credentials, and/or through informal 'contacts' established during the course of university training, and/or through information regarding job-openings and skills relevant to job interviews which is available to university students.

Dimensions of the duality of structure

At this point the type of analytical abstraction involved in the analysis of structure should be clear. As I have repeatedly stressed, the structural properties which are analysed in this way are abstracted from concrete modes of activities and relations. The warrant for this abstraction is provided by Giddens's conception of the duality of structure. Simply put, structural properties are recursively implicated in concrete modes of *praxis* as both the conditions agents require in order to reproduce institutionalised conduct, and as the reproduced outcomes of that conduct. In order to establish a comprehensive image of the reciprocal association between structure and concrete *praxis*, Giddens provides a schematic chart of the analytical dimensions of the duality of structure, which appears below in Figure 7.1 (see *NRSM*, p. 122; *SSPT*, p. 132; *CPST*, p. 82; *CS*, p. 29).

In order to properly understand Figure 7.1, three points of clarification must be made. First, I have substituted the term *'concrete praxis'* in place of Giddens's reference to interaction on the lowest row of the figure. This allows for activities undertaken by agents which do not involve face-to-face encounters in circumstances of co-presence. Second, the term 'modalities' in Figure 7.1 should be understood to refer to the inherent association that occurs in the structuration of practices and relations between concrete *praxis* on the one hand and structural properties on the other. Interpretative schemes, for example, form the core of agents' mutual knowledge regarding institutionalised practices and socially constituted contexts on the one hand, while when analysed as the semantic aspect of rules they appear implicated in structures of signification. Third, the middle column in Figure 7.1 compresses allocative and authoritative resources into a single category of structures of domination. Facilities then may be regarded either as structural resources or as capabilities of reaching outcomes exercised during the course of conduct.

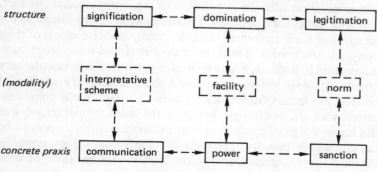

FIGURE 7.1

The double-headed arrows between columns in Figure 7.1 signify that no single aspect of the duality of structure exists apart from the other elements during the actual course of the production and reproduction of social life. The double-headed arrows between rows signify the recursive nature of the duality of structure. It shoud be noted that because the duality of structure places no analytical priority on either structure or conduct, the fact that structure appears on the top row has no analytical significance whatsoever. Indeed in certain instances Giddens inverts the rows so that concrete *praxis* (interaction) appears above structure (*NRSM*, p. 122; *CPST*, p. 82). Having said this, it may be useful to comment upon aspects of the duality of structure which move, analytically, from concrete *praxis* to structure. Here again I shall set aside the movement from power to domination since this was discussed in Chapter 5.

The left-hand column in Figure 7.1 analytically isolates the semantic aspect of rules in the connection between concrete *praxis* and structure. On the level of concrete *praxis* this aspect involves the identification of meaningful circumstances (practices, relations, contexts, events, and broader properties of social systems) which are generated during the institutionalised course of routine activities. The reference to communication here must be understood in a very broad manner (see *NRSM*, pp. 86–90; *CPST*, pp. 83–5). This follows from several insights. First, because all competent agents at least tacitly monitor their own conduct as well as the conduct of others and the physical, temporal, and social circumstances of context, both verbal and non-verbal interpretation and communication must be taken into account. Second, by equating communication with the generation of meaning in social conduct, Giddens allows for a distinction between what agents intend as the meaning of their utterances, and the communicative intent of their non-verbal activities. Third, in both verbal and non-verbal communication a distinction may be drawn between the perlocutionary quality of intended meaning, and the illocutionary quality of conduct as meaningful activity: i.e. what is intentionally communicated by an act, as distinguished from the conventional meaning of the act as a type of conduct in itself. Fourth, a distinction must be drawn, which broadly intersects the focal concern of symbolic interactionists, between how actors construe the meaning of what they say or do, and how other actors interpret these utterances or activities. Finally, a distinction must be drawn between meanings established in circumstances of co-presence versus meanings established via the production and hermeneutic reception of written texts and other cultural objects. The latter, of course, is of considerable importance in system integration, and it also serves as a basis for Giddens's recent remarks on cultural production (*STMS*, pp. 100–7).

All modes of the production and interpretation of meaningful conduct in institutionalised *praxis* involve tacit or self-conscious applications of interpretative schemes. These schemes, in turn, may be viewed in structural terms as properties of structures of signification. Giddens acknowledges the relevance of semiotic analyses of such structures (*CPST*, p. 98; see also *NRSM*, pp. 89–90). However, two closely related qualifications must be made. First, he departs from semiotic analyses by ascribing priority to the semantic meaning of signs, rather than treating signs as arbitrary signifiers which are interrelated with one another (*CS*, pp. 32–3; *CPST*, pp. 98–9). He thereby avoids a 'retreat into the code' which is characteristic of structuralist and post-structuralist traditions of thought. Second, the relational character of structures of signification is established with reference to the semantic aspects of the ordering of practices and relations in day-to-day life. But this should not be understood to imply that a single semantic code comprises a structure of signification. Rather, since signs may be employed in a variety of ways in different circumstances (for instance, alternative meanings of signs as used by members of different classes, ethnic groups, in public and private conduct, etc.), structures of signification may be comprised of a plurality of codes (*CPST*, p. 99). Following Paul Ricoeur, Giddens uses the concept of symbol to refer to polyvalent signs which appear in a variety of codes in a structure of signification (*CPST*, pp. 107–8; *CS*, pp. 32–3).

The right-hand column of Figure 7.1 analytically isolates the normative aspect of rules in the duality of structure (*NRSM*, pp. 108–10; *CPST*, pp. 85–8; *CS*, p. 30). In concrete *praxis* among agents norms are implicated in sanctioning procedures. But as modalities of structuration the same norms comprise aspects of structures of legitimation. As should be clear from remarks made in the chapter on administrative power, Giddens does not necessarily equate structures of legitimation with consensus based upon agents' 'internal' commitments to the realisation of normative rights and responsibilities. Lest this point be misunderstood, Giddens does not create a binary opposition between a utilitarian 'calculation' by agents of the liabilities and benefits of avoiding negative sanctions (and the advantages of pursuing positive sanctions) on the one hand, and a fully-fledged investment of personal allegiance to norms on the other. Rather:

> There is a range of possible 'shadings' between acceptance of normative obligations as a moral commitment, the type case of Durkheim, and conformity based on the acknowledgement of sanctions that apply to the transgression of normative prescriptions. (*CPST*, p. 87)

Structure and institutional orders

Having established the analytical dimensions of the duality of structure, attention now turns to the analysis of structural properties of collectivities, the principal objective of structural analysis. This analysis may proceed in two different ways, both of which involve categories on the top row of Figure 7.1. The first mode of structural analysis involves the identification of structures. *Structures* analytically represent configurations of structural properties *within* a structural dimension of the duality of structure (i.e. structures of signification, domination, and legitimation). The second mode of structural analysis involves the identification of institutional orders. Institutional orders analytically represent relations between properties *across* the structural dimensions of the duality of structure. Both modes of structural analysis are represented in Table 7.1.

All three of the categories of structure have been previously discussed: signification and legitimation in connection with the analytical dimensions of the duality of structure, and domination in Chapter 5 with regard to the role of resource in forms of rule and power relations. The only point that should be added here is that the study of each type of structure may be taken to comprise an analytically distinct *theoretical domain*. This is simply an acknowledgement of the professional division of topics of interest.

Table 7.1

Structure(s)	Theoretical domain	Institutional order
Signification	Theory of coding	Symbolic orders/modes of discourse
Domination	Theory of resource authorisation	Political institutions
	Theory of resource allocation	Economic institutions
Legitimation	Theory of normative regulation	Legal institutions

Paul Ricoeur, for example, is primarily concerned with issues in the theory of coding; Alford and Friedland's *Powers of Theory* (1985) is concerned with theories of resource authorisation and resource allocation; and Durkheim's *Suicide* is concerned with the theory of normative regulation.

Presuming that the categories under the headings of structures and theoretical domains are clear, some remarks are in order on the categories of institutional orders. The first step in the analysis of institutional orders is to decide which structural dimension (i.e. signification, domination with regard to authoritative resources, domination with regard to allocative resources, legitimation) is to be taken as the focal point of concern. Marxists, for example, generally are inclined to ascribe analytical priority to the role played by allocative resources, and *ipso facto* they will closely attend to the economic institutional order. The economic institutional order, however, involves more than the ordering of allocative resources in the structuring of social systems. The ordering of allocative resources in an economic institutional order is always related (through structural relations of conversion) with the ordering of authoritative resources (for example, as structural properties of state systems), as well as with the ordering of semantic and normative aspects of rules implicated in the practices through which resources are manipulated in day-to-day life.

Since there are four structural dimensions to which analytical priority may be ascribed (assuming a distinction between allocative and authoritative resources), there are four corresponding institutional orders as represented below (see *CPST*, p. 107; *CCHM*, p. 47; *CS*, p. 33).

S–D–L	Symbolic orders/modes of discourse
D(authorisation)–S–L	Political Institutions
D(Allocation)–S–L	Political Institutions
L–D–S	Law/modes of sanction

where s = signification, D = domination, L = legitimation

It should be repeated here that institutional orders are analytically abstracted from concrete social systems. Thus the identification of institutional orders does not presume the concrete differentiation of social systems. A tribal society may be analysed in terms of all four institutional orders to the same extent as a modern society.

Structural analysis: concluding remarks

Before closing on structural analysis something must be said about the nature and limits of the mode of theory construction Giddens employs. Unlike any other topic in structuration theory, Giddens develops structural analysis with a concern for the formal organisation and interrelation of conceptual categories. This strategy enables Giddens to make clear how all elements in the dimensions of the duality of structure are analytically abstracted from concrete forms of *praxis* (Figure 7.1), and to indicate the full set of options available in the analysis of structures and institutional orders (Table 7.1). Yet if formal theorising has the virtue of expository precision and clarity, it also has a decided disadvantage in so far as it creates an opening for the kind of enterprise in which the construction of an exhaustive system of complementary and interrelated analytical concepts becomes the primary method of social theory. In other words, it creates an opening for the kind of systematic, formal theorising which Talcott Parsons employs, and which more recently has been utilised by Jurgen Habermas (1987).

Giddens, I believe, has no intention whatsoever of developing structural analysis in this way. Indeed, it is noteworthy that nowhere either in his substantive writings or in his texts on structuration theory does he utilise the conceptual categories set forth in Figure 7.1 and Table 7.1 in a systematic and formal way.

Instead he virtually always maintains a clear-sighted recognition that structural analysis is a technique to be employed in order to understand properties of social systems which are reproduced in the *longue durée* through complex series and cycles of institutionalised activities and relations which 'stretch' across time and space. The extent to which structural analysis can yield formal models, therefore, does not depend upon the objectives of theory construction, but rather upon the degree of 'systematicity' which is evident in the constitution of the system or systems which comprise the subject-matter at hand (see above, pp. 18, 30). Considered in this light, the formally organised account of structural analysis in the preceding pages should be regarded as a propaedeutic to the development of substantive theory and research rather than as an invitation to carry structural analysis in the direction of 'grand theory'.

Societal systems: a non-unitary approach

Although Giddens refrains from engaging in 'grand theory', all of his works, both substantive and ontological, exhibit a pronounced concern for 'grand questions' (for a programmatic statement, see *STMS*, pp. 41–4). 'Grand questions', by definition, are concerned with large-scale collectivities, how they are constituted, and how they change. To entertain 'grand questions' therefore requires a conception of large-scale collectivities, or, more specifically, a conception of societies (and, ultimately, of inter-societal systems as well). Giddens has given a great deal of thought to the development of an adequate account of the constitution of societies, and he has introduced novel conceptions of structural principles and structural contradictions in this regard. However, the first order of business in explicating his views must be to consider societies as social systems.

Although Giddens characteristically qualifies each concept he introduces into structuration theory in a variety of ways, no single concept is more heavily qualified in his writings than that of society. The focal point of all of these qualifications is the need to avoid postulates which make it appear that societies are coherent, well-integrated, and clearly delimited social systems unto themselves, which, because of these qualities, may be assumed in all instances as the primary objects of social scientific interest (see *CCHM*, pp. 42–3; *CS*, pp. xxvi–xviii, 163–4; *NSV*, pp. 1–2, 17; *STMS*, pp. 33–4). Sociologists who make this assumption, Giddens argues, frequently, albeit often implicitly, maintain an image of societies which corresponds to modern nation-states. But while modern nation-states clearly *are* well-bounded and well-integrated systems, Giddens cautions against eliding the distinction between nation-states and modern societies. While nation-states may be unified as administrative systems – and even this is not clear in federated republics such as the United States – their administrative purview and their territorial domain generally are cross-cut by numerous other systems (e.g. capitalist systems of production and trade, systems of class and ethnic relations, etc.). In addition, various of these systems may not be fully incorporated within the politically defined boundaries of the state, but rather may extend beyond these boundaries as institutionalised activities and relations involved in the reproduction of inter-societal systems. But this still presumes the integrity of the nation-state as a well-defined system. *No other type of society throughout human history has included large-scale systems that were equally coherent or well organised.*

Giddens by no means is alone in recognising the empirical inadequacies of coherent conceptions of societal totalities. Indeed, while naive images of coherent societies are to be found in the works of Comte, Spencer, Durkheim and, in certain instances, Marx as well, and while for most sociologists the answer to the question 'what is sociology?' remains 'the study of society' (Frisby and Sayer, 1986, p. 121), various theorists (e.g. Weber, Simmel) have ignored coherent conceptions of societal collectivities, while others (e.g. Merton, 1968, pp. 79–84) have repudiated them, or refashioned them into analytical constructs which do not clearly refer to concrete systems (e.g. Parsons, 1966, pp. 9–10; Luhmann, 1982, pp. 76–82; Althusser, 1970, pp. 205–6 *passim*).

Among these diverse trends away from treating coherent societies as units of analysis, Giddens's views most closely correspond to those held by contemporary historical sociologists. Michael Mann – whose theoretical prologue to *The Sources of Social Power* (1986) converges with Giddens's views in structuration theory in many respects – epitomises the historical sociological position quite well when he asserts that societies are far *messier* than our theories of them. Human beings do not create unitary societies, but a diversity of networks of social interaction (Mann, 1986, pp. 4, 16). Charles Tilly substantiates Mann's claim from an empirical point of view:

> All of the standard procedures for delineating societies run into severe trouble when the time comes either to check the clarity and stability of the social boundaries thus produced or to describe the coherent structures and processes presumably contained within these boundaries. How? In many variants all the troubles return to two fundamental difficulties: *first*, how to make boundaries of the 'same' unit consistent in time, space, and personnel; *second*, how to determine whether the proposed boundaries do, in fact, delimit a distinct and coherent social entity. (Tilly, 1984, p. 22)

In subsequent remarks, Tilly (1984, p. 25) proposes that, given the absence of empirically effective criteria to delineate autonomous societies, we are better off simply abandoning the notion. In so far as the demarcation of coherent societal totalities is concerned, Tilly makes a very good case. But ultimately his proposal seems a bit too drastic. It might be justifiable to abandon the notion of society if other systems could be identified which were or are independent of one another in terms of their time–space articulation, as well as in terms of their personnel. We then would have systems which exhibit boundaries and coherence which societies lack. But there are very few systems of this kind to be found. Almost always, the systems to which we attend, be they based upon kinship, economic relations, military alliances, etc., intersect or overlap other systems. Determining the boundaries and the coherence of any of these systems therefore may be as difficult as doing so with regard to societies. Thus, if all social systems may be considered non-unitary collectivities in this sense, the fact that societies are not clearly bounded, coherent systems does not disqualify them from consideration. It is necessary, however, to define societies so as to accentuate their non-unitary characteristics as social systems.

The 'minimal' definition of societal totalities Giddens advances in structuration theory disavows all postulates regarding unity, bounded demarcations, and coherence:

All societies both are social systems and at the same time are constituted by the intersection of multiple social systems. Such multiple systems may be wholly 'internal' to societies, or they may cross-cut the 'inside' and the 'outside', forming a diversity of possible modes of connections between societal totalities and inter-societal systems . . .

Societies, then, in sum are social systems which 'stand out' in bas-relief from a background of other systemic relationships in which they are embedded. They stand out because definite structural principles serve to produce a specific overall 'clustering of institutions' across time and space. Such a clustering is the first and most basic identifying feature of a society . . .

It is important here to re-emphasize that the term 'social system' should not be understood to designate only clusters of social relations whose boundaries are clearly set off from others . . . I take it to be one of the main features of structuration theory that the extension and 'closure' of societies across time and space is regarded as problematic. (*CS*, pp. 164–5)

By conceiving the *praxis* extension and closure of societies as 'problematic', and by treating societies as constituted by the intersection of overlapping systems, Giddens adopts a position from which societies appear as both permeable and more or less loosely articulated across time and space. He therefore is free to suggest that societies need not be considered the only basic form of social systems in any given social inquiry (*CCHM*, p. 46), and his views also imply that societies should not be regarded in any event as the exclusive form of system at issue in any given investigation, if only because inter-societal systems must *always* be taken into account. Nevertheless, in so far as societies remain at issue, the image of intersecting systems must be complemented by criteria which may be used to identify societies. Giddens mentions four criteria in this regard. The first criterion refers to structural principles and institutional 'clusters'. As Giddens indicates, structural principles provide the most basic identifying feature of societies, and for this reason they must be discussed in some detail. Before doing so, however, it is worthwhile to comment briefly on three other identifying criteria. As will be evident, these criteria are quite loosely defined. Indeed, they reflect Giddens's view that what a 'society' is, admits no easy answer once unitary accounts of clearly delimited societal systems are set aside (*CS*, p. 250). Because societies are so difficult to define, Giddens stresses that they apply differentially in diverse empirical contexts (*CS*, p. 165, and the example presented on pp. 165–8).

Two of the criteria refer to societal locales. On the one hand, societies as social systems generally are associated with a specific territory of occupation. However, this need not imply that the territory must be 'fixed'. Not only is it possible that the frontiers of societies may be poorly defined as was the case prior to the era of the modern nation-state, but in the case of nomadic tribes it also is possible that societies may circulate across a territory rather than establishing an institutionalised settlement of some kind. On the other hand, societies may also be identified by normative claims to the legitimate occupation of the territory. Such claims are subject to dispute, and the modes of legitimation can be expected to vary between different societies (e.g. religious beliefs, rights of conquest, national myths, etc.).

The third criterion involves a substantial, albeit subtle alteration of conventional views of societies as cultural communities. Instead of referring to feelings of solidarity or acknowledgements of common interest, Giddens proposes that societies may be identified by an awareness of a *community of identity* among agents. Identity here denotes, at a minimum, nothing more than a formal association with the doings of other agents, which may be experienced or expressed tacitly as an aspect of the routine relations among social agents, or discursively in conversation or in formally established ceremonies (for example, rituals of citizenship in the modern nation-state, religious rituals in earlier forms of society). It also should be noted that the criterion of community of identity does not turn upon legal or politically imposed definitions. By refraining from references to solidarity, interest, or political/legal status, Giddens explicitly leaves open the question of whether members of a given society regard their societal identity as right and proper. The range of groups whose members may regard their societal identity with some degree of detachment includes refugees from war or famine, political exiles, indigenous religious, ethnic, or political minority groups, etc. Obviously, none of these groups necessarily share all of the same values, or commitments to goals, with other members of the societal community of identity.

Structural principles: ontological or historical?

As indicated above, structural principles serve to identify societies with reference to the 'clustering of institutions', which is their most basic feature from a structural point of view. The reason for using the term 'clustering of institutions' is that it admits substantial variations in the degree to which the chronically reproduced activities and relations that constitute societal totalities are systemically articulated and organised. However, it is more appropriate to speak of clusterings rather than a single cluster of institutions here. This is because, according to Giddens (*CS*, p. 276), structural principles actually refer to the factors involved in the overall institutional alignment of a specific society, or a categorical type of society. As will be evident in the discussion of societal types to be presented below, the overall alignment of institutions Giddens has in mind generally involves not one, but rather two distinct clusterings of activities and relations.

Of all the concepts in structuration theory, structural principles, and the related concept of structural contradiction which will be considered in due course, are the most difficult to expound in ontological terms. By an ontological conception of structural principles I mean a concept which ascribes priority to a given set of structural factors or properties which are to be of fundamental importance in the institutional alignment of societies of all kinds. Comte's (1893, vol. 1, p. 12) contention that all social mechanisms rest upon ideas which originate in philosophical systems, and Marx's (1970, pp. 20–21) briefly developed claim that the relations of production comprise the foundational structure which conditions the general processes of social, political, and intellectual life, provide useful examples in this regard.

From the standpoint of structuration theory, there are at least two problems that preclude the development of an ontological conception of structural principles. The first problem derives from the status of the social ontology set forth in structuration theory. As I indicated at length in Chapter 1, the hallmark of the structurationist ontology is an abiding respect for the human potential to generate historically specific variations in the constitution of social life, and a corresponding renunciation of concepts which impose theoretical restrictions upon the substantive analysis of the constitution of social life in historically specific domains. An ontological conception of structural principles would be thoroughly inconsistent with this point of view. To be sure, in hands of sophisticated theorists such as Comte and Marx, the postulation of a single set of factors that is fundamentally implicated in the organisation of societies of all kinds can admit a substantial degree of historical variation. Nevertheless, the conceptual priorities established through the postulation of these factors implicitly serve as theoretical restraints on the kinds of variation that may be proposed. For instance, Marx could not accept Comte's account of the centrality of theological ideas to the organisation of tribal societies, and conversely Comte could not accept Marx's account of the centrality of the exploitation of the proletariat by the bourgeoisie to the organisation of capitalist societies. Structuration theory, however, is prepared to accept that because tribal societies and capitalist societies differ so radically from one another, they may incorporate institutional alignments that cannot be subsumed under a single category of structural principles that is ontologically defined.

The second problem with ontological definition of structural principles arises in so far as most proposals of this kind ascribe priority to a given category of factors which are held to be generically fundamental to the evolution of societies. If nothing else, concentrating on a single category of factors across all types of societies permits evolutionary theorists to rank different societies in terms of their state or stage of evolutionary growth. In addition, the factors by which all forms of societies are defined are often held to be directly related to the mechanism through which evolutionary transitions are produced.

Giddens has no objection to ranking societies with reference to developmental criteria of various kinds (*CS*, p. 232). He accepts, for example, that societies may be compared in terms of their differentiation (*CS*, p. 323), their time–space distanciation (*CCHM*, p. 157), or their energy consumption (*CS*, p. 232). He also accepts the claim that certain technical developments or forms of social organisation may be prerequisites for others. But he refuses to employ any of these criteria as the basis for a theory of the institutional alignment in any and all societies. The most fundamental problem with the evolutionary mechanism and trajectories such rankings presume is empirical rather than theoretical. According to Giddens: 'Human history can be done serious harm by compressing it into one' (*CS*, p. 236; for a discussion of the kinds of harm that can be done, see *CS*, pp. 236–43).

The point is immediately relevant to the study of structural principles. As Giddens suggests (*CS*, pp. 238–9), contrary to evolutionary theory the pattern of the historical development of the human species at large is punctuated by discontinuities in societal forms. This is especially apparent when modern societies are contrasted with their historical predecessors. For example, no matter what set of factors evolutionary theorists may employ to define societal units of analysis, if one takes a prospective view of history based upon knowledge of the institutional alignment of European societies in, say, the latter part of the fourteenth century, it is almost impossible to foresee or deduce the radically different type of society that has been developed since the advent of capitalism and the nation-state. To employ an ontologically generic definition of structural principles appears in this light as an exceedingly difficult, and ultimately futile endeavour. Rather, if there are substantial discontinuities in historical types of societies, then theorists must be free to identify substantial differences in the structural principles, the alignment of institutions (or institutional clusters) between these disparate societal types.

Structural principles and societal types

The broadest possible application of the concept of structural principles, and the application which is most well-developed in Giddens's works, occurs with reference to the substantive analysis of categorically defined types of society. Drawing upon a wide array of historical studies, Giddens incorporates accounts of structural principles in a non-evolutionary typology of three forms of society: tribal, class-divided, and class societies (*CCHM*, p. 159; *CS*, pp. 181–2). These societal types, which will be introduced below, do not directly refer to individual societies. Rather each type is very broadly defined, and each allows considerable leeway for the specification of sub-categories. The structural principle which serves to identify each societal type is broadly defined to a similar extent. Hence the institutional alignment to which each principle refers covers a range of historical instances which may differ considerably from one empirical instance to the next. It should be kept in mind here that structural principles represent analytically abstract summaries of the properties of the most fundamental clusters of institutional activities and relations through which the reproduction of societies occurs. As I shall try to make clear during the following remarks, in reality these clusters of activities and relations are more or less well-organised and articulated across time and space.

Of the three basic societal types, tribal societies alone incorporate a structural principle abstracted exclusively from practices and relations conducted on a face-to-face basis. This is because, as indicated in Chapter 4, tribal societies were coordinated and controlled primarily through homeostatic modes of system reproduction. In keeping with established anthropological research, but in opposition to Marxist views on the centrality of material production and the control of allocative resources, Giddens proposes that the *structural principle of tribal societies involves the alignment of a kinship-based system of social relations with traditional modes of practice and belief.* The distinctive qualities of Giddens's formulation of this structural principle occur in his emphasis upon two points which effectively undermine the significance of tribal societies in evolutionary schemes of societal development. First, as opposed to evolutionary theories which accentuate the simplicity and lack of differentiation in tribal societies, Giddens stresses that kin networks may be exceedingly dense and complex, and that traditional practices may incorporate highly sophisticated linguistic codes, traditional rituals and art forms (*CCHM*, pp. 160–62; also 92–4; *CS*, p. 241). Second, as opposed to evolutionary theories which treat tribal societies as a 'stage' in societal development, Giddens observes that humankind has lived out most of its history on earth in tribal groupings (*CS*, p. 182). It also should be noted that the link between kinship and tradition established in the structural principle of tribal societies, by no means leaves political control and normative sanctions out of account, nor does it deny the transaction of various forms of trade. But these activities are conceived as embedded in the institutional structuration of kin-relations and traditional ways of life.

Class-divided societies, Giddens's second categorical type, occur in a variety of forms which range from city-states to agrarian empires to feudal systems. Giddens (*CCHM*, p. 108) uses the term 'class-divided' to indicate that while classes based upon the ownership of land may be found in these societies, their structural principles cannot be abstracted from the relations between dominant and subordinate classes. Rather, the most distinctive features of societal organisation hinge upon attempts (which appear rudimentary by modern standards) to develop centres of administrative power based in cities, which become, in effect, territorial 'power-containers'. However, while administered systems based upon modes of social integration can be established within cities, the absence of rapid and efficient modes of system integration forestalls the effective organisation of social activities beyond city walls. Whatever degree of administrative control is achieved in the hinterlands depends upon the application of military force. For the most part this force is insufficient to alter and reconfigure traditional practices and kinship-based systems institutionalised in communities in the hinterlands. *Hence, the structural principle in class-divided societies occurs in the loose alignment between the structured reciprocities involved in city-based domination and the structured forms of traditional ways of life in rural communities* (*CCHM*, pp. 162–4). The emphasis upon a loose alignment in this structural principle illustrates quite well why Giddens insists that the extension and 'closure' of societies across time and space must be regarded as problematic.

As previously mentioned, no proposal is more fundamental to Giddens's substantive writings than the claim that the structural principle characteristic of class society, his third categorical type, differ dramatically from the structural principles of class-divided or tribal societies (see *CCHM*, pp. 121–8, 157–66, 210–13; *NSV*, pp. 63–71, 134–7). For present purposes it will be sufficient to establish what this structural principle involves. Class society takes its name from the institutionalisation of modern capitalist economic systems. Within the manifold set of practices and relations which constitute modern capitalism, Giddens singles out the labour-contract between capitalists and workers as of fundamental importance to the structural principle of class societies. This, of course, sustains Marx's emphasis upon exploitative class relations, but there is something more involved in Giddens's formulation. A fundamental aspect of the labour-contract (as well as the institutionalisation of 'private property') is that the coordination and control of allocative resources and labour-power is reserved for the capitalist class, while the coordination and control of other institutionalised aspects of social life, including the legitimated control of the organised means of violence (i.e. the military and police forces) is reserved for the systemic activities of the nation-state. Thus the *structural principle of class society denotes the alignment between two massive, multi-systemic institutional 'clusters': capitalism and the nation-state*. This structural principle clearly moves beyond Marx, in so far as the state is conceived to be directly implicated in the overall organisation of modern capitalist societal systems, albeit in a manner that 'insulates' the capitalist sphere from direct control by the state, and 'insulates' the state from direct control by capitalist agents (*CCHM*, pp. 164–6).

Levels of abstraction in the structural analysis of societies

It must be underscored here that even within the brackets of institutional analysis the structural properties of societies cannot be conceived on the basis of structural principles alone. Indeed, it is fully consistent with Giddens's denial that societies comprise unitary or coherent systems that, at least with regard to class-divided and class societies, the systems which are aligned according to their respective structural principles may be more cohesively articulated and better organised than societal systems themselves. To facilitate the analysis of the more detailed structural properties of systems, Giddens specifies three levels of analytical abstraction which appear in descending order as: structural principles, structural sets, elements/axes of structuration (*CS*, pp. 188–90; *CCHM*, pp. 54–5). *Structural sets* may be conceived as either structures or institutional orders. In either case they may be defined in terms of conversion relations between rules and resources in the manner which was indicated earlier in this chapter. The study of structural sets is directly implied in the analysis of structural principles, in the sense that the institutional clusters aligned according to a structural principle may each be represented analytically as a structural set: for example, the capitalist economy in class societies, the city-based political order in class-divided societies. *Elements or axes of structuration* move to a lower level of analytical abstraction by focusing attention upon the structural properties (rules and resources) implicated in institutionalised activities which generally are reproduced in spatio-temporal delimited settings through modes of social integration (activities in circumstances of co-presence). Thus in the study of capitalism, an axis of structuration is formed by the structural properties of activities undertaken in a given type of manufacturing enterprise, while in class-divided societies an axis of structuration is formed by the structural properties of traditional ways of life carried out in a specific kind of rural community.

Although Giddens does not indicate as much, it seems far easier to analyse societies by proceeding from structural principles to lower levels of abstraction, than to proceed from the lower-level axes and structural sets to structural principles. One problem here is that any given axis or structural set may not reveal the overall societal alignment between institutional 'clusters', except in the case of homogeneous tribal societies. Another problem is that the lower-level axes and structural sets may manifest a great deal of variation without compromising the overall structural principle of a societal type. Thus, on the level of axes of structuration in class societies one may find capitalist enterprises in which relations between managers and workers are structured via union contracts, others in which relations are structured on the basis of individual contracts, and still others, especially in non-Western societies, in which paternalistic relations between capitalists and workers may be found. Similarly, the conversion of state-controlled authorita-tive resources into policing power may be far more important in some class societies (e.g. South Africa, Chile) than in others (e.g. Great Britain, Sweden). The conceptual point these examples bring to light is that in the analysis of structure the 'parts', i.e. axes or structural sets, never incorporate all aspects of the larger societal system (cf. *CCHM*, pp. 44–5).

Contradiction

Since societies are not conceived as unitary collectivities in struc-turation theory, to identify their fundamental institutional align-ments in terms of structural principles need not imply that they are structurally integrated systems in the sense that a compatibility exists between all institutionalised activities and relations. Well before Giddens published his first works on structuration theory, he already expressed strong reservations regarding the assumption of integration (expressed as 'consensus') which informs the works of theorists such as Comte, Durkheim, and Parsons (*SSPT*, pp. 223–4, 341ff). As opposed to these who would emphasise societal integration, Giddens sets forth a complex account of societal contradictions. One reason for the complexity of this account is that he deals with contradiction in two different forms: existential contradiction and structural contradiction. It is consistent with Giddens's emphasis upon discontinuities between historical types of society that these two forms of contradiction ultimately must be defined in substantive terms. However, before distinguishing these forms, and dealing with them from a substantive point of view, the generic idea of contradiction itself must be clarified.

All references to contradiction in social theory must begin by acknowledging the influence of Marx. However, while Giddens's views on contradiction are inspired by Marx, and while he does not disavow Marx's analysis of contradictions in the capitalist mode of production, his extended commentaries on the generic conceptions of contradiction employed by Marx and his successors make clear that he rejects the historical materialist implications of the term (*CPST*, pp. 130–45; *CCHM*, pp. 230–9). This rejection is a corollary of Giddens's opposition to the evolutionary trajectory of history which is associated with the way Marx employs contradictions in the development of his forces/relations of production scheme:

> I do not wish to question – and I accept as a basic theorem – the Marxian position that contradiction underlies the possibility of progressive movement in history ... But I do propose to interject also a concept of *system degeneration*: in other words, if we accept in full the contingency of history, we have to accept the possibility that contradiction can underlie or stimulate retrograde movements of historical change. (*CPST*, pp. 142–3)

The contingencies of contradictions with regard to social change involve a series of issues that will be addressed in subsequent remarks. For the moment, the point to be made is that by freeing himself from the historical materialist view of contradiction, Giddens establishes an opportunity to reconsider how the concept should be defined. As previously mentioned, Giddens ultimately distinguishes two kinds of contradiction. Since this is the case, the only way to speak of contradiction in generic terms is to define it as a logical relation which admits diverse conceptual interpretations. In the logical sense, contradiction appears as a definite relation between incompatible and irreconcilable sets of conditions. By virtue of the fact that incompatible sets of conditions are conjoined there will always be some tendency for the two to negate, subvert, or undermine one another. This tendency implies that if either set of conditions (counterfactually) could completely overtake the other it would mean that the other would be completely abolished. This much is evident in Giddens's writings. However, I believe that one further implication of defining the logical form assumed by all contradictions should also be drawn out. In my view, because contradiction implies an antagonistic relation between incompatible and irreconcilable sets of conditions, contradictions of all kinds always are expressed as tensions in at least some aspects of the position-practices or position-practices relations through which societal systems are organised and reproduced. These tensions, however, may be dealt with by agents in historically contingent ways. Thus, the organisation and reproduction of societal systems may be stabilised for greater or lesser historical intervals where accommodations to contradictory tensions are established and maintained. Conversely, where accommodations are not reached, contradictions may generate tensions which destabilize societal systems, thereby contributing to the likelihood that conflict and change may occur. (There will be more to say on this point below.)

Existential contradiction

Although existential contradiction is most directly implicated in the structuring of tribal societies, it fundamentally pertains to the generic relation between human social life on the one hand, and the material/organic aspects of the human condition on the other. The existential contradiction may be summarised by saying that human life is both predicated upon nature, yet it does not conform entirely to the natural order, and therefore is set off against it (cf. *CPST*, pp. 161–2; *CCHM*, pp. 236–7; *CS*, p. 193). Thus, on the one hand, human beings as *homo sapiens* both are a natural species and must deal in some way with the irrevocable rhythms and unavoidable conditions of the material and biological foundations of human life. On the other hand, human beings as participants in social life engage in activities which are not naturally preordained. References to the existential contradiction refer to the fact that at least some of these activities will encounter naturally ordained limits which cannot be surpassed. This is true regardless of whether one adopts a materialist or an idealist position. Even the most modern forms of material technology, for example, must deal with the fact that the regularities of the physical and chemical constitution of the natural order are not inherently designed to accommodate human plans. By the same token, any attempt to confer 'meaning' upon natural circumstances and events ultimately encounters imponderable 'mysteries', questions for which the natural order *per se* supplies no answers.

Giddens's account of the existential contradiction is fundamentally inconsistent with the instrumental view of nature, assumed by Marx and many non-Marxists alike, which emphasises the human capacity to intervene in and exploit the natural environment (see *CCHM*, pp. 59–60, 245). Without gainsaying modern advances in the technological harnessing of natural regularities to suit human ends, the existential contradiction means that certain natural rhythms are beyond human control. Giddens favours the example of the biologically established finitude of human existence. Whether or not, as Giddens suggests (*CPST*, p. 161), the finitude of human beings set off against the apparent infinity of nature in time–space stands at the heart of all religions, it is true that birth, death, and the somatic vulnerability of humans to illness and aging always are mediated in social life by institutionalised frames of meaning which presume that there are limits to the extent to which the biological conditions of human life can be bent to human ends. This is, perhaps, why Giddens speaks with qualified approval of suggestions that a 'search for meaning' may be centrally involved in supplying a basis for a philosophical anthropology of human culture (*CCHM*, p. 156).

But if the existential contradiction applies to human social life at large, its consequences do not intrude to the same extent into the structuring of all types of society. In Giddens's view the influence of the existential contradiction is particularly evident in the structural principle of tribal society. Assuming a position which he explicitly contrasts with evolutionary theories of environmental adaptation (*CCHM*, p. 237; *CS*, p. 194), Giddens proposes that tribal societies, precisely because they engage in direct and, for the most part, technologically unmediated relations with nature make a distinctive accommodation with nature through mutually acknowledged symbolic modes of representation and moral codes. These accommodations ultimately are bound up in mythic 'world views' in which homologies are established between contrasting categories of natural and social aspects of human existence. In this way the rhythms of nature and social life are interwoven in the traditions and kin-networks which serve to structure the (homeostatic) organisation and reproduction of tribal systems. One need not subscribe to 'primitivist' doctrine (*CCHM*, p. 251) to appreciate this point. Even staunch advocates of the virtues of modernity must accept that the moral and cognitive proximity to nature in tribal societies is unparalleled in contemporary modes of social organisation.

Structural contradiction

Whereas existential contradiction stems from inconsistencies in the conjunction of the natural and social aspects of human existence, structural contradiction occurs through inconsistencies in the institutional alignments of societal systems. Structural contradictions are structural in the sense that the inconsistencies to which they refer are conceived analytically as chronically reproduced properties of societies. As will be indicated in the following section, any given societal system may incorporate two kinds of structural contradiction: primary and secondary. Primary contradictions, i.e. those which enter into the constitution of societal totalities (*CS*, p. 193), will be at issue in the present remarks.

Giddens's generic definition of structural contradictions is clear and consistent throughout his writings. However, this definition introduces a certain amount of confusion which must be dealt with from the start. Giddens explicitly wishes to absorb into his conception of structural contradiction Marx's notion that such contradictions manifest immanent forms of order stimulated by an existing one (*CPST*, p. 136). This is not a teleological notion: i.e. Giddens proposes that immanent forms of order are contingent possibilities rather than necessary developments. But to entertain this notion Giddens defines structural contradictions as oppositions, or contradictory alignments between *two* structural principles in the organisation of societal systems (*NRSM*, p. 125; *CPST*, p. 141; *CCHM*, p. 231; *CS*, pp.˙ 193, 372). That is, societies, or types of society, in which (primary) structural contradictions exist involve an intrinsic interrelationship between two 'clusters' or spheres of institutionalised activities, each of which only exists in virtue of its relation to the other, yet each of which tends to undermine or subvert its counterpart.

Now the problem with this definition of structural contradiction does not involve the contradictory relation in the alignments between institutional spheres in societal systems. It is, rather, that Giddens defines each of those institutional spheres as organised in terms of a separate and distinct structural principle. As much as this preserves the notion that alternative forms of social order may be immanent in an existing society, this definition suggests that societies *qua* systems are not organised in terms of a single structural principle of their own. However, Giddens elsewhere fails to honour this point. He speaks, for example, of the *dominant* structural principle of class-divided societies as interrelating urban areas (city-based administrations) to their rural hinterlands (tradition-bound communities), and of the *distinctive* structural principle of class societies of modern capitalism as involving the disembodying, yet interconnecting, of state and economic institutions (*CS*, pp. 182–3). Giddens's formulations here propose that each of these types of societies is organised according to a *single* structural principle. So the question is: should societies be said to be institutionally aligned in terms of a single structural principle, or in terms of two structural principles? And if the first option is preferred what then becomes of structural contradiction? In my judgement it makes sense to speak of societies, or societal types, with reference to a single structural principle. This is because, despite all contradictions, societies or categorical types of society remain at least loosely organised as systems themselves. Indeed, if societies were *not* organised according to single structural principle the intrinsic relation between institutional spheres or 'clusters' which oppose one another would not make sense. Instead it would be possible to suggest that this alignment involved only a *contingent* relation: for example, a contingent relation between the capitalist institutional order and the state in class societies. It is my view, then, that *a structural principle may, in itself, denote the existence of a structural contradiction*. But to adopt this view in no way denies that this contradiction manifests an immanent social order stimulated by the order which presently exists. The latter point may be preserved by regarding each of the institutional clusters or spheres as an institutional order, one of which may include conditions (i.e. structured activities and relations) which might serve as the basis for the development of new forms of society.

Structural contradictions and societal types

In order to illustrate the association between structural principles and structural contradictions, which I have set forth above in abstract, conceptual terms, it is useful at this point to turn to Giddens's categorical typification of class-divided and class societies. It will be recalled that the structural principle in class-divided societies involves the institutionalised connection between the city as an administrative 'power container', and the hinterland communities which are loosely articulated with the city via the imposition of military force. It is immediately apparent that this relation simultaneously denotes both a type of societal organisa-tion, and a structural contradiction as well:

> In class-divided societies [structural – IJC] contradiction is located in the city–countryside relation. Agrarian states involve an antagonistic fusion of two modes of social organisation, the rural community on the one hand, and the city-based institu-tions on the other. Structural contradiction here is not strictly 'economic', and sustains ties with the existential contradiction of tribal societies. (*CCHM*, p. 137; see also *CS*, p. 196)

The structural principle of class-divided societies involves a structural contradiction by virtue of the intrinsic alignment between the city-based administrative sphere and the ways of life in rural communities. Rural communities sustain ties to the existential contradiction in so far as their agricultural and social routines still conform to traditions geared into natural conditions and the rhythms of natural events. In the city, however, the exercise of administrative power involves quite different forms of institutionalised conduct organised to serve the purposes of upper-level rulers and officials. The alignment between city and countryside occurs in so far as each institutional sphere is, to some extent, dependent upon the other. Thus, the city-based administrative order imposes itself militarily upon rural communities both in order to extract material goods ('surplus') and in order to maintain the territorial perimeters of its dominion, while the rural communities come to anticipate that city-based rulers will provide military protection from potential invaders, and material support in times of shortage. This alignment is contradictory, however, because city-based institutions, if generalised to the countryside, would subvert traditional ways of life, and conversely, traditional ways of life, if generalised, would undermine the institutional activities through which power is exercised by city-based officials.

Class societies differ, *inter alia*, from class-divided societies in that neither of the institutional spheres aligned according to the dominant structural principle involves tradition-bound acknowledgements of the existential contradiction. This is because capitalism, with its novel and disruptive commodification of time, space, and labour-power, and its reliance upon industrial production techniques, presumes a thoroughly instrumental relation with the natural circumstances of the human condition (cf. *CCHM*, p. 238; *NSV*, pp. 312–13). This instrumental relation is never entirely without significant consequences, as modern ecological social movements remind us today. Nevertheless, neither capitalism, nor the modern nation-state with which it is aligned in class societies, associate their respective modes of the administration of social activities and relations to the underlying natural order.

The structural principle of class societies involves the disembedding, yet interconnecting, of capitalistic economic institutions and the institutional order of the modern nation-state. Once again this structural principle directly involves a structural contradiction. Focusing upon how this contradiction appears from the standpoint of the nation-state, Giddens describes it in the following terms:

The primary contradiction of the capitalist (nation)-state is to be found in the modes in which a 'private' sphere of 'civil society' [i.e. the realm in which capitalist accumulation occurs, as

Giddens makes clear in adjacent remarks – IJC] is created by, but is separate from and in tension with, the 'public' sphere of the state . . . The contradiction between civil society and state [is] at least roughly parallel to the classical formulation of the capitalist contradiction between 'private appropriation' and 'socialized production'. The capitalist state as a socializing centre representing the power of the community at large, is dependent upon mechanisms of production and reproduction which it helps bring into being but which are set off and antagonistic to it. (*CS*, p. 197; see also pp. 315–16)

Primary contradiction, secondary contradiction

To understand the distinction between primary contradiction and secondary contradiction a loose geological analogy may be drawn. Just as in geology a primary 'fault line' between tectonic plates may lead to secondary 'fault lines', so too primary structural contradictions in a societal system may lead to secondary structural contradictions between institutional spheres. A distinctive feature of secondary contradictions as structural 'fault lines' in societies, however, is that they may involve institutional spheres which are 'internal' to societal systems, or they may involve institutional spheres which cross-cut societies by virtue of their articulation with inter-societal systems (*CPST*, p. 145; *CCHM*, p. 232; *CS*, p. 193). Another distinctive feature of secondary contradictions is that they may converge with (i.e. operate to compound the tensions generated by) primary contradictions, or they may diverge from (i.e. operate so as to dissipate the tension generated by) primary contradictions.

Given these two kinds of variation, the connections between primary and secondary contradictions always involve historical contingencies. But Giddens provides a clear-cut illustration of a secondary contradiction in his account of capitalistic class societies (*CPST*, p. 143; *CS*, pp. 197–8). Here the primary contradiction between the sphere of capitalistic control of 'private property' and the 'public sphere' of the state is associated with a secondary contradiction between the internationalisation of markets and enterprises to form a capitalist world-economy, and the simultaneous consolidation of nation-states, which results, in part, from the formation of a global state system and an international military order (see *NSV*, ch. 10). This example serves as yet another reminder of the non-unitary nature of societies in structuration theory. It suggests that any major change in the capitalist world-economy (e.g. the migration of capital, international business cycles) may generate tensions which state administrators must 'manage' in some way. Conversely, any major change in international relations (from military affairs, to 'trade wars' between states) may generate tensions which impinge upon the activities of capitalist firms and markets which operate within the administrative purview of given states. Frequently, of course, changes in both the capitalist world-economy and international relations may occur simultaneously, and interact in highly complex ways. Secondary contradictions also may be discerned *within* the structural alignment of societies. A well-known example here would be the inconsistency between formal legal codes enforced by the state which define and prescribe equal rights for all citizens, and the substantive inequalities of class which are a concomitant of the control of private property in the capitalist institutional order.

Contradiction, conflict, and the duality of structure

Throughout Giddens's writings the concept of structural contradiction is both distinguished from, and then contingently related to, social conflict (*CPST*, p. 131; *CCHM*, p. 232; *CS*, p. 198; see also *NRSM*, p. 125; *SSPT*, pp. 127–8; and the qualification in *CPST*, p. 276, n. 23). The distinction between the two turns upon a matter of definition in so far as contradiction is defined in structural terms – i.e. as conditions of societal reproduction conceived within the brackets of institutional analysis – while conflict is defined as confrontation or struggle in the conduct of activity – i.e. as practices carried out *in situ* by agents either as individuals, as aggregates, or in organised groups. Having said this, however, Giddens also observes that while the existence of contradictions in no way guarantees that conflicts must occur, and while conflicts may occur which are not immediately associated with contradictions, structural contradictions and outbreaks of conflict do tend to coincide. While this coincidence is fully consistent with the duality of structure, it poses an issue that differs substantially from the way Giddens typically frames his discussions of the latter concept. Whereas the duality of structure more often is represented with reference to the tacit reproduction of routine forms of *praxis* which draw upon and regenerate institutionalised structural conditions of action, here the contradictory structural conditions of action are linked to conflictual activities which, in general, are disruptive of established routines.

Two related questions arise at this point: first, how are structural contradictions implicated in outbreaks of conflict? second, what circumstances forestall or delimit the likelihood that contradictions will provoke social conflict? The answer to the second question clearly depends upon the answer to the first. However, I do not believe that the way Giddens deals with the first question is acceptable as it stands. The closest he comes to establishing a link in the duality of structure between contradiction and conflict is in his reformulation of insights into perverse effects which originate in the works of Jon Elster (1978) and Raymond Boudon (1982). Structural contradictions, in this sense, establish conditions of action that lead to unintended consequences of a multiplicity of acts which diminish the likelihood that the objectives actors pursue in these acts will be achieved. These 'perverse outcomes' are likely to generate resentments, and thereby create opportunities for struggles to mobilise. This line of thought is quite plausible as far as it goes, but Giddens recognises that it is by no means a generic link between contradiction and conflict: on the one hand, contradiction may *not* lead to 'perverse consequences' in many situations; on the other hand, perverse consequences may not stimulate conflict (*CS*, p. 317; and, more generally, pp. 310–19; see also *CPST*, pp. 139–41).

At this juncture it might be expected that Giddens would provide at least a programmatic, generalised link between contradiction and conflict conceived from the standpoint of the duality of structure. However, instead of doing so he relies on a claim which involves an association between contradiction and agents' interests. From this vantage point, the reason why contradiction and conflict tend to coincide is that: 'contradictions tend to involve divisions of interest between different groupings or categories of people (including classes but not limited to them)' (*CS*, p. 198; see also pp. 317–18). The problem with this insight extends beyond Giddens's failure to address the link between contradictory structural conditions and outbreaks of conflict. As indicated in Chapter 5 with regard to exploitation, a more fundamental difficulty is that the concept of interest is a meta-theoretical term when such interests are not acknowledged by social agents: i.e. interests need not exist in the minds of actors in order to be imputed to them by social theorists (Giddens acknowledges that such is the case in a footnote to one central discussion of the connections between contradiction, interest, and conflict. See *CCHM*, p. 282, n. 5.)

Now, as is the case with regard to exploitation, in so far as actors recognise the interests imputed to them by social analysts there is no problem in accepting that structural contradictions are associated with divisions of interest which may lead to conflict. But considered as a generic, conceptual link between contradiction and conflict, references to interests which actors do not acknowledge simply will not do, because unacknowledged interests imputed to agents by theorists simply do not exist as salient aspects in the reality of social life. Theoretical representations of unacknowledged interests are, by definition, counterfactual proposals. Hence, at best, the conceptual sequence which moves from structural contradiction to interests to conflict is incomplete. What is required, I believe, is a more secure conception of the link between contradictions, conditions of action, and the likelihood that actors will recognise that their interests lie in conflict rather than adhering to routine, institutionalised modes of conduct.

My references to tensions stimulated by contradictory structural alignments earlier in this chapter anticipate an account of the reason why contradiction and conflict tend to coincide. The most basic insight here is that contradictions always involve oppositions between interrelated institutional spheres. While accommodations can be achieved for certain historical periods, there is an inherent tendency not only for 'perverse outcomes' to occur, but also for other kinds of instability in the reproduction of societal systems. In class-divided societies, for example, the amount of resources required by city-based rulers can be expected to fluctuate depending upon political and military vicissitudes of various kinds. Coercive extraction of taxes, rents, and tributes etc., therefore also will vary. While these variations may occur in different ways in different class-divided societies, the general point is that because of these variations, the relations between city-based administrative activities and rural communities ultimately will be unstable and tense. Similarly, in class societies the contradictory alignment of the capitalistic 'private sphere' and the 'public sphere' of the state may generate instabilities including recurrent cycles of inflation and recession, which can result from capitalistic business cycles (managed through Keynesian policies instituted by state agencies), or from state expenditures (e.g. on military forces) which throw the business cycle into expansion or decline.

Marxist and like-minded theorists may wonder why the link I wish to draw between structural contradiction and social conflict involves instabilities and tensions in the conditions of action rather than exploitation or oppression. In the first instance this is because exploitation and oppression sometimes can be institutionalised and organised in stable routines which may be reproduced, with only a minimum of conflict, for considerably historical periods. In such situations agents may become sufficiently accustomed to their established ways of life that they come to take them for granted. But where agents experience instabilities in their routinised activities and social relations, the 'givenness' of social life is necessarily disrupted. These disruptions are experienced as insecurities or anxieties, and these psychic tensions can lead agents to develop an interest in participation in conflict, or to be 'mobilised' for participation in organised movements which engage in conflict. Of course, disruptions of established routines fostered by structural contradictions generally will provoke the most insecurity among those who are most exploited and oppressed. But in certain situations, even politically or economically dominant groupings of agents may be moved to engage in conflict as the result of contradiction-induced disruptions. This was, for example, clearly the case in the pre-revolutionary periods studied by Theda Skocpol in *States and Social Revolutions* (1979). As Skocpol demonstrates, contradictions involved in the alignment between aristocracies engaged in international military affairs and the propertied classes which extracted material support for these aristocracies, led to a disruption of routine relations between these groups. These disruptions, in turn, led members of the propertied classes to doubt the reliability of the aristocratic rulers, and to engage in conflict by withdrawing their support. This disruption of upper-level activities and relations, subsequently, created further disruptions in the conditions of action in exploited and oppressed groups who thereby became candidates for mobilisation in revolutionary movements.

The foregoing depiction of the link between contradiction and conflict could be expanded in greater detail by tracing out the manner in which instabilities generated by contradictions disrupts the reproduction of position-practices and position-practice relations. However, enough has been said to establish the manner in which contradiction may lead to conflict through the duality of structure. Given this point, it must be re-emphasised here that the link between contradiction and conflict always involves historical contingencies from the standpoint of structuration theory. Hence it is necessary now to consider circumstances that may dissipate the likelihood that conflict induced by contradiction will occur. Giddens proposes three circumstances in this regard (*CS*, pp. 318–19; *CPST*, pp. 144–5), and I shall deal with them *seriatim*.

The first circumstance, the imposition, or the threat to impose, direct repression, is both obvious and widely employed. Yet it also is frequently overlooked. Direct repression hinges upon the control of the means of violence by administrators or rulers committed to maintaining the established order in a societal system. Direct repression is a generic technique, and it is in no way tied to the suppression of conflicts stemming from structural contradiction. Indeed Giddens's example of the repression of potentially profound conflict in South Africa (*CS*, p. 319) does not appear to turn upon contradictions inherent in class society, since a white socialist regime might still institutionalise many practices of oppression associated with *apartheid*. Nevertheless, the incidence of conflict associated with contradiction undoubtedly is diminished whatever agents prone to conflict must consider the likelihood of the physical harm to themselves that may result from their actions.

Giddens's second circumstance, the dispersal of contradictions, is the only suppressor of conflict that is directly tied to contradiction *per se*. The dispersal of contradictions refers to the degree to which primary and secondary contradictions are disengaged from one another, as opposed to circumstances in which multiple contradictions coincide. For example, in a class-divided society the primary contradiction between city-based administrative power and tradition-bound rural communities may be cross-cut by rural actors' devotion in practice and belief to a religious system (e.g. the Roman Catholic church) which maintains institutionalised relations with state officials, but ultimately extends across societal. bounds. Church–state relations here can be regarded as a secondary contradiction which may be partially disengaged from its primary counterpart. Hence, if tensions develop in city–hinterland relations, say on the basis of an increase in taxation demands, this need not be accompanied by changes in church–state relations. Conversely, city–hinterland relations may remain stable while tensions develop between state rulers and church officials. The overall result of this dispersal of contradictions may be to create a balance between tension and stability which reduces the number of agents who are willing to engage in conflict. However, were these contradictions to converge so that tensions in city–hinterland relations are associated with tensions in church–state relations, then the likelihood of large-scale conflict would increase.

The 'opacity' of action is the final circumstance Giddens cites which inhibits the likelihood that conflict will occur. Giddens's remarks here closely parallel his account of ideology (*CPST*, p. 144), and, like the latter, the 'opacity' of action refers to the suppression of actors' recognition of theoretically imputed interests, except that in this case the further inference is drawn that if actors acknowledged these interests they would be more inclined to engage in conflict against groupings of agents who are committed to preserve and defend the status quo.

As I have previously suggested, the theoretical imputation of unacknowledged interests poses problems that remain to be solved in structuration theory. However, the imputation of such interests may be less problematic in certain instances where the 'opacity' of action is linked to conditions stemming from structural contradictions, than in many other situations. The instances I have in mind occur when the structural contradictions lead to the disruption of established routines: for instance, when the administered organisation of state activities breaks down in class-divided societies, or when a capitalist depression occurs in class societies. In these circumstances the fact that agents whose day-to-day activities have been disrupted already experience tension and anxiety may be assumed to provoke their interest in restructuring the systemic conditions that led to this disruption. But this interest can only be provoked *providing* agents have an adequate understanding of how the system works. The 'opacity' of action here refers to the ideological aspects of symbolic modes of discourse and normative legitimating codes which have the effect of obscuring agents' awareness of the contradictions inherent in the societal system that ultimately led to the disruptions in their lives. It is noteworthy that interests in societal restructuring may develop and be shared by many agents even when ideology has these effects. For example, in so far as ideology disposes agents to accept the sectional interests of the dominant powers-that-be as their own, one possible result of disruption generated through contradictions may be that agents will be inclined to support the plans promulgated by dominant leaders to restore the routine operation of the societal system. In addition, as Giddens observes, the disruption of routines in 'critical situations' may create dispositions among agents to invest their loyalty and trust in charismatic leaders who propagate and manipulate symbols in a demagogic manner. Charismatic leaders, of course, may establish conflict-oriented social movements designed to bring about societal change. But, as is illustrated by the charismatic leadership of Franklin Delano Roosevelt in the United States during the 'Great Depression' (see Willner, 1984, pp. 111–17 *passim*), charismatic leaders may also exploit prevailing symbols and legitimating codes to preserve the confidence of followers in the viability of a contradictory system.

Societal change: a conjunctural approach

The preceding discussion of the contingent relation between contradiction and conflict already suggests that structural contradictions are fundamentally important in so far as they establish conditions which, in certain situations, may contribute to the development of large-scale episodes of societal change. Yet it would be to misunderstand Giddens's position on societal change (i.e. transitions from one type of society to another) to concentrate exclusively on his view of contradictions. To the contrary, Giddens actually upholds a conjunctural view of change; a view which emphasises that historical variations in several different kinds of circumstances may intersect and interact to influence the production of differing forms and outcomes of societal transitions (cf. *CS*, p. 245).

One of the foremost reasons why Giddens adopts a conjunctural approach is to forestall the kinds of 'endogenous' theorising that leads social scientists committed to evolutionary analyses of change to concentrate exclusively on mechanisms or factors 'internal' to societies. 'Endogenous' theories of change have deep-seated origins in the works of classical evolutionists such as Comte, Spencer, Durkheim, and Marx. However, in recent years a contrasting emphasis upon 'exogenous' factors implicated in societal change has been advanced, most notably in Immanuel Wallerstein's all-encompassing organic conception of world-systems, and also in Robert Nisbet's less programmatic stress upon the effects of 'external' tensions and instabilities. Giddens's conjunctural approach to change denies the efficacy of 'endogenous' accounts. But at the same time he also believes that 'exogenous' accounts of the conditions implicated in change overstate their case (see *CPST*, pp. 222–6; *CCHM*, pp. 166–7; *NSV*, pp. 161–71). The conjunctures of conditions he has in mind always involve both 'endogenous' and 'exogenous' circumstances. Structural contradictions represent the most fundamental 'endogenous' factor involved in these conjunctures. The 'exogenous factors' he has emphasised to date include *inter-societal systems*, *time–space edges*, and *world-time*. Each of these concepts requires clarification.

Turning first to *inter-societal systems*, it is rather easy to see that even if two societies were to be 'internally' identical in all relevant aspects, substantially different conditions for change might exist based upon both their respective intersections with inter-societal systems and their time–space distantiation *vis-à-vis* other societies in the context of inter-societal systems. The notion of time–space distantiation is particularly important in non-modern (i.e. tribal and class-divided) societies where rapid and effective means of system integration across time and space did not yet exist. Inter-societal systems in these circumstances were relatively fragmentary by comparison with their modern counterparts (to which the term 'world-system' is truly appropriate for the first time in history; *CS*, pp. 184–5). Thus, societies at great distance from one another rarely were in position to exercise a direct influence on their respective forms of change.

In discussing the role of inter-societal systems in fostering change in non-modern societies, Giddens lays particular stress upon contact between societies of different types, i.e. societies aligned according to diverse types of structural principles. Such contacts involve what Giddens terms *time–space edges* (*CCHM*, pp. 23, 83, 167–9; *CS*, pp. 164, 244). Time–space edges should not be equated with zones of diffusion, i.e. the gradual transfer of institutions from societies of one type to societies of another (see *CCHM*, p. 166). They rather involve tensions and instabilities which may induce societal change in historically contingent ways depending, *inter alia*, on the nature of relations between the societies involved. In the most dramatic, but not infrequent, situations, time–space edges may involve warfare, invasion, or threats of attack of various kinds. Even when attacks do not materialise, the mobilisation of forces may induce societal change. Time–space edges also may involve relations of inter-dependence through military alliances, trade, and in more recent times the establishment of capitalist facilities for the extraction of resources and/or the manufacture of commodities in tribal or class-divided societies. The novel institutions and systems thereby introduced may destabilise established routines, and thereby establish conditions in which episodic transitions from one type of society to another may occur in a manner less violent than war or invasion, but no less effective in the long run.

One consequence of the formation of the modern world-system has been the formation of time–space edges which have led to the impending demise of non-modern societal types (*CCHM*, pp. 168–9). However, here again, conjunctures between societies and the modern world-system are sufficiently complex to foster different kinds of change. This is not only because of the positioning of societies in the capitalist world-economy as Wallerstein suggests. In his substantive writings Giddens expresses strong objections to the economic reductionism at the centre of Wallerstein's account. The modern world-system, if it is to be spoken of as a single system at all, not only is unevenly developed, but is highly disaggregated as well. In addition to the world capitalist economy, Giddens suggests that a world military order, a global state system, and a world information order must be taken into account (*NSV*, pp. 167–71, 276–7, ch. 10 *passim*). Thus even if a group of societies may be subject to similar structural conditions *vis-à-vis* the world capitalist economy, they may be subject to dissimilar conditions *vis-à-vis* any or all of the other three world-systemic orders. Given these conditions, episodes of change may be far more diverse than Wallerstein's monolithic model of the capitalist world economy would suggest.

Among factors included in Giddens's conjunctural view of change, readers are likely to be least familiar with the notion of *world-time*. Giddens adopts this term from the works of Wolfram Eberhard (*CCHM*, pp. 24, 167; *CS*, p. 251; see also Eberhard, 1965, pp. 13ff). Eberhard uses the concept 'world-time' to establish the resolutely non-evolutionary idea that even apparently similar sequences of processes and events leading to change may have dissimilar implications and effects. The so-called 'leapfrog' idea of change can be used to illustrate the point (see *CPST*, pp. 229–30). The leapfrog effect occurs when a society which is 'advanced' at one point in time may be superseded by an initially 'less advanced' society which undergoes change at a later date. In such cases the timing of societal change appears to influence the nature and extent of development when similar kinds of transition occur. Another way to consider the influence of world-time is by noting that dissimilar sequences of change may yield broadly similar results. For example, while France and Great Britain presently share roughly similar forms of parliamentary-democratic governments, and capitalist economies which are similar in many basic respects, they arrived at these similar institutional orders in different ways and at different times.

Obviously world-time itself is a notion that stands in place for a variety of historically more specific conjunctions of circumstances and events. The old saying that timing *per se* does not account for change continues to apply. But, expanding upon Eberhard, Giddens proposes that one fundamental factor involved in the influence of world-time is that leaders of social movements, and others who institute change, can and do monitor the nature and history of change in other societies. This knowledge, Giddens observes, may be used to avoid errors committed in the past (*CPST*, p. 230), and, of course, it may also be used to adopt those changes that have proven to be worthwhile. This 'historicity' of change (*CS*, pp. 203, 374) is most evident in the modern world where administered systems are specifically designed to make use of information of all kinds which is relevant to leaders' policies and plans. However, Giddens argues that the 'historicity' of change is in no sense confined to modernity. To buttress this claim he notes that there is much evidence indicating that agents in supposedly 'primitive' societies have known a great deal about 'superior' civilisations, and have used this knowledge to resist incorporation within them (*CCHM*, pp. 22–3).

Structuration theory and historical sociology

As opposed to theories that embody an evolutionary trajectory and accentuate a trans-historical mechanism of social change, Giddens's conjunctural approach exhibits an unqualified appreciation for the complex permutations of conditions, and the varying responses of agents to these conditions that serve to distinguish one sequence of change from another. Since both the course and outcomes of change are regarded, in principle, as subject to so many circumstantial variations, from the standpoint of structuration theory the only viable accounts of change are those which are limited to historically specified circumstances and processes.

Does this emphasis upon historical specificity entail a demand for straightforward idiographic research? This most definitely is not the case if by idiographic research is meant a chronologically organised narrative of historical events. Substantive theory and general concepts have a more significant role to play in the organisation of empirical accounts than those committed to narrative historical methods recognise or allow. This is especially the case in so far as the structural conditions of change must be taken into account (see *CS*, pp. 359–60). Narrative historians typically accentuate the doings of agents. But in doing so they underplay the role of the duality of structure. The influence of structural contradictions, the positioning of societies in intersocietal systems, and other structural circumstances, at one and the same time foster instabilities and tensions which provoke actors into the activities and projects through which change occurs, and establish a range of enablements (i.e. practical possibilities for change) as well as a range of constraints which together may not determine the course of change, but nevertheless shape that course to a significant extent. Since it cannot be presumed that the agents whose *praxis* serves to bring change about recognise and acknowledge all of these structural conditions, theories and concepts developed by social scientists on a second-order basis play a necessary part in organising the analysis of change.

Structuration theory also does not necessarily entail an idiographic view of historical change where idiographic history denotes an exclusive concern for individual 'case studies'. Generalisations based upon comparative historical inquiries are very much in order provided that the difficulties inherent in comparative analysis are taken into account. As is evident, for example, in Barrington Moore's (1966) influential study of the origins of dictatorship and democracy, the differences between sequences of change which share broad similarities may be as salient as the conditions which these instances share in common. Having said this, the 'grand questions' at issue in historical sociology today (for example, the origins of capitalism, the modern nation-state, and the various dimensions of the modern world-system) clearly require generalisations which transcend the limitations of idiographic research. Although I shall not recapitulate the details here, an example of how the concepts in structuration theory may be applied to the development of historical generalisations appears in the analysis of the anthropological origins of states Giddens sets forth in *The Constitution of Society* (pp. 244–56).

Before concluding, there is one essential point to be made regarding historical sociology. In the works of evolutionary theorists, as indeed in the works of many historians, history itself is equated with change. This equation is repudiated in structuration theory (*CPST*, pp. 7–8). It must not be overlooked that the structural conditions that influence the course and outcome of even the most massive instances of change are themselves properties of institutionalised systems which were reproduced many times over in the preceding era. Of equal importance, as I have indicated in earlier chapters, no transitional change, regardless of how epoch-making it may be, sweeps away all of the institutional forms of *praxis* carried out in the past. The analysis of stable and highly routinised activities and systemic relations therefore is as much at issue in historical analysis as the circumstances and events through which change is brought about.

8
Closing Remarks: Beyond Ontology

In the introduction to this book I said that my efforts would be directed to the clarification and explication of the ontology of social life initiated in Giddens's writings on structuration theory. That task is now complete. But it would be misleading to leave the impression that structuration theory itself should be regarded as a fully-developed project. Giddens has given no indication that the concepts and insights which presently are incorporated in the structurationist ontology are complete as they stand. Moreover, the reception of these concepts and insights by well-informed critics leaves many issues unaddressed and others on which much remains to be said. It should be noted that Giddens harbours no illusions that his ontological lines of thought somehow will be immune from criticism. Indeed, he regards persistent disagreement about the nature of human conduct as integral not only to social theory, but to social life at large (*CPST*, p. 239).

But the present account of structuration theory also leaves many issues open that extend beyond the realm of ontology *per se*, and in these closing remarks I would like to indicate the nature of these issues, and say something about how they might be developed in the future. The issues I have in mind pertain to the implications of the ontology of structuration theory for social research and critical theory. Giddens has been sensitive to these issues throughout his writings on structuration theory. In fact, while each of his major works on structuration theory centres upon conceptual themes, Giddens reserves one chapter in each for a discussion of the nature and applications of the knowledge which social scientists produce (*NRSM*, ch. 4; *CPST*, ch. 7; *CS*, ch. 6). The chapter in *The Constitution of Society* is particularly important, not only because it represents the most fully-developed exposition of Giddens's views to date, but also because it incorporates commentaries upon a series of empirical studies designed to illustrate the utility of concepts in structuration theory for social research.

I shall not attempt a comprehensive examination of the nature and implications of Giddens's ideas on social research and critical theory here. The problem is not that there is little to say. To the contrary, my first essay on structuration theory was devoted to these issues (Cohen, 1984), and I am well aware that many topics in this area remain to be explored. The problem is, rather, that to develop these issues to the same extent as I have dealt with structuration theory's ontological concepts would require a volume of approximately the same length as the present work. I shall indicate below some of the purposes I believe such a volume should serve, and how it might be organised to these ends. In lieu of a full-scale discussion at this point, I shall address my remarks to three programmatic issues in the development of structuration theory beyond the ontological realm. These issues are: (i) the question of whether structuration theory can serve as the basis of a research programme; (ii) the development of the implications of the ontology of structuration theory for social research; (iii) the development of critical theory in light of Giddens's reflections on the nature and significance of the double hermeneutic.

The question of whether or not structuration theory can serve as the basis for a research programme is particularly relevant, since during the course of Chapter 1 I drew upon views of Kuhn, Lakatos, and other post-positivist philosophers of science in order to establish the status of structuration theory as an ontology of potentials. In Kuhn's notion of 'paradigms' and Lakatos's image of 'research programmes', ontological postulates serve as one basis for the formation of a community of investigators. Members of a community devoted to a programme of research draw upon these postulates, in conjunction with a range of methodological practices and with an eye toward exemplary studies, to develop and pursue an agenda of themes which, when successful, leads to the cumulative growth of a body of knowledge. Ultimately this body of knowledge may be consolidated into scientific theory in its conventional form, i.e. layers of generalisations which are supported and connected by logical inferences and empirical findings.

In all likelihood, structuration theory will not serve as the basis for a research programme of this kind. There are two reasons why this should be so; one is practical, the other is a matter of principle. In practical terms, the formation of a research programme typically requires a concerted effort to attract students and scholars into a scientific community – for example, through the establishment of a research centre, the promotion of conferences, the creation of a journal dedicated to the advancement of the research programme, etc. However, neither Giddens nor anyone else has undertaken the tasks required to develop structuration theory in this way.

But the more important point here is that, in principle, structuration theory does not easily lend itself to the cumulative development of social scientific knowledge. Giddens (*STMS*, pp. 42–4) has expressed serious reservations about the kind of theory construction that occurs, among other occasions, when the body of knowledge in research programmes is consolidated into a coherent form. The fundamental problem here reverts to issues regarding generalisations discussed in Chapter 1. Theory construction, as I indicated above, typically involves multiple levels of generalisations. At the apex of these levels the generalisations involved apply to an indefinite range of circumstantially distinguishable cases, which is to say that they refer to universal or trans-historical regularities. But as I have argued at some length (see pp. 18–26), the principle of the uniformity of nature which is presupposed in the pursuit of trans-historical regularities is considered inapplicable to social life from the standpoint of structuration theory. This is because the potential for the alteration of established regularities is conceived in structuration theory as an ineradicable potential of the exercise of agency in social life, albeit a potential which may remain open to a lesser or greater extent. Since the *praxis* through which agency is exercised potentially may serve to alter the articulation, organisation, and structural properties of systems, there can be no trans-historical regularities in these aspects of social life as well. In principle, then, all generalisations in the social sciences must be delimited with reference to historically and spatio-temporally circumscribed domains. Research programmes designed to culminate in trans-historical generalisations therefore appear out of the question (see *CS*, pp. 343–7).

But as I indicated at the close of Chapter 7, if structuration theory does not lend itself to the development of a scientific programme of research, it is well-suited to inform the kinds of substantive studies pursued by historical sociologists today. That is to say, research projects informed by structuration theory are more likely to be driven by investigator's substantive themes, and their concern for social life in a given set of historical circumstances, rather than by the advancement of social scientific knowledge at large. This in no way implies a disregard for historically bounded regularities, nor does it rule out cumulative research projects within historically delimited domains of inquiry. In addition, as is evident in Giddens's own substantive writings on modernity, questions of a considerable historical scale, which have been at issue in the social sciences since the classical era, are quite consistent with the principles of structuration theory. But it bears repeating that no matter how historically far-reaching social research may be, it is set in motion by the investigator's thematic concerns with the subject-matter at hand. This is why Giddens ('Comments', p. 77) insists that the historically oriented research programme envisaged in his substantive writings cannot be directly inferred from the concepts he develops in his writings on structuration theory.

The second issue in the development of structuration theory beyond ontology that I wish to address, involves the bearings of structuration theory for the production of social research, the selection of themes and the analysis of data. Any ontology of social life implies a set of heuristic guidelines for the kinds of themes that are consistent with its principles, and the kinds of themes that are inconsistent as well. For example, it should be evident at this point that studies which attribute teleological powers of coordination and control to collectivities, or a trans-historical trajectory or teleology to the course of human history, are unacceptable in research informed by structuration theory. Conversely, presuming appropriate brackets are invoked (i.e. the brackets involved in the analysis of strategic conduct, systems analysis, and institutional analysis), structuration theory both approves of, and has much to offer to, historical investigations of day-to-day *praxis*, the articulation of systems across time and space, and the structural properties of systems. Diverse forms of data produced by 'qualitative' and 'quantitative' research techniques may be usefully employed on different levels of analysis. But, given the historical orientation of research informed by the ontology of structuration theory, the most significant studies frequently will integrate different levels of analysis, thereby combining 'qualitative' and 'quantitative' methods of research. Indeed, given the emphasis upon *praxis* performed by knowledgeable agents, all studies consistent with the principles of structuration theory, even those conducted within the brackets of systems analysis or institutional analysis, necessarily must include some insights into the practical understanding agents maintain with regard to their own conduct and the conduct of others, and how they make sense of the social circumstances in which that conduct occurs (cf. *CS*, pp. 333–4).

Much of the chapter on social research in *The Constitution of Society* is devoted to issues such as those touched upon above. Still it is fair to say that much work remains to be done before structuration theory has as much relevance for researchers as it presently does for theorists. In my view, now that most of the basic concepts regarding the constitution of social life have been established, nothing would do more to persuade researchers of the virtues of structuration theory than a book devoted exclusively to their concerns. Nigel Thrift (1985, p. 621) proposes that a book of this kind should be developed as an empirical research project, and that its purpose should be to show how structuration theory can be used as a basis for challenging existing interpretations of historical events. While I agree with Thrift that a book on the implications of structuration theory for social research should incorporate pieces of research that illustrate its capacity to inspire original themes and insights, I also think that the project should be developed in a somewhat different way from that which he suggests.

Thrift's proposal amounts to a call for a 'demonstration project', such as Durkheim developed in *Suicide*, although Durkheim, of course, pursued other objectives in that book as well. However, Durkheim did not spell out his views on research-oriented issues in *Suicide*, preferring instead to develop them in *Rules of Sociological Method*. The kind of work I believe structuration theory needs, which might involve a collaboration between Giddens and someone whose career has been devoted to the conduct of research, would integrate general guidelines for research derived from the ontology of structuration theory with a series of empirical studies. Ideally all studies would focus on different elements of the same historical theme. But the reason why a series of studies is required is that the guidelines for research in structuration theory can be expected to vary depending upon which level of analysis is involved and the methodological brackets appropriate to that level. The culmination of the study would involve the consolidation of findings from all levels of analysis, and a demonstration of the capacity of structuration theory to stimulate inquiries which challenge prevailing points of view on the thematic topic in question.

The third, and final, issue I wish to discuss involves the elaboration of structuration theory with regard to the development of critical theory and empirical critique. Here, again, Giddens already has made inroads into the problems involved. This is nowhere more evident than in the development of his thoughts on the double hermeneutic. As I have previously indicated, according to the double hermeneutic all social theory and research ultimately must take account of lay actors' knowledge and beliefs, while the insights and findings of social theory and research conversely have direct implications of a practical and critical nature for the same lay implications and beliefs they take into account. These practical and critical implications arise because social scientific knowledge always departs from lay knowledge in a variety of ways, which, depending on the study, may involve redescriptions of institutionalised practices and events in ethnographic works, as well as far-ranging second-order analyses of systems articulated and organised across time and space, and the structural properties of these systems. Giddens makes the same point in the following terms·

[T]he development of theoretical ⁓
cialization demanded ⸀⸀
social life ens⸀⸀⸀
merge⸀
:

for further discussion of the double hermeneutic, see *CS*, pp. 334–43, 348–54)

The implications of social scientific knowledge cannot be confined to social critique alone. As Giddens (*STMS*, p. 21) observes, it is in the nature of organisations in modern social life to rely heavily upon information of various kinds (see above, Chapter 5). In this regard the practical applications of social scientific knowledge are as profound as they are inescapable. Theories of bureaucracy, statecraft, and the capitalist system infiltrate and influence the practices of the powerful in numerous ways, and statistical studies conducted by social scientists do so to an even greater extent.

But the practical connotations of social scientific knowledge take a more critical turn when they challenge and undermine the commonsense beliefs which underlie lay agents' mutual knowledge of the nature and consequences of their own conduct and social relations. Giddens has begun to examine the connection between mutual knowledge and commonsense beliefs, and the critical role social scientific knowledge can play in fostering new points of view (see again, *CS*, pp. 234–43; and Cohen, 1984). But the development of the critical implications of structuration theory must be worked out in other areas as well. One problem, to which I already have referred (see above, pp. 188–93) is the imputation of unacknowledged interests to social actors, without which the concepts of exploitation and ideology, which are highly relevant to critical theory, remain incomplete. As matters stand in Giddens's writings, the empirical status of such imputations remains unsecured.

The status of unacknowledged interests, however, is part of a more global problem in critical theory at large regarding the grounds on which social agents are likely to accept social scientific insights that challenge their beliefs. One option available to Giddens in this regard would be to join hands with Habermas's efforts to anchor the reception of critical theory in the liberating potentials of human discourse. However, Giddens has expressed serious reservations concerning the 'linguistic turn' in Habermas's works (*STMS*, pp. 244–7), and there are no indications in his own writings that he intends to develop lines of thought in critical theory that are consistent with the implications of Habermas's approach. To the contrary, instead of pursuing a secure basis for critical theory, in linguistic potentials or anywhere else, Giddens insists that critical theory must be stripped of all guarantees, and that a more appropriate way to proceed is to identify the contingent opportunities and tendencies that exist in historically specific settings. This, in turn, is connected to his call for the development of counterfactual utopias:

> What we should envisage is . . . a process of critique that does not recoil from connecting material possibilities of social reform with an utopian element . . . All social analysis . . . is implicitly social critique and also has transformative implications for whatever it describes. These provide the 'grounding' of critical theory, but do not in and of themselves indicate how immanent possibilities in a given set of circumstances can be actualized, or what connections that actualization might bear to more inclusive goals. The 'utopian moments' of critical theory are necessary where what is immanent does not disclose a practical means of researching those more inclusive goals. (*NSV*, p. 337)

Giddens's approach to critical theory 'without guarantees' has much to commend it for future development. It may lack the philosophical appeal of Habermas's alternative, but it brings us closer to questions concerned with how viable critiques can be produced. Still there is an area of critical theory that remains unaddressed in Giddens's work, namely how the 'more inclusive goals' to which he refers in the preceding passage are to be identified. Whether or not Habermas's works yield a practicable solution to this problem, he clearly has recognised that the determination of the goals for social change, or at least the nature of the dialogue through which these goals are determined, is a matter of no small importance to the grounding of critical theory and the way it will be received by lay agents. Unless one set of goals can command assent from those who would bring about social change, as well as those who are expected to benefit from the changes involved, social reform and reconstruction can result in the substitution of one set of inequities and iniquities for another as easily as it can result in a set of social arrangements more satisfactory to those involved than the present state of affairs. The dilemma not only for Giddens but for the prospects of critical theory at large, is that, while diagnoses of the oppressive and ominous problems of our time – including the unprecedented potential for nuclear annihilation – are in no short supply, and while proposals exist to check oppression and forestall these dangers, no one has advanced more positive goals that might attract widespread support for social reform and reconstruction. Whether or not Giddens can do so remains to be seen. To date, the only inklings of his thoughts in this area appear in his brief references to the need for a philosophical anthropology to complement structuration theory (see Livesay, 1985, for a comparison between Habermas and Giddens in this regard.)

It is, I believe, a sign of the fertility of structuration theory that many issues remain to be addressed. The most significant contributions to social theory always leave as many unsettled issues as those which they explicitly confront. But in saying this it is important not to lose sight of what Giddens already has accomplished. When Giddens entitled his first work on structuration theory *New Rules of Sociological Method*, his objective to reconstruct the foundations of social theory clearly was uppermost in his mind. The title invites comparison to Durkheim's classic work only in an ironic sense; for Giddens clearly meant to establish a set of concepts far removed from Durkheim's account of 'social facts' (cf. *NRSM*, p. 159). It should be evident by now that in structuration theory there are no 'social facts' *sui generis*. Social agents, through their *praxis*, make 'social facts', albeit they make them in circumstances they inherit from the past. Fifteen years ago this insight seemed incidental to the concerns of most social theorists. *New Rules* was one of the very first works to bring the production of social life as it occurs in social *praxis* into the centre of theoretical discourse. Thus it is, in some measure, a mark of Giddens's accomplishments that today even theorists who are committed to positions at some distance from structuration theory, and with whom Giddens would be inclined to disagree, now assume that the production of social life must be regarded as one of the central problems in the discipline(e.g. Alexander, Giesen, Münch and Smelser, 1987, Coleman, 1986).

Throughout his writings Giddens has sought not simply to overturn the classical inheritance of theorists such as Durkheim, but to renew the ambitions that informed their works as well. It is fitting, then, to close this book by proposing that for all of

Giddens's many departures from Durkheim on conceptual matters, they ultimately share an objective in common. At the turn of the century, in *Rules of Sociological Method*, Durkheim advanced a proposition that many social scientists in subsequent generations have been inclined to ignore:

> Before beginning the search for the method appropriate to the study of 'social facts' it is important to know what are the facts termed 'social'. (Durkheim, 1982, p. 50)

If Durkheim's reference to the facts termed 'social' is properly understood, he is proposing that the very first order of business in social theory should be to entertain questions regarding the ontological qualities of social life; the qualities, that is, of the subject-matter which is the common concern of all social scientists. Giddens, I believe, at least implicitly recognises the wisdom in Durkheim's proposal. His writings on structuration theory, in effect, reinvigorate Durkheim's classical ambition, while simultaneously providing a new point of departure. Perhaps, in an era when new points of departure are very much in order, this may be judged no small accomplishment indeed.

Bibliography

Alexander, J. C. (1984) 'Social-Structural Analysis: Some Notes on Its History and Prospects', *The Sociological Quarterly*, 25 (1), pp. 5–26.

Alexander, J. C. (1985) 'Introduction', in *Neo-Functionalism*, ed. J. C. Alexander, Beverly Hills, Sage Publications, pp. 7–18.

Alexander, J. C., Giesen, B., Münch, R. and Smelser, N. J. (1987) *The Micro-Macro Link*, Berkeley, University of California Press.

Alford, R. R. and Friedland, R. (1985) *Powers of Theory: Capitalism, the State, and Democracy*, Cambridge, England, Cambridge University Press.

Althusser, L. (1970) *For Marx*, trans. B. Brewster, New York: Vintage.

Archer, M. S. (1982) 'Structuration versus Morphogenesis: On Combining Structure and Action', *British Journal of Sociology*, 33 (4), pp. 445–83.

Barnes, J. A. (1979) 'Network Analysis: Orienting Notion, Rigorous Technique, or Substantive Field of Study?', in *Perspectives in Social Network Research*, eds P. W. Holland and S. Leinhardt, New York, Academic Press, pp. 403–23.

Bershady, H. (1973) *Ideology and Social Knowledge*, Oxford, Basil Blackwell.

Bhaskar, R. (1978) *A Realist Theory of Science*, Sussex, Harvester.

Bhaskar, R. (1979) *The Possibility of Naturalism: A Philosophical Critique of the Contemporary Human Sciences*, Atlantic Highlands, Humanities Press.

Bhaskar, R. (1983) 'Beef, Structure and Place: Notes from a Critical Naturalist Perspective', *Journal for the Theory of Social Behavior*, 13, pp. 81–95.

Blau, P. M. (1974) 'Parameters of Social Structure', *American Sociological Review*, 39 (5), pp. 615–35.

Blau, P. M. (1975) 'Parallels and Contrasts in Structural Inquiry', in *Approaches to the Study of Social Structure*, ed. P. Blau, London, Open Books, pp. 1–20.

Blau, P. M. (1977a) *Inequality and Heterogeneity: A Primitive Theory of Social Structure*, New York, Free Press.

Blau, P. M. (1977b) 'A Macrosociological Theory of Social Structure', *American Journal of Sociology*, 83 (1), pp. 26–54.

Blau, P. M. (1981) 'Diverse Views of Social Structure and Their Common Denominator', in *Continuities in Structural Inquiry*, eds P. M. Blau and R. K. Merton, Beverly Hills, Sage Publications, pp. 1–23.

Blau, P. M. (1982) 'Structural Sociology and Network Analysis: An Overview', in *Social Structure and Network Analysis*, eds P. Marsden and N. Lin, Beverly Hills, Sage Publications, pp. 273–9.

Blumer, H. (1969) *Symbolic Interactionism: Perspectives and Method*, Englewood Cliffs, Prentice-Hall.

Boorman, S. A. and White, H. C. (1976) 'Social Structure From Multiple Networks: Part II: Role Structures', *American Journal of Sociology*, 81 (6), pp. 1384–446.

Boudon, R. (1971) *The Uses of Structuration*, trans. M. Vaughn, London, Heinemann.

Boudon, R. (1982) *The Unintended Consequences of Social Action*, London, Macmillan.

Buckley, W. (1967) *Sociology and Modern Systems Theory*, Englewood Cliffs, Prentice-Hall.

Burawoy, M. (1979) *Manufacturing Consent: Changes in the Labor Process under Monopoly Capitalism*, Chicago, University of Chicago Press.

Burt, R. S. (1980) 'Models of Network Structure', *Annual Review of Sociology*, 6, pp. 79–141.

Burt, R. S. (1982) *Toward A Structural Theory of Action: Network Models of Stratification, Perception, and Action*, New York, Academic Press.

Buttell, F. H. (1987) 'New Directions in Environmental Sociology', *Annual Review of Sociology*, 13, pp. 465–88.

Callinicos, A. (1985) 'Anthony Giddens', *Theory and Society*, 14 (2), pp. 133–66.

Camic, C. (1987) 'The Making of a Method: A Historical Reinterpretation of the Early Parsons', *American Sociological Review*, 52 (4), pp. 421–39.

Campbell, C. (1982) 'A Dubious Distinction? An Inquiry into the Value and Use of Merton's Concept of Manifest and Latent Function', *American Sociological Review*, 47 (1), pp. 29–44.

Carlstein, T. (1980) *Time, Resources, Society and Ecology*, Lund, Department of Geography.

Carlstein, T. (1981) 'The Sociology of Structuration in Time and Space: A Time-Geographic Assessment of Giddens's Theory', *Svensk Geografisk Arsbok*, 57, pp. 41–57.

Catton, W. R. and Dunlop, R. E. (1978a) 'Environmental Sociology: A New Paradigm', *The American Sociologist*, 13, pp. 41–9.

Catton, W. R. and Dunlop, R. E. (1978b) 'Paradigms, Theories, and the Primacy of the HEP–NEP Distinction', *The American Sociologist*, 13, pp. 256–9.

Cicourel, A. V. (1964) *Method and Measurement in Sociology*, New York, Free Press.

Cohen, G. A. (1979) *Karl Marx's Theory of History: A Defense*,

Princeton, Princeton University Press.

Cohen, G. A. (1982) 'Reply to Elster', *Theory and Society*, 11 (4), pp. 483–95.

Cohen, I. J. (1981) 'Max Weber on Modern Western Capitalism: Introduction to the Transaction Edition', in *General Economic History*, M. Weber, New Brunswick, Transaction Press, pp. xv–lxxxiii.

Cohen, I. J. (1984) 'Participant Observation and Professional Sociology: Transposing and Transforming Descriptions of Everyday Life', *Current Perspectives in Social Theory*, 5, pp. 71–100.

Cohen, I. J. (1985) 'The Underemphasis Upon Democracy in Marx and Weber', in *A Weber–Marx Dialogue*, eds R. J. Antonio and R. M. Glassman, Lawrence, University of Kansas Press, pp. 274–99.

Cohen, I. J. (1986) 'The Status of Structuration Theory: A Reply to McLennan', *Theory, Culture & Society*, 3 (1), pp. 123–34.

Cohen, J., Hazelrigg, L. E. and Pope, W. (1975) 'DeParsonizing Weber: A Critique of Parson's Interpretation of Weber's Sociology', *American Sociological Review*, 40 (2), pp. 229–41.

Coleman, J. S. (1986) 'Social Theory, Social Research, and a Theory of Action', *American Journal of Sociology*, 91 (6), pp. 1309–35.

Collins, R. (1981a) 'Micro-translation as a Theory-building Strategy', in *Advances in Social Theory and Methodology: Towards an Integration of Micro- and Macro- Sociologies*, eds K. Knorr-Cetina and A. V. Cicourel, London, Routledge & Kegan Paul, pp. 81–108.

Collins, R. (1981b) 'The Micro-Foundations of Macro-Sociology', *American Journal of Sociology*, 86 (5), pp. 984–1014.

Collins, R. (1986) 'Is 1980s Sociology in the Doldrums?', *American Journal of Sociology*, 91 (6), pp. 1336–55.

Comte, A. (1893) *Positivist Philosophy*, ed. and trans. H. Martineaus, 2 vols, London, Routledge & Kegan Paul.

Coser, L. A. (1981) 'Review of *Central Problems in Social Theory* by A. Giddens', *American Journal of Sociology*, 86 (6), pp. 1435–6.

Dickie-Clark, H. F. (1984) 'Anthony Giddens's Theory of Structuration', *Canadian Journal of Political and Social Theory*, 8 (1–2), pp. 92–110.

DiTomaso, N. (1982) '"Sociological Reductionism" From Parsons to Althusser: Linking Action and Structure in Social Theory', *American Sociological Review*, 47 (2), pp. 14–28.

Durkheim, E. (1982) *The Rules of Sociological Method and Selected Texts on Sociology and its Method*, ed. S. Lukes, trans. W. D. Halls, London, Macmillan, and New York, Free Press.

Durkheim, E. (1984) *The Division of Labour in Society*, trans. W. D. Hall, London, Macmillan, and New York, Free Press.

Eberhard, W. (1968) *Conquerers and Rulers*, Leiden, Brill.

Elster, J. (1978) *Logic and Society: Contradictions and Possible Worlds*, New York, Wiley.

Faia, M. A. (1986) *Dynamic Functionalism: Strategy and Tactics*, Cambridge, Cambridge University Press.

Foucault, M. (1980) *Power/Knowledge: Selected Interviews and Writings 1972–77*, ed. C. Gordon, New York, Pantheon.

Frisby, D. and Sayer, D. (1986) *Society*, New York, Tavistock.

Gane, M. (1983) 'Anthony Giddens and the Crisis of Social Theory', *Economy and Society*, 12 (4), pp. 368–98.

Garfinkel, H. (1967) *Studies in Ethnomethodology*, Englewood Cliffs, Prentice-Hall.

Garfinkel, H. and Sacks, H. (1970) 'On Formal Structures of Practical Actions', in *Theoretical Sociology*, eds J. C. McKinney and E. A. Tiryakin, New York, Appleton-Century-Crofts, pp. 326–38.

Goffman, E. (1959) *The Presentation of Self in Everyday Life*, Garden City, Doubleday Anchor.

Gouldner, A. (1959) 'Reciprocity and Autonomy in Functional Theory', in *Symposium on Sociological Theory*, ed. L. Gross, Evanston, Row, Peterson & Co., pp. 241–70.

Gouldner, A. (1960) 'The Norm of Reciprocity: A Preliminary Statement', *American Sociological Review*, 25, pp. 161–79.

Granovetter, M. S. (1973) 'The Strength of Weak Ties', *American Journal of Sociology*, 78 (6), pp. 1360–80.

Granovetter, M. S. (1979) 'The Theory-Gap in Social Network Analysis', in *Perspectives on Social Network Research*, eds P. W. Holland and S. Leinhardt, New York, Academic Press, pp. 501–18.

Gregory, D. and Urry, J. (eds) (1985) *Social Relations and Spatial Structures*, London, Macmillan, and New York, St Martin's Press.

Habermas, J. (1984) *The Theory of Communicative Action: Volume One: Reason and the Rationalization of Society*, trans. T. McCarthy, Boston, Beacon.

Habermas, J. (1987) *The Theory of Communicative Action: Volume Two: Lifeworld and Systems: A Critique of Functionalist Reason*, trans. T. McCarthy, Boston, Beacon.

Hägerstrand, T. (1970) 'What About People in Regional Science?', *Papers of the Regional Science Association*, 24, pp. 7–21.

Hägerstrand, T. (1975) 'Space, Time, and Human Conditions', in *Dynamic Allocation of Urban Space*, eds A. Karlquist, L. Lundquist and F. Snickars, Farnborough, Saxon House, pp. 3–14.

Haines, V. (1985) 'From Organist to Relational Human Ecology', *Sociological Theory*, 3 (1), pp. 65–74.

Hanson, N. (1969) *Perception and Discovery: An Introduction to Scientific Inquiry*, San Francisco, Freeman, Cooper & Co.

Hempel, C. G. (1965) 'The Logic of Functionalist Analysis', in *Aspects of Scientific Explanation*, C. G. Hempel, New York, Free Press, pp. 297–330.

Heritage, J. (1984) *Garfinkel and Ethnomethodology*, Cambridge, England, Polity Press.

Hochschild, A. R. (1983) *The Managed Heart: Commercialization of Human Feeling*, Berkeley, University of California Press.

Holland, P. W. and Leinhardt, S. (1979) 'The Advanced Research Symposium on Social Networks', in *Perspectives on Social Network Research*, eds P. W. Holland and S. Leinhardt, New York, Academic Press, pp. 1–10.

Homans, G. C. (1974) *Social Behavior: Its Elementary Forms*, 2nd edn, New York, Harcourt Brace Jovanovich.

Kiessling, B. (1988) *Kritik der Giddensschen Sozialtheorie: Ein Beitrag zur Theoretisch-methodischen Grundlegung der Sozialwissenschaften*, Frankfurt, Peter Lang.

Kuhn, T. S. (1970) *The Structure of Scientific Revolutions*, 2nd edn, Chicago, University of Chicago Press.

Lakatos, I. (1978) *The Methodology of Scientific Research Programmes*, 2 vols, Cambridge, Cambridge University Press.

Landes, D. S. (1983) *Revolution in Time: Clocks and the Making of the Modern World*, Cambridge, MA, Harvard University Press.

Laudan, L. (1977) *Progress and its Problems: Towards a Theory of Scientific Growth*, Berkeley, University of California Press.

Laumann, E. W. (1973) *Bonds of Pluralism: The Form and Substance of Urban Social Networks*, New York, Wiley Press.

Laumann, E. W. (1979) 'Network Analysis in Large Social Systems: Some Theoretical and Methodological Problems', in *Perspectives on Social Network Research*, eds P. W. Holland and S. Leinhardt, New York, Academic Press, pp. 379–423.

Lawrence, P. R. and Lorsch, J. W. (1969) *Developing Organizations: Diagnosis and Action*, Reading, Mass., Addison-Wesley.

Layder, D. (1981) *Structure, Interaction and Social Theory*, London, Routledge & Kegan Paul.

Layder, D. (1985) 'Power, Structure, and Agency', *Journal for the Theory of Social Behavior*, 15 (2), pp. 131–49.

Leach, E. R. (1954) *Political Systems of Highland Burma: A Study of Kachin Social Structure*, Boston, Beacon.

Levine, D. N. (1981) 'Sociology's Quest for the Classics: The Case of Simmel', in *The Future of the Sociological Classics*, ed. B. Rhea, London, George Allen & Unwin, pp. 60–80.

Levine, D. W., Carter, E. and Gorman, E. M. (1976) 'Simmel's Influence on American Sociology. I', *American Journal of Sociology*, 81 (4), pp. 813–45.

Lévi-Strauss, C. (1963) *Structural Anthropology*, trans. C. Jacobsen and B. G. Schoepf, New York, Basic Books.

Livesay, J. (1985) 'Normative Grounding and Praxis: Habermas, Giddens, and a Contradiction Within Critical Theory', *Sociological Theory*, 3 (2), pp. 66–76.

Livesay, J. (forthcoming) 'Structuration Theory and the Unacknowledged Conditions of Action, *Theory, Culture and Society*.

Lockwood, D. (1964) 'Social Integration and System Integration', in *Explorations in Social Change*, eds G. K. Zollschan and W. Hirsch, Boston, Houghton Mifflin, pp. 244–57.

Luhmann, N. (1982) *The Differentiation of Society*, trans. S. Holmes and S. Laramore, New York, Columbia University Press.

McLennan, G. (1984) 'Critical or Positive Theory? A Comment on the Status of Anthony Giddens's Social Theory', *Theory, Culture & Society*, 2 (2), pp. 23–9.

McLennan, G. (1988) 'Structuration Theory and Post-empiricist Philosophy: A Rejoinder', *Theory, Culture & Society*, 5 (1), pp. 101–9.

McNeil, W. H. (1982) *The Pursuit of Power: Technology, Armed Force, and Society Since A.D. 1000*, Chicago, University of Chicago Press.

MacCannell, D. (1976) 'The Past and Future of Symbolic Interactionism', *Semiotica*, 16, pp. 99–114.

Maines, D. R. (1977) 'Social Organization and Social Structure in Symbolic Interactionist Thought', *Annual Review of Sociology*, 3, pp. 235–59.

Malinowski, B. (1961) *Argonauts of the Western Pacific: An Account of Native Enterprise and Adventure in the Archipelagoes of Melanesian New Guinea*, New York, Dutton Press.

Mandelbaum, M. (1955) 'Societal Facts', *British Journal of Sociology*, 6, pp. 305–17.

Mann, M. (1986) *The Sources of Social Power: Volume 1: A History of Power From the Beginning to A.D. 1760*, Cambridge, England, Cambridge University Press.

Marx, K. (1963) *The Eighteenth Brumaire of Louis Bonaparte*, New York, International.

Marx, K. (1967) *Capital: A Critique of Political Economy: Volume 1: The Process of Capitalist Production*, trans. S. Moore, E. Aveling, ed. F. Engels, New York, International Publishers.

Marx, K. (1970). *A Contribution to the Critique of Political Economy*, trans. S. W. Ryazanskaya, New York, International Publishers.

Marx, K. (1973) *Grundrisse: Introduction to the Critique of Political Economy*, trans. M. Nicolaus, New York, Vintage.

Marx, K. (1975) *Karl Marx: Texts on Method*, trans. and ed. T. Carver, Oxford, Basil Blackwell.

Mayhew, B. H. (1980) 'Structuralism Versus Individualism: Part I: Shadowboxing in the Dark', *Social Forces*, 59 (2), pp. 335–75.

Mayhew, B. H. (1981) 'Structuralism Versus Individualism: Part II: Ideological and Other Obfuscations', *Social Forces*, 59 (3), pp. 627–48.

Maynard, D. W. and Wilson, T. P. (1980). 'On the Reification of Social Structure', *Current Perspectives in Social Theory*, 1, pp. 287–322.

Meltzer, B. W., Petras, J. W. and Reynolds, L. T. (1975) *Symbolic Interactionism: Genesis, Varieties and Criticisms*, London, Routledge & Kegan Paul.

Merton, R. K. (1968) *Social Theory and Social Structures*, enlarged edn, New York, Free Press.

Mitchell, J. C. (1979) 'Network, Algorithms, and Analysis', in *Perspectives on Social Network Research*, eds P. W. Holland and S. Leinhardt, New York, Academic Press, pp. 425–51.

Moore, B. (1966) *Social Origins of Dictatorship and Democracy: Lord and Peasant in the Making of the Modern World*, Boston, Beacon.

Mullins, N. C. (1973) *Theories and Theory Groups in Contemporary American Sociology*, New York, Harper & Row.

Mumford, L. (1934) *Technics and Civilization*, New York, Harper.

Münch, R. (1981) 'Talcott Parsons and the Theory of Action: The Structure of the Kantian Core', *American Journal of Sociology*, 86 (4), pp. 709–39.

Nadel, S. F. (1957) *The Theory of Social Structure*, Glencoe, Free Press.

Nagel, E. (1967) 'A Formalization of Functionalism with Special Reference to its Application in the Social Sciences', in *System, Change, and Conflict*, eds N. J. Demerath and R. A. Peterson, New York, Free Press, pp. 77–98.

Oakes, G. (1980) 'Simmel's Problematic', in G. Simmel, *The Problems of the Philosophy of History: An Epistemological Essay*, New York, Free Press, pp. 1–37.

O'Connor, J. (1973) *The Fiscal Crisis of the State*, New York, St Martins Press.

Parkes, D. and Thrift, N. (1980) *Time, Space, and Places*, Chichester, Wiley.

Parsons, T. (1935) 'Sociological Elements in Economic Thought: II: The Analytical Factor View', *Quarterly Journal of Economics*, 49, pp. 646–67.

Parsons, T. (1951) *The Social System*, New York, Free Press.

Parsons, T. (1961) 'An Outline of the Social System', in *Theories of Society: Foundations of Modern Sociological Theory*, vol. 1, eds T. Parsons, E. Shils, K. D. Naegele and J. R. Pitts, New York, Free Press, pp. 30–79.

Parsons, T. (1966) *Societies: Evolutionary and Comparative Perspectives*, Englewood Cliffs, Prentice-Hall.

Parsons, T. (1968) *The Structure of Social Action*, New York, Free Press.

Parsons, T. (1969) *Politics and Social Structure*, New York, Free Press.

Perinbanayagam, R. S. (1985) *Signifying Acts: Structure and Meaning in Everyday Life*, Carbondale, Southern Illinois University Press.

Perrow, C. (1984) *Normal Accidents: Living with High-Risk Technology*, New York, Basic Books.

Polanyi, K. (1944) *The Great Transformation: The Political and Economic Origins of Our Time*, Boston, Beacon.

Popper, K. R. (1968) *The Logic of Scientific Discovery*, New York, Harper & Row.

Rawls, A. W. (1987) 'Interaction Order Sui Generis, Goffman's Contribution to Social Theory', *Sociological Theory*, 5 (2), pp. 136–49.

Schnaiberg, A. (1980) *The Environment*, New York, Oxford University Press.

Schudson, M. (1984) 'Embarrassment and Erving Goffman's Idea of Human Nature', *Theory and Society*, 13 (5), pp. 633–48.

Schutz, A. (1962) *Collected Papers: Vol. 1: The Problem of Social Reality*, ed. M. Natanson, The Hague, Martinus Nijhoff.

Selznick, P. (1949) *TVA and the Grass Roots*, New York, Harper & Row.

Shaw, M. (ed.) (1984) *War, State, and Society*, London, Macmillan.

Simmel, G. (1950) *The Sociology of Georg Simmel*, ed. K. H. Wolff, New York, Macmillan.

Simmel, G. (1959) 'The Problem of Sociology', in *Georg Simmel, 1858–1918*, ed. and trans. K. Wolff, Columbus, Ohio State University Press.

Skocpol, T. (1979) *States and Social Revolutions: A Comparative Analysis of France, Russia, and China*, Cambridge, England, Cambridge University Press.

Smith, J. W. and Turner, B. S. (1986) 'Constructing Social Theory and Constituting Society', *Theory, Culture & Society*, 3 (2), pp. 125–33.

Spencer, H. (1873) *The Study of Sociology*, London, Kegan Paul, Trench.

Spencer, H. (1905) *The Principles of Sociology*, 3rd edn, New York, D. Appleton & Company.

Spencer, H. (1977) *Herbert Spencer*, ed. S. Andreski, London, Thomas Nelson.

Stinchcombe, A. (1968) *Constructing Social Theories*, New York, Harcourt Brace & World.

Thompson, J. B. (1984) *Studies in the Theory of Ideology*, Berkeley, University of California Press.

Thrift, N. (1985) 'Bear and Mouse or Tree and Bear? Anthony Giddens's Reconstruction of Social Theory', *Sociology*, 19 (4), pp. 609–23.

Tilly, C. (1984) *Big Structures, Large Processes, Huge Comparisons*, New York, Russell Sage Foundation.

Toulmin, S. (1961) *Foresight and Understanding: An Enquiry into the Aims of Science*, New York, Harper & Row.

Touraine, A. (1977) *The Self-Production of Society*, Chicago, University of Chicago Press.

Turner, J. H. (1986) *The Structure of Sociological Theory*, 4th edn, Chicago, Dorsey.

Turner, J. H. and Maryanski, A. (1979) *Functionalism*, Menlo Park, Benjamin/Cummings.

Turner, R. H. (1962) 'Role Taking: Process Versus Conformity', in *Human Behavior and Social Processes: An Interactionist Approach*, ed. A. R. Rose, Boston, Houghton Mifflin, pp. 20–40.

Udy, S. H. (1968) 'Social Structure: Social Structural Analysis', in *International Encyclopedia of the Social Sciences*, vol. 14, ed. D. Sills, New York, Free Press.

Vico, G. (1968) *The New Science*, Ithaca, Cornell University Press.

Wallace, W. L. (1969) 'Overview of Contemporary Sociological Theory', in *Sociological Theory: An Introduction*, ed. W. L. Wallace, Chicago, Aldine, pp. 1–59.

Wallace, W. L. (1983) *Principles of Scientific Sociology*, New York, Aldine.

Weber, M. (1946) *From Max Weber*, eds H. H. Gerth and C. W. Mills, New York, Oxford University Press.

Weber, M. (1968) *Economy and Society: An Outline of Interpretative Sociology*, eds G. Roth and C. Wittich, New York, Bedminster.

Wellman, B. (1983) 'Network Analysis: Some Basic Principles', *Sociological Theory 1983*, San Francisco, Jossey Boss, pp. 1201–31.

White, H. C., Boorman, S. A. and Breiger, R. L. (1976) 'Social Structure from Multiple Networks: 1: Blockmodels of Roles and Positions', *American Journal of Sociology*, 81 (4), pp. 730–80.

Whitehead, A. N. (1925) *Science and the Modern World*, New York, Free Press.

Willer, D. and Willer, J. (1973) *Systematic Empiricism: Critique of a Pseudo-Science*, Englewood Cliffs, Prentice-Hall.

Williams, R. (1983) *Keywords: A Vocabulary of Culture and Society*, revised edn, New York, Oxford.

Willis, P. (1977) *Learning to Labor*, New York, Columbia University Press.

Willner, A. R. (1984) *The Spellbinders: Charismatic Political Leadership*, New Haven, Yale University Press.

Wilson, T. P. (1984) 'On the Role of Mathematics in the Social Sciences', *Journal for Mathematical Sociology*, 10, pp. 221–39.

Wilson, T. P. and Zimmerman, D. H. (1979–80) 'Ethnomethodology and Social Theory', *Humboldt Journal of Social Relations*, 7, pp. 52–83.

Winch, P. (1958) *The Idea of Social Science and its Relation to Philosophy*, New York, Humanities Press.

Wolf, E. R. (1969) *Peasant Wars of the Twentieth Century*, New York, Harper.

Wright, E. O. (1983) 'Giddens's Critique of Marxism', *New Left Review*, 138 (April), pp. 11–35.

Wright, E. O. (1985) *Classes*, London, Verso.

Zeruvabel, E. (1981) *Hidden Rhythms: Schedules and Calendars in Social Life*, Chicago, University of Chicago Press.

Index of Names

Index of Subjects